The Imprint of the Picturesque on Nineteenth-Century British Fiction

Alexander M. Ross

"Despite the negative criticism directed at its sentiment, its heartlessness, its superficiality, the picturesque remained in both art and fiction of Victorian
England a mode of seeing that even the greatest of the
artists and novelists relied upon from time to time so
that their viewers and readers could rejoice in the
instant recognition of place and character distinctly
limned and sometimes subtly enough to elicit sympathy" (Preface).

After briefly tracing the development of the
theory of the picturesque in the eighteenth-century
writings of William Gilpin, Sir Uvedale Price, and
Richard Payne Knight and examining how
nineteenth-century novelists accommodated aesthetic theory to the practice of fiction, Ross focuses on the
use of the picturesque in the works of Sir Walter Scott,
Charlotte Brontë, Charles Dickens, George Eliot, and
Thomas Hardy. The persistence of the picturesque
through novels ranging from *Waverley* to *Jude the
Obscure* and in writers like Dickens and Eliot, who
had little respect for its conventions, attests to its
strength and attraction in nineteenth-century literature.

*Alexander Ross retired in 1978 from the Department
of English at the University of Guelph.*

The Imprint of the Picturesque on Nineteenth-Century British Fiction

Alexander M. Ross

Wilfrid Laurier University Press

Canadian Cataloguing in Publication Data

Ross, Alexander M., 1916-
   The imprint of the picturesque on nineteenth-
century British fiction

Bibliography: p.
Includes index.
ISBN 0-88920-191-9

1. Picturesque, The, in literature.   2. English
fiction – 19th century – History and criticism.
I. Title.

PR861.R67 1986   823'.7'09   C86-094301-1

Copyright © 1986
WILFRID LAURIER UNIVERSITY PRESS
Waterloo, Ontario, Canada   N2L 3C5

86 87 88 89 4 3 2 1

Cover design by Polygon Design Limited

Printed in Canada

For Celia

Contents

List of Illustrations

ix

Sources and Abbreviations

Throughout the text, quotations from the major novelists are identified by title and chapter.

The editions used for these novelists are as follows: Sir Walter Scott (Frowde, Oxford University Press); Charlotte Brontë (Thornton Edition); Charles Dickens (Oxford Illustrated Dickens); George Eliot (Cabinet Edition); Thomas Hardy (Wessex Edition).

When reference is made to published letters, the abbreviated title, *Letters*, appears in the text followed by roman numerals for the volume, if more than one, and arabic for the page reference.

Preface

This book looks at the effect which the theory and practice of the picturesque had upon some representative major British novelists of the nineteenth century. It was an effect which may be discerned not only in the novels examined in this study but also in hundreds of others of that century, especially those in the area of "minor fiction." The use and popularity of the picturesque owed much to the fact that, for the artist or novelist, it provided a way of showing landscapes and their contents to viewers or readers in a fashion that seemed to them organized and sensibly pictorial. It was by and large how they considered the world should look when seen within picture frames or within the covers of a novel: representative and recognizably pleasant.

As much as possible I have tried to take my directions from eighteenth-century theorists and, in particular, from meanings which nineteenth-century novelists attached to the word "picturesque." For my illustrations, I have relied extensively upon the novelists' own use of the term as I found it in their fiction.

For many of the novelists and even for some of the theorists, the picturesque was a rather vague aesthetic classification which seemed to bridge the gap between Burke's two concepts of beauty and sublimity. Because it possessed, for example, intricacy, irregularity, and roughness, it appeared to be distinct from either the vastness and gloom of Burke's sublime or the delicateness and smoothness associated with his concept of beauty. Unlike the sublime, which drew upon terror for its effect, the picturesque, like beauty, produced pleasure. Because of the vagueness of its classification, however, the qualities assigned to it often encroached upon those normally characteristic of both the sublime and the beautiful.

As it is important to try to clarify the meanings that cluster about the term, my introductory chapter presents a summary of the development of the theory of the picturesque with particular reference to the work of William Gilpin, Sir Uvedale Price, and Richard Payne Knight. Chapter 2 moves into the nineteenth century to show how novelists accommodated the theory to the practice of fiction and how usage extended the meaning of the term.

To some readers my choice of novelists—Sir Walter Scott, Charlotte Brontë, Charles Dickens, George Eliot, and Thomas Hardy—will appear both capricious and limited. My defense for such a course is that I preferred first to treat major British novelists who rank high among my own favourites; second to avoid the risk of needless repetition on my subject; and third to choose fiction that offered a reasonably inclusive coverage of the nineteenth century. For those who remain dissatisfied with this defense, I hope that their dissatisfaction may encourage them to continue the search for the fictional picturesque—particularly in those directions beyond my competence to explore.

My selection of authors has perhaps one distinguishing merit and that is that not all of them are fervent admirers of the picturesque. Two of them—Charles Dickens and George Eliot—had deep suspicions about an aesthetic which seemed so indifferent and incongruous whenever its vision included poor and suffering people. Their use of this aesthetic is at times hesitant, even reluctant, and, with Dickens, frequently ironic in its application. But although Dickens and George Eliot distrusted picturesque representation, they very seldom moved beyond this convention in their own appreciation of fine art. Throughout their lives both of them enjoyed painting that was essentially of this kind.

In fact, Dickens and George Eliot, like Scott, Charlotte Brontë, and Hardy, found the conventions of the picturesque exceedingly useful for descriptions particularly of place, character, and architecture. Here, of course, they had the assistance of Victorian painters who offered innumerable examples of how to adapt the theory to the practice. What the painter did in pigments the novelist tried to do in words. It was a process, too, that often worked in reverse as when artists like J. M. W. Turner and George Cattermole provided illustrations for Scott and Dickens. Under the canopy of the picturesque, art and fiction throughout the nineteenth century were often seen comporting together and frequently to each other's artistic advantage.

The appeal to readers was very great because, for the average ones in the rapidly burgeoning Victorian middle class, picturesque vision was a way of seeing landscape and character with which they were likely to be very familiar. Not until the end of the century, when

Pre-Raphaelitism and Impressionism had won acceptance, was the vision in any way significantly dimmed or supplanted.

And so, despite the negative criticism directed at its sentiment, its heartlessness, its superficiality, the picturesque remained in both art and fiction of Victorian England a mode of seeing that even the greatest of the artists and novelists relied upon from time to time so that their viewers or readers could rejoice in the instant recognition of place and character distinctively limned and sometimes subtly enough to elicit sympathy.

I was encouraged to write this book by the late Professor Lionel Stevenson of Duke University who heard me read a paper on the subject at the Eighth Conference of the International Association of Professors of English held at Istanbul in 1971. My indebtedness to other scholars is, I hope, obvious in my bibliography and references. Not so obvious is the consideration and kindness which has been extended to me by librarians: those in the British Library, the Victoria and Albert Museum, the University of Guelph, and, for the last few years, those in the Douglas Library of Queen's University. I like especially to think of this work as a final audit of my obligations to Canada Council, whose awards in the past assisted me greatly in my research.

This book has been published with the help of a grant from the Canadian Federation for the Humanities, using funds provided by the Social Sciences and Humanities Research Council of Canada.

Plate 1
William Gilpin, *Landscape*

Plate 2
William Gilpin, *Tintern Abbey*

Plate 3

J. M. W. Turner, *Interior of Tintern Abbey*
The Victoria and Albert Museum, London

Plate 4

William Gilpin, *A Blasted Tree on a Heath*

Plate 5

Salvator Rosa, *Landscape*

Plate 6
William Gilpin, *Approach to Wells*

Plate 7

Peter Paul Rubens, *Landscape with a View
of the Château de Steen*

Plate 8
John Constable, *Dedham Vale*
National Galleries of Scotland, Edinburgh

Plate 9

Paul Sandby, *Gate of Coverham Abbey, Coverdale, Yorkshire*
Reproduced by courtesy of the Trustees of the British Museum, London

Plate 10
Paul Sandby, Dumbarton Castle
The National Gallery of Canada, Ottawa

Plate 11
William Gilpin, *Dumbarton Castle*

Plate 12
Thomas Gainsborough, *Open Landscape with Wood-gatherer,*
Peasant Woman with Her Baby on a Donkey, and Peasants
Seated round a Cooking Pot on a Fire
The Tate Gallery, London

Plate 13
Thomas Gainsborough, *The Cottage Door*
The Henry E. Huntington Library and Art Gallery,
San Marino, California

Plate 14
Jacob van Ruisdael, *A Waterfall in a Rocky Landscape*
Reproduced by courtesy of the Trustees, The National Gallery, London

Plate 15

Philip James de Loutherbourg, Travellers Attacked by Bandits

The Tate Gallery, London

Plate 16
John Constable, *A Boat Passing a Lock*
Courtesy of Sudeley Castle, Gloucestershire

Plate 17

George Fripp. *Kilchurn Castle*
Royal Library, Windsor Castle

Plate 18
J. M. W. Turner, *The Falls of the Clyde* (1802)
The Walker Art Gallery, Liverpool

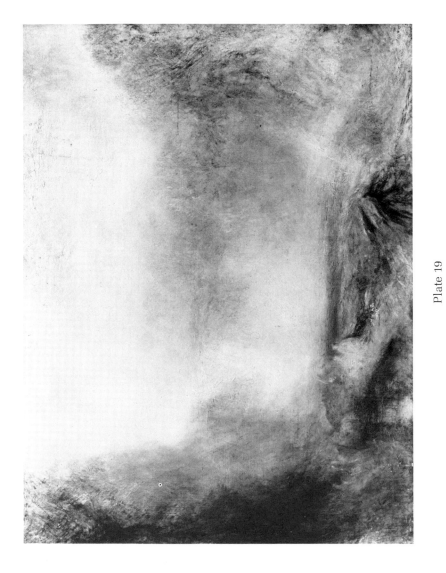

Plate 19

J. M. W. Turner, *The Falls of the Clyde* (c. 1835)
The Walker Art Gallery, Liverpool

Plate 20

Thomas Rowlandson, *Dr. Syntax at a Review*

Plate 21

William Gilpin, *Broken Lines in a Landscape*

Plate 22
Clarkson Stanfield, *The Dogana and Church of the Salute, Venice*
Reproduced by courtesy of the Trustees of the British Museum, London

Plate 23
Peter de Wint, *Ruins of the Bishop's Palace, Lincoln*
The Tate Gallery, London

Chapter 1

A Backward Glance

[T]he eye is a mere window. It is a pane of glass, through which the imagination is impressed by the notices it receives of outward objects.

William Gilpin, *Forest Scenery*

No artistic movement has had so much impact upon the English novel as that associated with the picturesque. This may be explained by the popularity of the movement during the last decades of the eighteenth century, when educated men and women were seeing the landscape around them by means of its conventions, were designing their estates and homes with its principles in mind, adding to their libraries handsomely bound works of its theorists, and reading novels whose authors were quite willing to promote picturesque vision for the sake of the new, interested public.

Historical reasons can be advanced for the acceptance of this mode of seeing landscape, the buildings in it, and the people who lived upon it. Not least of these in Britain was the nature of the rather ancient, wealthy, landed aristocracy which, by the end of the eighteenth century, was able to demonstrate its very considerable interest in estate improvement. "Improvers" like Vanbrugh, Bridgeman, Switzer, Kent, Repton, and Brown gave a new look to the face of England and created homes and estates that attracted very considerable attention. The names of some of these properties appear in every worthwhile tourist guide today; Castle Howard, Blenheim, Stowe, Rousham, Corsham Court, and Chatsworth may be taken as representative of how interested estate owners were in the theories advanced by landscape gardeners and architects throughout the eighteenth

1

century. The theories depended essentially upon a visual approach
that was supposed to owe much to the sister art of painting which
offered hundreds of examples of how artists as far apart as Claude and
Gainsborough saw and organized the countryside to suit their artistic
ends.

For those who were interested in studying the subject, the exercise was not a demanding one because examples, framed and unframed, were always at hand. The theorists themselves made good use
of the same examples as they went about convincing their patrons of
the need for change. As the eighteenth century moved into the
nineteenth, most private libraries of note among the landed class must
have held at least one copy of a book that could be used as a reference.
The choice was wide: essays of Addison; poetry of Pope, Dyer, and
Thomson; philosophical monographs by Shaftesbury, Burke, and
Alison; discourses on art by Reynolds and on rhetoric by Blair; travel
books by Arthur Young and William Gilpin; the journal of Thomas
Gray; books on gardening by Stephen Switzer, Batty Langley, Thomas
Whately, William Mason, Sir William Chambers, and Horace Wal-
pole; and books devoted to the theory of landscape architecture by Sir
Uvedale Price, Humphry Repton, and Richard Payne Knight.

And, of course, it is hardly possible to overemphasize the effect
which travel abroad had had upon the eighteenth-century English
tourists. From the time they left London until their return from Rome,
they experienced a variety of real landscapes: the gardens of Le Nôtre,
the views of the Alps, the classical scenes and formal gardens of Italy,
the ruins of the Roman Forum and Paestum. To this experience the
travellers added another dimension as they viewed paintings in Paris,
Florence, Rome, and Venice and—like Beckford of Fonthill and
Richard Colt Hoare, whose grandfather had designed Stourhead—
bought art they admired and carried it back to England to add distinction to the paintings already hanging in their galleries. Beckford had
two Claudes to remind him of ideal landscape; Richard Colt Hoare
brought back Cigoli's *Adoration of the Kings* to accompany his grandfather's paintings by Carlo Maratta and Mengs. On either side of the
fireplace in the library at Stourhead, until 1883, were ten views by
Canaletto.[1] Multiply these travel experiences and purchases of art by
the number of Britons who completed their education by taking the
Grand Tour, and some idea emerges of how tremendously important

1   Kenneth Woodbridge, *Landscape and Antiquity, Aspects of English Culture at
    Stourhead, 1718 to 1838* (Oxford, 1970), pp. 150-51.

this travel adventure was in shaping eighteenth-century cultural attitudes and, in particular, the interest of the aristocracy in the appearance of their country estates.

Opinion among the landed classes was particularly favourable to those who had ideas about how they might improve their homes and estates. By 1750 a visitor to their residences saw changes worthy of comment. One such visitor, a rather obscure, quiet Anglican curate named William Gilpin, wrote an anonymous description of the gardens at Stowe under the title *A Dialogue upon the Gardens of the Right Honourable The Lord Viscount Cobham at Stow* [sic] *in Buckinghamshire* (1748). Modelled upon the narrative form of Shaftesbury's "The Moralists," Gilpin's *Dialogue* has two friends, Polython and Callophilus, discuss the nature of the scenery at Stowe. Both men comment upon what they see in a conversation of some detail which seems now too wooden to be at all realistic. But their comments remain historically important.

Perhaps because of the presentation, it is by no means easy to decide to what extent Gilpin himself accepted the opinions of either of the two speakers. Certainly at Stowe the later Gilpin would have been critical of the fake ruin, the temple of Bacchus, the clutter of emblematic detail, and such sights as the hermitage, the pyramid, the equestrian statue, St. Austin's cave, the "Piece of Satyr," the grotto with its profusion of mirrors, and the Palladian bridge. He probably would have described it, as he did Stourhead in 1775, where he found "a littleness in the execution," buildings that were "too numerous and too sumptuous," simplicity everywhere "too much wanting." But the *Dialogue* should not be taken too literally, for its naive enthusiasms hide ironic undertones which the reader hears as Gilpin puts Pope's couplet in the mouth of the ardent Callophilus: "But treat the goddess like a modest fair, / Nor overdress, nor leave her wholly bare"; or when Gilpin has Polython quote from "L'Allegro," where Milton is obviously praising natural landscape untrammelled by "noble Productions of Art." Polython, however, comes close to scoffing at some of these: the "horrid pieces of Rock-Work," the "impertinent hedge," the "jolly figure" who represents drunkenness, the wretched scrawling of the Necromancer, the stagnant serpentine river, the whimsical appearance of the Chinese house, the use of chequered marble in busts, the overall ostentation which Gilpin was later to condemn at Fountains in Yorkshire.

Generally, however, the two friends agree about some characteristics of the park and scenery, which Gilpin was later to incorporate into his theory of the picturesque. Polypthon asserts that the ruin at Stowe enhances the beauty of the lake. "There is," he asserts, "something so vastly picturesque, and pleasing to the Imagination in such Objects, that they are a great Addition of every Landskip." Callophilus agrees and says that although "a regular Building perhaps gives us very little pleasure . . . yet a fine Rock, beautifully set off in *Claro-obscuro*, and garnished with flourishing Bushes, Ivy, and dead Branches, may afford us a great deal; and a ragged Ruin, with venerable old Oaks, and Pines nodding over it, may perhaps please the Fancy yet more than either of the other two Objects."[2] By the end of the *Dialogue*, the reader has met most of the characteristics of the picturesque: irregularity, contrast, roughness, kinship to the real world, variety, use of light and shade, novelty, and pictorial organization.

William Templeman's identification in 1939 of William Gilpin as the author of the *Dialogue* was important because of its date of publication: eight years before Burke's *A Philosophical Enquiry into the Origin of Our Ideas of the Sublime and Beautiful* and twenty years before the publication of Dr. John Brown's famous letter to Lord Lyttelton, which Christopher Hussey described as "being the earliest critical and comparative examination of romantic scenery."[3] The *Dialogue*, then, is a forerunner of great importance in the evolution of the picturesque. Here, for example, Gilpin hints at the primacy of natural scenery for the landscape artist, cavils at whatever is regular and artificial, stresses the value of composition and drawing, makes use of painting technique to describe what he sees, emphasizes the pleasure offered by distant prospects, accents the use of light and shade for contrast, and gives a role to imagination and the fancy which on occasion may have to censure Nature's own too profuse composition and yet must never become "impertinent" in so doing.

If a novelist like Sir Walter Scott were in search of a method whereby his reader could visualize a scene, the *Dialogue* offered helpful illustrations of how to make "a noble Picture" in prose. Polypthon, who, like Gilpin himself, came from the north of England, describes the scenery upon the banks of the River Eden near Penrith in Cumberland in this way:

2   [William Gilpin], *A Dialogue Upon the Gardens of the Right Honourable The Lord Viscount Cobham at Stow in Buckinghamshire* (1748; rpt. Los Angeles: The Augustan Reprint Society, 1976), p. 6.

3   Christopher Hussey, *The Picturesque, Studies in a Point of View* (London, 1967), p. 99.

There is the greatest Variety of garnished Rocks, shattered Preci-
pices, rising Hills, ornamented with the finest Woods, thro' which
are opened the most elegant Vales that I have ever met with: Not to
mention the most enchanting Views up and down the River, which
winds itself in such a manner as to shew its Banks to the best
Advantage, which, together with very charming Prospects into the
Country, terminated by the blue Hills at a Distance, make as fine a
Piece of Nature, as perhaps can any where be met with.[4]

Here in Gilpin's early prose are many of the ingredients that the reader
associates with the Scottish scenery of the Waverley novels which
appeared over half a century later.

Although the word "picturesque" had been used as early as 1705
in England, it was not until the publication of Gilpin's *Dialogue* that
its meaning was explained at length.[5] As the *Dialogue* passed through
three editions and was plagiarized in 1750 by George Bickham,[6] it
must have been fairly widely known long before Gilpin published his
*Three Essays: on Picturesque Beauty; on Picturesque Travel; and on
Sketching Landscape* (1792); and before his six tours appeared (1782-
1809). The *Three Essays* were written about 1776, and the texts for the
tours were also in manuscript at least a decade before publication. As
many of the books were sent in manuscript to his friends for comment,
Gilpin's ideas about picturesque scenery—aside from those in the
anonymous *Dialogue* of 1748—were recognized and known, before
their publication, by men of letters as distinguished as Thomas Gray
and Sir Joshua Reynolds.

Their place in time underlines their seminal nature and makes
clear their independence of the work of both Sir Uvedale Price and
Richard Payne Knight. Because a great part of *An Essay on the Picturesque* (1794) had been written before Price saw "that of Mr. Gilpin on
picturesque beauty,"[7] Price's *Essay* owes little to Gilpin's *Three Essays* of 1792. But another link with Gilpin exists. What Price had read
were Gilpin's "other works" which included the "very ingenious
work on Forest scenery"[8] and presumably three of the six tours. These

4   Gilpin, *Dialogue*, p. 25.
5   See William D. Templeman, *The Life and Work of William Gilpin, 1724-1804*
    (Urbana, Illinois, 1939), pp. 113-30.
6   Templeman, *William Gilpin*, pp. 128-29.
7   Sir Uvedale Price, *An Essay on the Picturesque as Compared with the Sublime and
    the Beautiful; and, on the Use of Studying Pictures, for the Purpose of Improving
    Real Landscape*, new ed. (London, 1796), I, p. 391.
8   Price, *An Essay on the Picturesque* (1796), I, p. 401.

"other works" also preceded Richard Payne Knight's poem, *The Landscape* (1794), and his book, *An Analytical Inquiry into the Principles of Taste* (1805).

Although both Price and Knight moved well beyond Gilpin's powers as an aesthetician, nonetheless it was Gilpin in his essays "On Picturesque Beauty" and "On Sketching Landscape" who was the first to attempt to explain to readers how they could distinguish "between such objects as are *beautiful*, and such as are *picturesque*—between those, which please the eye in their *natural state*; and those, which please from some quality, capable of being *illustrated in painting*."[9] Enlarging upon the ideas contained or hinted at in his *Dialogue*, Gilpin had much to say that proved of considerable importance to nineteenth-century novelists intent upon presenting easily recognized landscape description to their readers.

It is often remarked that picturesque art is imitative, a copy simply of a striking outdoor scene. Gilpin would deny that this is so. "The picturesque eye, it is true, finds it's [sic] *chief* objects in nature; but [he continues] it delights also in the images of art."[10] Rather than making a copy, artists represent "those ideas, which have made the most impression," sometimes by a "short-hand scrawl" of their pen. In language that brings Wordsworth's "Tintern Abbey" to mind, Gilpin asserts that "there may be more pleasure in recollecting, and recording, from a few transient lines, the scenes we have admired, than in the present enjoyment of them." He parts company with Wordsworth, however, when he adds this qualifier: "If the scenes indeed have *peculiar greatness*, this secondary pleasure cannot be attended with those enthusiastic feelings." Still he is close to the "Preface" of the *Lyrical Ballads* as he argues that the process of recollection brings "a calmer species of pleasure" which is "more uniform, and uninterrupted."[11]

Further, a striking landscape "rising before the eye" may appeal to us

> beyond the power of thought—when the *vox faucibus haeret*; and every mental operation is suspended. In this pause of intellect; this *deliquium* of the soul, an enthusiastic sensation of pleasure over-

9   William Gilpin, *Three Essays: on Picturesque Beauty; on Picturesque Travel; and on Sketching Landscape: to Which is Added a Poem, on Landscape Painting* (London, 1792), p. 3.
10 Gilpin, *Three Essays*, p. 27.
11 Gilpin, *Three Essays*, pp. 51-52.

spreads it, previous to any examination by the rules of art. The general idea of the scene makes an impression, before any appeal is made to the judgment. We rather *feel*, than *survey* it.[12]

In his emphasis here upon "impression" and "feeling" as being prior to intellect and the "rules of art," Gilpin's aesthetic is modern. And it should also be noted that the feeling which he experiences is far removed from the kind of sentiment that so often afflicts picturesque representation in Victorian narrative art.

Gilpin's theorizing sometimes brings the real and the ideal into contrasting relationships. Admitting the importance of imagination in the creative process—especially in representing "scenes of fancy," not linked directly to the external world—he asserts: "The imagination becomes a camera obscura, only with this difference, that the camera represents objects as they really are; while the imagination, impressed with the most beautiful scenes, and chastened by rules of art, forms it's [sic] pictures, not only from the most admirable parts of nature; but in the best taste."[13] Here and elsewhere Gilpin reveals how divided his allegiance is between the classical tendencies of the eighteenth century and the romanticism of the nineteenth. At times the tension between what is general and what is particular, what is an objective view and what is a subjective one, is nearly in balance. Against the "Nature" of Alexander Pope, with its emphasis upon the rules of the ancients and its objectivity, we have the boundless variety and peculiarities of the world of the Romantic where "the province of the picturesque eye is to *survey nature*; not to *anatomize matter*."[14] In "Essay on Picturesque Travel," Gilpin also reminds us emphatically that "Nature is the archetype." But because nature is "too vast for picturesque use," liberties may be taken with it providing it is done "with caution." For this task his eighteenth-century good sense comes to his rescue:

> We do not mean
> With close and microscopic eye, to pore
> On ev'ry studied *part*: The practis'd judge
> Looks chiefly on the *whole*; and if thy hand
> Be guided by true Science, it is sure
> To guide thy pencil freely. Scorn thou then
> On *parts minute* to dwell: The *character*
> Of objects aim at, not the *nice detail*.[15]

12 Gilpin, *Three Essays*, pp. 49-50.
13 Gilpin, *Three Essays*, p. 52.
14 Gilpin, *Three Essays*, p. 26.
15 Gilpin, "On Landscape Painting, a Poem," in *Three Essays*, p. 19.

This is advice which Gilpin also offers in prose when writing about the lakes of Cumberland and Westmoreland: "he who works *from imagination*—that is, he who culls from nature the most beautiful parts of her productions—a *distance* here; and there a *foreground*—combines them artificially; and removing every thing offensive, admits only such parts, as are *congruous*, and *beautiful*; will in all probability, make a much better landscape, than he who takes all as it comes."[16] In such a pronouncement, Gilpin parts company with many later nineteenth-century landscape artists and sides with Gainsborough whose early landscapes, like Gilpin's, are seldom copies of particular scenes. Gilpin's own books often display made-up scenes such as the attractive sketch which he inserted in his "Essay on Picturesque Travel" to illustrate "a *simple mode* of tinting a drawing" (Pl. 1).

For Gilpin the picturesque ranges well beyond mere landscape description: "The picture, the statue, and the garden [he states] are all the objects of it's[sic] attentions."[17] Even the human face in old age is picturesque: "What is it, but the forehead furrowed with wrinkles? the prominent cheek-bone, catching the light? the muscles of the cheek strongly marked, and losing themselves in the shaggy beard? and, above all, the austere brow, projecting over the eye . . . in a word, what is it, but the *rough* touches of age?"[18] And finally, in this connection, Gilpin observes that the human figure itself may be picturesque "when agitated by passion" and more so when we see it in action. For this reason, he says, we "admire the Laocoon more than the Antinous." Gilpin's admiration for the "*spirited* action" which, he says, belongs to antique statues like "the Laocoon, the fighting gladiator, and the boxers . . . the Apollo Belvidere—Michael Angelo's Torso—Arria and Paetus—the Pietas militaris . . . the Alexander, and Bucephalus"[19] is interesting because it may account for the extension of the word "picturesque" by authors like Scott, Dickens, and Stevenson to qualify historical or fictional narrative that is particularly animated or spirited in its presentation.

16   William Gilpin, *Observations, Relative Chiefly to Picturesque Beauty, Made in the Year 1772, on Several Parts of England; Particularly the Mountains, and Lakes of Cumberland and Westmoreland* (London, 1786), I, pp. xxvi-xxvii.

17   Gilpin, *Three Essays*, p. 45.

18   Gilpin, *Three Essays*, pp. 10-11.

19   Gilpin, *Three Essays*, p. 13n.

Perhaps remembering the "good effect" that the ruin at Stowe presented to Callophilus and Polypthon, Gilpin expands upon their remarks in his "Essay on Picturesque Travel":

> But among all the objects of art, the picturesque eye is perhaps most inquisitive after the elegant relics of ancient architecture; the ruined tower, the Gothic arch, the remains of castles, and abbeys. These are the richest legacies of art. They are consecrated by time; and almost deserve the veneration we pay to the works of nature itself.[20]

In thus putting his stamp of approval upon the effect of ruins, Gilpin set an example that contributed to the emphasis that novelists from Scott to Hardy put upon "the relics of ancient architecture." What it was that they emphasized may be seen in J. M. W. Turner's water colour, *Interior of Tintern Abbey* (ca. 1794). It is a scene which Gilpin himself saw in the summer of 1770 (Pl. 2) and which he sketched and described in his *Observations on the River Wye*. So unlike Gilpin's rendering of the abbey, Turner's water colour (Pl. 3) gives romantic charm to a dilapidated, mouldering ruin and presents much of the detail that Gilpin noted in his prose: the broken outline of Gothic arches, the ivy and shrubbery growing out of the walls, the rough fragments of shattered stone, the framing arch, the perspective that leads the eye under other arches to the hills along the Wye, and in the half-light of the foreground, to the two tourists surveying, in Gilpin's language, this "very enchanting piece of ruin." Visual representation of this sort did much to develop a sensitivity and liking for picturesque architecture throughout the nineteenth century.

William Gilpin's aesthetic umbrella—if unreliable psychologically—was a very commodious one judging from the number of nineteenth-century authors who found no trouble sheltering either themselves or their readers under its canopy. Its commodiousness, of course, was the result, as Richard Payne Knight pointed out, of the vagueness which attached to the word "picturesque," and especially to Gilpin's compound term "picturesque beauty." Because Gilpin and Price both admitted that picturesque elements were often to be found in scenes that were essentially either sublime or beautiful, they thereby further ensured that the circumference of the umbrella was even larger and of great interest to those novelists who felt compelled to fit their characters and their actions into plausible but unusual settings.

20 Gilpin, *Three Essays*, p. 46.

The effect of Gilpin's theorizing in the *Three Essays* was very much amplified by the popularity of his tours and his sketches of scenes he had admired. Sometimes, too, the sketches, especially those of trees and animals in *Forest Scenery*, were designed to show other would-be travellers how either to recognize or to draw picturesque objects. In fact, it would be difficult to overestimate the influence of the observations, for example, in the first volume of *Forest Scenery* about the blasted oak and Gilpin's illustration of it standing alone on a desolate heath (Pl. 4). In this instance, Gilpin drew upon his own extensive knowledge of the woods and scenery of New Forest in Hampshire and turned to Salvator Rosa to illustrate the effectiveness of "the *withered top*" and "*curtailed trunk*" of trees[21] (Pl. 5). And such "splendid remnants of decaying grandeur [says Gilpin] speak to the imagination in a stile of eloquence"; in some scenery the shattered tree is essential: "When the dreary heath is spread before the eye, and ideas of wildness and desolation are required, what more suitable accompaniment can be imagined, than the blasted oak, ragged, scathed, and leafless; shooting it's [sic] peeled white branches athwart the gathering blackness of some rising storm?"[22] This blasted tree and its accompaniments are perhaps the most frequently met landmarks in picturesque landscape description. Scott, Charlotte Brontë, and Hardy all make use of this device in a variety of circumstances.

Throughout the many volumes of his tours, Gilpin offered hundreds of detailed descriptions in prose to support his theories about the delights of travel and landscape portraiture. In his account of his approach to Wells in 1775, as well as in his aquatint of the scene (Pl. 6), Gilpin made his descriptive process obvious:

> Our approach to Wells, from the *natural* and *incidental* beauties of the scene, was uncommonly picturesque. It was a hazy evening; and the sun, declining low, was hid behind a deep purple cloud, which covered half the hemisphere, but did not reach the western horizon. Its lower skirts were gilt with dazzling splendor, which spread downwards, not in diverging rays, but in one uniform ruddy glow; and uniting at the bottom with the mistiness of the air, formed a rich, yet modest tint, with which Durcote-hill, projecting boldly on the left, the towers of Wells beyond it, and all the objects of the distance, were tinged; while the foreground, seen against so bright a

21 William Gilpin, *Remarks on Forest Scenery and Other Woodland Views* (London, 1791), I, p. 9.
22 Gilpin, *Forest Scenery*, I, p. 14.

piece of scenery, was overspread with the darkest shades of evening. The whole together invited the pencil, without soliciting the
imagination. But it was a transitory scene. As we stood gazing at it,
the sun sunk below the cloud, and being stripped of all its splendor
by the haziness of the atmosphere, fell, like a ball of fire, into the
horizon; and the whole radiant vision faded away.[23]

This is the sort of scenic prose which could serve as the prototype of
hundreds of settings which novelists in the eighteenth and
nineteenth centuries prepared for their readers.

It should be remarked, too, that Gilpin's tours concerned a real
countryside whose villages, towns, ruins, castles, and stately homes
could be found on a map. His verbal descriptions of Wookey Hole near
Wells, of the ruins of the Austin Friary in Canterbury, of Lidbroke on
the Wye, of the great forges of the Carron Works near Falkirk, and of
the ruins of Loch Leven Castle are examples of the kind of realism
which supported his writing.

At the same time his tours appealed to romantic taste. His interest in "old, unhappy, far-off things, / And battles long ago" was very
pronounced. The Castle of Lewes brings to his mind the battle which
"decided the great cause between Henry III and the barons"; Dynevor
Castle, near Llandeilo, in Wales reminds him of Spenser's Cave of
Merlin: Holyroodhouse in Edinburgh means Mary Queen of Scots and
the ill-fated Rizzio; the grandeur of Stonehenge "brings a train of
wondering ideas . . . into the mind" which for some pages concern
ancient methods of burial; and in the Portsmouth dockyard "the
careening of a ship" brings an account of fire at night and recalls to
Gilpin Shakespeare's description of the campfires of the English and
the French and how "the *paly* flames just *umber* the faces that watch
round them." This associative process is one of the most pronounced
features of the picturesque. What a place brings to mind is often as
important as its physical appearance. It is a process that Sir Walter
Scott makes considerable use of as characters like Jonathan Oldbuck
and the Baron of Bradwardine solemnly pronounce upon the antiquities of Monkbarns or Tully-Veolan.

The popularity of Gilpin's travel books has been well docu-
mented by William Templeman and Carl Paul Barbier. The extent of
this popularity and something of its significance may be grasped in
William Wordsworth's description of the picturesque in *The Prelude*

23 William Gilpin, *Observations on the Western Parts of England, Relative Chiefly to
    Picturesque Beauty*, 2nd ed. (London, 1808), pp. 129-30.

as "a strong infection of the age";[24] he was not exaggerating. Of course, by 1805, when *The Prelude* was complete, Gilpin's theories were even more widely known than earlier because of the work particularly of Sir Uvedale Price and Richard Payne Knight; further-more, the numerous rancorous debates which attended the Price-Repton controversy made the picturesque a lively literary and aesthet-ic subject in the earlier years of the century, even stimulating satiric treatment. *The Tour of Doctor Syntax in Search of the Picturesque* (1812), *Sense and Sensibility* (1811), and *Headlong Hall* (1816) serve nicely as examples of how this new cult excited interest and ridicule in the literary world.

Sir Uvedale Price's work appeared in two separate volumes: the first, *An Essay on the Picturesque* in 1794; the second, *Essays on the Picturesque* in 1798. His works were published in 1810 in three vol-umes bearing one title, *Essays on the Picturesque*, and continuing on with the rest of the title of the earlier volumes, *as Compared with the Sublime and the Beautiful; and, on the Use of Studying Pictures, for the Purpose of Improving Real Landscape*. His theories, like Gilpin's, owe much to Burke's *Enquiry* of 1757 but are much more particular in their application. Like Gilpin, Price gives precedence to nature over art. The word "picturesque," he says, may be "applied to every object, and every kind of scenery, which has been, or might be represented with good effect in painting."[25] His definition is close to the one that Gilpin offered in 1768: "a term expressive of that peculiar kind of beauty, which is agreeable in a picture."[26] Unlike Gilpin, Price de-votes much space to censuring the school of landscape gardening founded upon the work of Capability Brown. In so doing he is careful to explain in 1796 how his own ideas would be an improvement upon the monotony of Brown's lawns, clumps, and his serpentine lines: "Upon the whole, it appears to me, that as intricacy in the disposition, and variety in the forms, the tints, and the lights and shadows of objects, are the great characteristics of picturesque scenery; so monotony and baldness are the greatest defects of improved places" (I, pp. 26-27). Sir Uvedale favours the retention of as much of the natural landscape as possible: the roots of trees, the paths of sheep, lanes, high banks, old quarries, and chalk and gravel pits overgrown

---

24   William Wordsworth, "The Prelude," Bk. XII, l. 113.
25   Price, *An Essay on the Picturesque* (1796), I, p. 46.
26   [William Gilpin], *An Essay upon Prints: Containing Remarks Upon the Principles of Picturesque Beauty* (London, 1768), p. x.

with climbers and weeds. Rather than Brown's artificial lakes, Price prefers running water: "all water whose surface is broken, and whose motion is abrupt and irregular, as universally accords with our ideas of the picturesque; and whenever the word is mentioned, rapid and stony torrents and cataracts, and the waves dashing against rocks, are among the first images that present themselves to the imagination" (I, pp. 68-69). Like the author of *Forest Scenery*, Price admires old oak or elm trees and finds such trees highly picturesque if their limbs have been "shattered by lightning or tempestuous winds." And like that author, too, he admires the worn and shaggy cart horse more than he does the "pampered steed."

For support for his arguments on the subject of picturesque landscape, Sir Uvedale turns to painters like Rosa, Claude, Poussin, Mola, Rubens, and Gainsborough. In their paintings he can find many illustrations of how these artists composed into pleasing wholes the details of their countrysides; as well, they offer examples of how passion and strong emotion affect the human figure picturesquely. Rubens's landscapes "are full of the peculiarities, and picturesque accidents in nature; of striking contrasts of form, colour, and light and shadow: sun-beams bursting through a small opening in a dark wood—a rainbow against a stormy sky—effects of thunder and lightning—torrents rolling down trees torn up by the roots, and the dead bodies of men and animals; with many other sublime and picturesque circumstances" (I, p. 153) (Pl. 7). From some seventeenth- and eighteenth-century landscapes, Price also finds much to say about the appearance of beggars and gypsies.

On such humankind, the picturesque eye looked with much pleasure. This Price makes clear in his "Dialogue on the Distinct Characters of the Picturesque and the Beautiful" which was a reply to Knight's charge that the distinction Price made in his *Essays* between the beautiful and the picturesque was an imaginary one. In his "Dialogue" Price has three friends conveniently come upon a gypsy encampment. The resulting description illustrates nicely the qualities which appealed to those in search of the picturesque and incidentally, too, how their vision could isolate visual qualities that gave pleasure from the human squalor that would have disturbed a novelist like Dickens or George Eliot. Before them, the three gentlemen—Mr. Howard, Mr. Hamilton (who represent Knight and Price), and Mr. Seymour—see

> a ruinous hovel on the outskirts of a heathy common. In a dark corner of it, some gypsies were sitting over a half-extinguished fire,

which every now and then, as one of them stooped down to blow it, feebly blazed up for an instant, and shewed their sooty faces, and black tangled locks. An old male gypsey stood at the entrance, with a countenance that well expressed his three-fold occupation, of beggar, thief, and fortune-teller; and by him a few worn-out asses: one loaded with rusty panniers, the other with old tattered cloaths and furniture. The hovel was propt and overhung by a blighted oak; its bare roots staring through the crumbling bank on which it stood. A gleam of light from under a dark cloud, glanced on the most prominent parts: the rest was buried in deep shadow: except where the dying embers "Taught light to counterfeit a gloom".

    The three friends stood a long while contemplating this singular scene: but the two lovers of painting could hardly quit it: they talked in raptures of every part; of the old hovel, the broken ground, the blasted oak, gypsies, asses, panniers, the catching lights, the deep shadows, the rich mellow tints, the grouping, the composition, the effect of the whole; and the words beautiful, and picturesque, were a hundred times repeated. The uninitiated friend [Mr. Seymour] listened with some surprise.[27]

The eighteenth century's acceptance of a rigid class system may account for Price's indifference to the social and economic lot of picturesque poor people like the gypsies. It was what Dickens protested against and what we in the twentieth century like to consider intolerable—at least in the Western world. It is also one of the reasons why art critics look upon picturesque treatment of a subject as either sentimental or downright superficial.

    But Mr. Howard, Mr. Hamilton, and Mr. Seymour were only interested in the scene as a manifestation of the picturesque: in its irregularities, its contrasting lights, the grouping of the gypsies about the campfire, and its overall composition. In one sense theirs was a superficial viewing, but in another they were seeing as Constable saw when he sketched the foreground of Dedham Vale in 1828 with its frame of towering trees and gnarled pollarded trunks, its coarse vegetation, the rough banks of the roadway that leads the eye to the tent of the gypsy mother and child crouched before a smouldering fire and nearly hidden in the chiaroscuro which contrasts so gloriously with the Constable sky over the sunlit meanderings of the Stour (Pl. 8). The eye here, as Gilpin pointed out in another context, has

---

27   Sir Uvedale Price, "A Dialogue on the Distinct Characters of the Picturesque and the Beautiful, in Answer to the Objections of Mr. Knight," in *Essays on the Picturesque, as Compared with the Sublime and Beautiful; and, on the Use of Studying Pictures, for the Purpose of Improving Real Landscape* (London, 1810), III, pp. 262-63.

"nothing to do with *moral sentiments*, and is conversant only with visible forms."[28] Mr. Howard and Mr. Hamilton would have no difficulty in recognizing the merit of *Dedham Vale*.

From paintings and from the illustrations used by Gilpin, Price, and Knight, the novelist could learn much about landscape when seen in various lights. For the Vicar of Boldre "the *going off* of mists and fogs is among the most beautiful circumstances ... While the obscurity is only *partially* clearing away, it often occasions a pleasing contrast between the *formed* and *unformed* parts of a landscape."[29] This is the device Scott used to show his readers in *Waverley* the two armies before the engagement at Prestonpans. In writing about autumn, Sir Uvedale Price explains how "all is matured; and the rich hues of the ripened fruits, and of the changing foliage, are rendered still richer by the warm haze, which on a fine day in that season, spreads the last varnish over every part of the picture."[30] Sir Uvedale is here recalling light that suffuses so many paintings of the Venetian School. Richard Payne Knight also observes how "candle-light, moon-light, and twilight melt every thing into one mild hue; through the harmonising medium of which, things the most offensively glittering, gaudy, and harsh, become beautifully rich, splendid, and mellow."[31] From Gilpin, too, there was more advice as he exhorts the youthful artist to give his view "more ample range" and explore

> The vast expanse of ocean; see, when calm,
> What Iris-hues of purple, green, and gold,
> Play on its glassy surface; and when vext
> With storms, what depths of billowy shade, with light
> Of curling foam contrasted. View the cliffs;
> The lonely beacon, and the distant coast,
> In mists array'd, just heaving into sight
> Above the dim horizon; where the sail
> Appears conspicuous in the lengthen'd gleam.[32]

It is worth noting that Gilpin, Price, and Knight are not far away from some of the values of Impressionism with, for example, the light that

28   William Gilpin, *Three Essays: on Picturesque Beauty; on Picturesque Travel; and on Sketching Landscape: with a Poem, on Landscape Painting. To These Are Now Added Two Essays, Giving An Account of the Principles and Mode in Which the Author Executed His Own Drawings*, 3rd ed. (London, 1808), p. 164.
29   Gilpin, *Observations on the Western Parts of England*, p. 162.
30   Price, *An Essay on the Picturesque* (1796), I, pp. 201-202.
31   Knight, *An Analytical Inquiry into the Principles of Taste*, 4th ed. (1808; rpt. Westmead, Farnborough, 1972), pp. 97-98.
32   Gilpin, "On Landscape Painting, a Poem," in *Three Essays*, p. 3.

melts "every thing into one mild hue" in Monet's *Haystacks: Snow Effect* (1891) or with the "Iris-hues of purple, green, and gold" in Turner's *Yacht Approaching the Coast* (1835-40). Some of the Impressionist effect often attributed to Hardy's *Woodlanders* could reasonably have its genesis in earlier art and theory. The "luminous lavender mist" that shrouded the apple-rich prospect of Sherton Abbas is an example.

The link between colour and the picturesque is acceptable because both relate to the visual process. But Price in 1796 makes a less obvious connection when he introduces music saying that it may possess picturesqueness if, in its movements, there are "sudden, unexpected, and abrupt transitions,—from a certain playful wildness of character, and an appearance of irregularity" (I, p. 56). For his examples Price cites any "capricious movement of Scarlatti or Haydn" and supports his stand by saying that there is "a general harmony and correspondence in all our sensations when they arise from similar causes." If we accept Price's argument, it is reasonable to think that this application of the word "picturesque" to a quality of sound could equally well be applied to what Thomas Hardy heard as he listened to the "treble, tenor, and bass notes" of the wind ricocheting over the "pits and prominences" of Egdon Heath. It is also tempting—and perhaps reasonable—to extend the meaning of the word to spoken language and especially to the peculiarity of the sound of dialectal words—to what may be referred to as a region's linguistic landscape.

In Part II of his first volume (1796), Price builds upon his preceding chapters and goes on to discuss to what extent the improvers have heeded the examples of great landscape artists. The improvers— Walpole, Kent, and Brown—fare badly at his hands. Chapter 2 is given over to a detailed exposition of the place of trees in a landscape, and chapter 3, the last, is devoted to the general effects of water in a landscape.

After essays entitled "Artificial Water" and "Decorations" in Volume II, Price closes his work with one on scenery called "Architecture and Buildings." To begin with, he is emphatic that both building and landscape should "peculiarly suit, and embellish each other" (II, p. 212). In fact, throughout both volumes, Price reminds his readers how important it is that all the parts of landscaped scenery should blend into "one striking, and well-connected whole" (II, p. 201). A house must not have the "insulated look" that belonged to so many in Capability Brown's landscapes. To support his statement

Price refers to Sir Joshua Reynolds's thirteenth "Discourse" in which Reynolds praises the work of Vanbrugh for its "painter-like effects" and cites Blenheim Palace as forming "a well-combined whole" (II, p. 252). Interestingly, Sir Uvedale refers to the effect that the raised decorations on the roof make and how the architect makes use of light and shadow to give "more elegance and congruity to the parts." And this leads him to praise the town of Tivoli in Italy, where the buildings advance or retire "from the eye, according to the nature of their situation; while the happy mixture of trees completes the whole" (II, p. 260).

That contemporary people of taste were influenced by Price's theories is widely recognized. Sir Walter Scott is one who, having read Price thoroughly, was determined to put his ideas into practice at Abbotsford. Thomas Hope offers another very interesting illustration as he applied picturesque principles to Deepdene, an estate he purchased in 1807. His concern about the relation of his house to the surrounding landscape may be seen in the sketches which the young William Henry Bartlett made from the terrace.[33] The irregularities of the house, especially its roofline, and the effect produced by light and shadow and trees are evident in the designs which Hope and William Atkinson, his architect, made of the house. Specific descriptions of picturesque roof and house outlines exist throughout nineteenth-century fiction.

In spite of the fact that Price can find little evidence in the paintings of Rosa, or Claude, or Poussin to support his contention that Greek and Roman ruins and those, more recent, of abbeys, castles, and old mansion houses are often highly picturesque, he pursues his argument vigorously: "All external objects affect us in two different ways; by the impression they make on the senses, and by the reflections they suggest to the mind (II, p. 282). This reliance upon the principle of association enables Price to make a stronger case for the effect of classical ruins than for "a beautiful scene in some obscure district." He also favours Greek or Roman ruins because "the character of beauty still lingers about their forms" (II, p. 286). Like Gilpin's, his picturesque accommodates easily both the sublime and the beautiful of Burke's *Enquiry*.

Unlike Gilpin, however, Price devotes very little attention to the role of the imagination. He is much more concerned with detailed and

---

33 See David Watkin, *Thomas Hope, 1769-1831, and the Neo-Classical Idea* (London, 1968), chaps. 5, 6.

accurate representation than is the Vicar of Boldre. If imagination has any role to play, it is in Sir Uvedale's emphasis upon the need for unity and harmony in a landscape. Generally, he does not want to disturb or move the objects in his landscapes. If ruinous, old mansion houses with their walled terraces and ivy-covered summer houses can be restored, "too much caution," asserts Price, "cannot be used in disturbing their ancient character and accompaniments, by clearing away those disguises and intricacies, which the hand of time has slowly created" (II, p. 302). His emphasis here is, of course, on the practice of landscaping and not, as Gilpin's was in *Three Essays*, upon observing and sketching landscape.

The two men differ markedly about "cottages, mills, outhouses, and hovels," many of which, says Price, "are in their entire state extremely picturesque, and almost all become so in decay" (II, p. 302). Here, of course, Sir Uvedale could draw upon many Netherlandish painters like David Teniers, Adriaen van Ostade, or Philips Wouwerman to sustain his theory. But Gilpin never mentions these homes of the poor in *Three Essays* other than to warn the amateur painter to avoid "the mean and trivial." A cottage, if it embellishes a scene, if it is a place where happiness resides, may please the eye. But in a forest scene, for example, it offends. "It should be a castle, a bridge, an aquaduct, or some other object that suits it's [sic] dignity."[34] Carl Paul Barbier suggests that Gilpin's predilection was for the sublimities in the natural scene, rather than for sentimental portrayal of rustic cottages and peasants in the style of the early Gainsborough. The low vulgarisms of day-to-day living, which the Flemish and Dutch artists so liked to paint, simply did not appeal to William Gilpin. Furthermore, there is a hint in his *Dialogue upon the Gardens . . . at Stow* that his reluctance to include the dwellings of the poor was related to a moral question. Polython wonders why men are more taken by "Prospects of this ruinous kind than with Views of Plenty and Prosperity." Callophilus can only answer that they have to make "a distinction between natural and moral Beauties," that, in fact, they get more pleasure from what is irregular than regular, from a "fine rock . . . in Claro-obscuro," from a "ragged Ruin," or from old oaks and pines. And so he concludes that the old Hermitage in the wilderness at Stowe is to be admired. But the moral question has been evaded. It reappears in notable dress over a century later in chapter 17 of *Adam Bede*. Barbier contends that "the subject of cottages brings

34 Gilpin, *Forest Scenery*, I, p. 217.

out clearly the nature of [Gilpin's] conception of the Picturesque, which is austere and idealistic, and runs counter to the general attitude of his age."[35]

But Gilpin's concern is not shared by Price who continues in his last chapter to give a place to "very singular and striking effects" produced by wooden bridges in alpine scenery; domes, pyramids, obelisks, and towers on buildings; the intricacy of water mills seen in the paintings of Ruisdael, Waterlo, and Hobbema; the inside details of Dutch kitchens and the exterior of Dutch cottages as shown by Ostade and Wouwerman; the effect of thatch on a cottage, even when "mossy, ragged, and sunk in among the rafters in decay" (II, p. 398); the characteristic features of country churches; and the attractiveness of village dwellings which, like those in Hardy's Casterbridge, possessed "picturesque irregularity" with tints of "that rich, mellow, harmonious kind, so much admired by painters" (II, p. 407).

Throughout this chapter—and indeed in everything he wrote—Price's contention is that the landscape gardener should in his work be guided by the principles of the art of painting which although "really founded in nature, and totally independent of art, are, however, most easily and usefully studied in the pictures of eminent painters."[36] Price's psychology, like Edmund Burke's, assumes that there are "certain qualities, which uniformly produce the same effects in all visible objects, and according to the same analogy, in objects of hearing and of all the other senses."[37] In speaking about the kind of beauty, for instance, that attaches to ruins, Price argues that the mind associates with ruins the ideas of "age, decay, and abandonment." This association comes about because of what the senses tell us about the external world; of these senses, sight is the most important. What we associate with what we see will have force depending upon our store of ideas and our power to draw upon them. Those who can associate Claude, for example, with the ruins they see will have distinguished proof of how the ruins may be arranged to provide beauty of a picturesque kind. This awareness of relationships between the external world and the world of art is one which always brings pleasure to the viewer. Such, in brief, is Price's aesthetic. Within its limitations it made sense and provided generations of

35 Carl Paul Barbier, *William Gilpin, His Drawings, Teaching, and Theory of the Picturesque* (Oxford, 1963), p. 113.
36 Price, *Essays on the Picturesque* (1810), II, p. vi.
37 Price, *Essays on the Picturesque* (1810), I, p. 47.

impressionable men and women with a working theory whereby their experience of the external world was very considerably enriched.

It was in 1801 that Price published a reply to Richard Payne Knight's criticism of his theories which appeared in the second edition of Knight's *The Landscape, a Didactic Poem* (1795). In a lengthy footnote, Knight had taken issue with the idea that picturesque qualities existed in external objects. For Knight the "picturesque is merely that kind of beauty which belongs exclusively to the sense of vision; or to the imagination, guided by that sense." This is so, he states, because "the eye, unassisted, perceives nothing but light variously graduated and modified . . . and as the eye has learnt by habit to perceive form as instantaneously as colour, we perpetually apply terms belonging to the sense of touch to objects of sight."[38] Consequently, Knight asserts that Price makes throughout "the otherwise able and elegant *Essays on the Picturesque*," a "fundamental error" in "seeking for distinctions in external objects, which only exist in the modes and habits of viewing and considering them."[39] It will not serve here to expand upon the Knight-Price aesthetic difference because it was not consequential enough to affect nineteenth-century fiction. On the whole the novelists were quite prepared to accept the picturesque as they discerned it in the works of Gilpin and Price. Despite the strictures of Richard Payne Knight upon the psychology of sensation and perception—as accepted by Burke, Gilpin, and Price—his subtle explication of the role of association and the imagination, his conclusion that "the beauties of light, shade and colour are all that affect the eye, or make any impression upon organic sense and perception," Knight accepted the picturesque as a mode of vision, a mode very dependent upon what he called "the habitual association of ideas"[40] and the perceiver's ability to view and receive pleasure from fine pictures and similar "objects" in nature. His work, in brief, was a scholarly refinement and extension in psychological terms of the work already done by Gilpin and Price.

But because Knight was, like them, essentially a person in search of what was picturesque, his work also contributed to the popularity of this way of seeing. Had he, as Christopher Hussey maintains, carried his thinking a bit further and been able to establish " 'the

---

38 Richard Payne Knight, *The Landscape, a Didactic Poem in Three Books, Addressed to Uvedale Price, Esq.*, 2nd ed. (London, 1795), p. 19.
39 Knight, *Analytical Inquiry*, p. 196.
40 Knight, *Analytical Inquiry*, pp. 152-58.

visible appearance' of things as the primary concern of painting,"[41] then he might have anticipated the Impressionism of J. M. W. Turner. But this he did not do, with the result that picturesque theory was confined to paintings that had a subject which could be easily associated with other ideas and with the physical facts of the external world; as a theory it was closely related to a reasoning process rather than an intuitive one. This limitation was one, however, that suited the needs of novelists writing for nineteenth-century readers who expected rational connections and who were far more interested in the real world around them than they were, for instance, in Turner's abstract vision of it. To make their readers see, the novelists turned naturally to description that relied heavily upon the conventions of the picturesque.

When the novelists looked as well at eighteenth-century landscape art, they found in the work of English painters like Richard Wilson (1714-82) a picturesqueness which antedated the three theorists just mentioned and which had its origin in seventeenth- and eighteenth-century Italian and Dutch art. Wilson's *Snowdon from Llyn Nantlle*, painted about the time Gilpin was beginning his tours, shows a landscape that Gilpin would have admired: the foreground with its blasted tree; the ruffled light from the lake; the side screens; the rugged outline of mountains in the middle ground, setting off the bulk of Snowdon in the background; the varied and irregular parts harmonizing in the autumnal unity of one splendid prospect.

Paul Sandby (1730?-1809), like his contemporary Richard Wilson, also had a strong topographical sense and an admiration for landscape that can best be described as picturesque. He was an artist, as Martin Hardie has said, "of his age and gave it what it liked and could understand."[42] The titles and the content of many of his pictures reveal at once the importance of place in his art, for example: *Gate of Coverham Abbey, Coverdale, Yorkshire* (1752) (Pl. 9); *Pont y Pair over the River Conway above Llanrwst in the County of Denbigh* (1775); and *In Windsor Park* (1802). It is with good reason that Christopher Hussey places Paul Sandby among "the most eminently picturesque English painters."[43]

Some time between 1745 and 1751, while employed in the Military Survey of Scotland, Paul Sandby painted a view in gouache of

41   Hussey, *The Picturesque*, p. 78.
42   Martin Hardie, *Water-colour Painting in Britain*, I: *The Eighteenth-Century* (London, 1967), pp. 109-10.
43   Hussey, *The Picturesque*, p. 251.

Dumbarton Castle (Pl. 10). To the left is a peasant and his two-wheeled cart on a rough, rutted roadway. In the centre middle ground, gentlemen on horseback are conversing, while a rather nondescript mounted pedlar looks on; to the far right are the bayonets and heads of a column of soldiers. A broken tree with twisted roots appears in the foreground, and in the background, high up on the rock, the castle terminates the view. If the castle seems too well preserved to be called picturesque, the overall scene deserves the epithet. In fact, the rock itself, because it was a "natural ruin" struck William Gilpin in 1776 as having "a wonderful appearance." He also thought that the "form of the fortress" was "very picturesque" as was the contrast between the two summits, the broken, craggy sides of the rock and the "amusing views" it offered from its summit, where close at hand Gilpin admired the tints of the *lychen geographicus.*

The contrast between one of Gilpin's two sketches of Dumbarton Castle (Pl. 11) and Sandby's painting reveals at once how devoid of particulars Gilpin's sketches were, how anxious he was to present his own imaginative impression of the scene so as to give a unified, harmonious blend of land, water, and sky. His scenes become idealized, almost classic, when compared with Sandby's water colour in which there is so much romantic detail that the overall effect is one of clutter and lack of control. Gilpin reserves narrative detail for his prose account that accompanies the sketches.[44] Dumbarton rock and Dumbarton Castle fill his mind with many literary associations from Virgil, Sallust, Caesar, Buchanan, and the life of Mary Queen of Scots. His account of the capture of Dumbarton in 1571 is a picturesque action in prose of the kind that Sir Walter Scott so much admired.

The emphasis which picturesque art from the seventeenth century on placed upon the delineation of place, on the recognizable representation of real landscape, and upon scenery which was often associated with stirring events in the past attracted the attention of novelists concerned to make their characters seem to belong to a fictional landscape. This art also emphasized for them the advantages of selecting telling detail from a scene and of highlighting the selection by use of contrast. Novelists, especially nineteenth-century ones, could, if they wished, learn just as much from studying landscape painting as they could from reading the works of those who theorized about it.

---

44 William Gilpin, *Observations, Relative Chiefly to Picturesque Beauty, Made in the Year 1776, on Several Parts of Great Britain; Particularly the High-Lands of Scotland* (London, 1789), II, pp. 43-53.

In many of his early landscapes, Thomas Gainsborough (1727-88), whom Christopher Hussey has described as "the founder of the 'rough' picturesque,"[45] left work of great interest both for painters and novelists. An unfinished painting (c. 1753-54) by this artist of peasants before a fire (Pl. 12) could serve to illustrate the gypsy camp which drew the attention of Price's Mr. Hamilton and Mr. Howard on their walk. A later engraving by J. Ward of this scene appears in John Hayes's *Gainsborough* (Pl. 113) and illustrates even better than the original what it was that so fascinated Mr. Hamilton and Mr. Howard. Of the theoretical statements on the picturesque, only Gilpin's *Dialogue upon the Gardens . . . at Stow* (1748) is earlier than Gainsborough's painting which could have been seen at least forty years before the major publications of Gilpin, Price, Repton, and Knight appeared. This fact needs to be emphasized because it is a reminder of how important the examples of picturesque art in England may have been in forming the popular taste not only of the theorists but also of nineteenth-century novelists interested in placing characters in settings that were distinctive and yet visually credible. As well, Gainsborough impresses viewers because of his ability to put figures in a landscape and then cast over his pictures a dominant mood that appeals emotionally. In his *Cottage Door* (1780), which was very well known by the turn of the century, Gainsborough combines highly picturesque qualities with an underlying nostalgia for the past,[46] the sort of romantic backward look that can be found in the fiction of both Charles Dickens and George Eliot. In the grouping and attitudes of the mother and children, *The Cottage Door* (Pl. 13) is sentimental in a mid-Victorian way; elsewhere its visual aspect supports the theorizing of Gilpin and Price: the gaunt remains of the blasted tree, the uneven ground, the rough thatched cottage embowered by great wind-tossed trees, the rough outlines of the wooden bridge over the fast water of the stream, and the contrast of dark and light, above and below—all point to the picturesque of the late eighteenth century.

It is a mode, of course, which appealed to many painters of the seventeenth century in the Netherlands, France, and Italy where it is easily discerned in the work, for example, of Rubens, Rembrandt, Adriaen van Ostade, Teniers the Younger, Wouwerman, Allart van Everdingen, Pynacker, Ruisdael (Pl. 14), Claude, Dughet, and Rosa.

---

45 Hussey, *The Picturesque*, p. 246.
46 I am indebted for this idea to John Hayes, *Gainsborough, Paintings and Drawings* (London, 1975), p. 46.

In the painting of these artists, the eighteenth-century connoisseurs could find an abundance of blasted oaks, pollarded willows, irregular rock faces, ruined castles, caves inhabited by banditti,[47] dramatic use of light and shade, waterfalls broken by rocks, ragged peasants by old thatched houses, mills driven by water power, and—in the background of many pictures—outlines of mountain peaks or the gently receding prospect of a river valley.

To the list of the artists we have already mentioned, eighteenth-century Britain contributed many more whose art illustrated the vogue of the picturesque: Alexander Cozens, Robert Adam, Philip James de Loutherbourg, Michael "Angelo" Rooker, Thomas Hearne, Francis Nicholson, Thomas Rowlandson, Alexander Nasmyth, Julius Caesar Ibbetson, George Morland, Thomas Barker, and James Ward. With the examples which such artists provided (see de Loutherbourg, Pl. 15), a novelist like Mrs. Ann Radcliffe could, without travelling abroad, draw upon a wide variety of painted landscapes to illustrate the wild fictional terrain on which characters like Emily St. Aubert and Montoni played out the melodrama of their lives. "No other novelist," notes Elizabeth Manwaring, "is so closely a follower of painted scenery" as is Mrs. Radcliffe.[48] But her scenery, as Sir Walter Scott complained, has a "haze" over it which does not communicate "any absolute precise or individual image to the reader."[49] It was in the fiction of Scott and those who came after him that we find landscape described, not as set pieces, but particularized and integrated fully into the fabric of the novel.

47 Paintings like de Loutherbourg's *Travellers Attacked by Bandits* (1781), the origins of which go back to Salvator Rosa, helped promote the popularity of the brigand theme in both painting and melodrama in the early nineteenth century. See especially Martin Meisel, *Realizations, Narrative, Pictorial, and Theatrical Arts in Nineteenth-Century England* (Princeton, 1983), pp. 111-15.

48 Elizabeth Wheeler Manwaring, *Italian Landscape in Eighteenth Century England* (London, 1925), p. 217.

49 Sir Walter Scott, *The Miscellaneous Prose Works of Sir Walter Scott*, III: *Biographical Memoirs of Eminent Novelists* (Edinburgh, 1834), p. 379.

Chapter 2

Theory to Practice

With scarcely an exception every painter was more or less
picturesque till the Pre-Raphaelites began painting tracts,
and, in our own times, the movements of the later
nineteenth century in France made themselves felt.
Christopher Hussey, *The Picturesque*

As landscape art and fiction moved from the eighteenth century into
and through the nineteenth, their affinities remained noticeable, if
not obvious: painters and novelists made use of the topography of
country and town and of the people who frequented them; both
painters and novelists were concerned to make their viewers and
readers see what they saw as they selected and arranged the details of
their visual experience; both strove for the contrasts which light and
shadow could give to their subject matter; both were often attracted by
ruins and the associations that clung about them; and like novelists,
painters often displayed in their art a narrative element.

In some respects, despite the limits of a frame and a moment in
time, painters were often more successful than novelists for the artists' scenes could be immediately recognized and nearly always
geographically defined. By their art, too, painters made their viewers
see not only the variety but also the charm of their countryside. This,
at a glance, novelists could not do. Their strength lay, however, in the
greater complexity which words could contribute to their descriptions of setting and in the illusion they could create of time passing
and effecting changes. At the same time, however, they remained very
much aware of how artists were achieving their effects. Because the
conventions which defined a picturesque landscape were so widely

known, novelists found it both reasonable and convenient to rely upon them frequently in order to gain their readers' acceptance of their fictional setting.

This trend was noticeable by the end of the eighteenth century when English novelists like Mrs. Radcliffe demonstrated how useful it was to adapt the techniques of the sister art of painting to that of fiction. Henry Mackenzie, for instance, had looked carefully at Salvator Rosa's art when he described the scene where his hero, Harley, found the old soldier:

> He was one of those figures which Salvator would have drawn; nor was the surrounding scenery unlike the wildness of that painter's back-grounds. The banks on each side were covered with fantastic shrub-wood, and at a little distance, on the top of one of them, stood a finger-post, to mark the directions of the two roads which diverged from the point where it was placed. A rock, with some dangling wild flowers, jutted out above where the soldier lay; on which grew the stump of a large tree, white with age, and a single twisted branch shaded his face as he slept.[1]

Mackenzie's references to Salvator's wild backgrounds, to the rock, the single twisted branch, and to the reclining figure of the old soldier make clear the origin of his descriptive technique, an origin which William Gilpin often referred to as he sought support for his theory of the picturesque.

In 1788, seventeen years after the publication of *The Man of Feeling*, Mrs. Charlotte Smith drew a picture in words to show her readers what her heroine, Emmeline, saw as she looked back at Mowbray Castle in its "gothic magnificence," making "one of the most magnificent features of a landscape." From the vantage point of her carriage, Emmeline noticed the stream that "washed the castle walls, foaming over fragments of rock." Through a wood she saw the ruins of a monastery which "reared it's [sic] broken arches . . . marked by grey and mouldering walls" that were linked to the castle itself. The background of the picture concluded the "charms of the prospect":

> Farther to the West, beyond a bold and rocky shore, appeared the sea; and to the East, a chain of mountains which seemed to meet the clouds; while on the other side a rich and beautiful vale, now variegated with the mellowed tints of the declining year, spread its enclosures, 'till it was lost again among the blue and barren hills.[2]

---

1   Henry Mackenzie, *The Man of Feeling* (New York, 1958), p. 59.
2   Charlotte Smith, *Emmeline, the Orphan of the Castle* (London, 1971), p. 37.

This is the sort of landscape which appealed to George Lambert, Richard Wilson, and Julius Caesar Ibbetson. As a prospect it is more fully described than Mackenzie's: foreground, middle distance, and background with a suggestion of side screens and of the frame made by the carriage window. Its scenic organization, too, is more obvious than Mackenzie's—more in accordance with picturesque composition. But both novelists illustrate in these passages their awareness of this kind of artistic composition. As well as showing their readers scenes which "would be agreeable in a picture," they emphasized ruin and age, foaming torrents and mouldering walls, variety of mellow tints, and the contrast afforded by cloud-touching mountains and fertile valleys.

By the end of the eighteenth century, English novelists could look back nearly three centuries and find persistent examples of landscape art whose subject matter and form were sufficiently picturesque to offer them hints on how to make their own settings easily comprehensible to their readers. Despite the satirical treatment meted out to it in fiction, verse, and cartoon, the picturesque in art also flourished, as Christopher Hussey said it did, throughout the nineteenth century.[3] Many names could be used to document the argument: John Thomson, Samuel Prout, Copley Fielding, J. D. Harding, James Holland, George Cattermole, Thomas Shotter Boys, and William Callow may suffice. All of these and many more continued to provide picturesque views that one suspects were of much greater value to the novelist than were the dry, sometimes verbose, and often contradictory statements of the theorists.

Hussey's statement at the head of this chapter implies that we need not worry about associating the picturesque, that "strong infection of the age," with the art of a Constable or even a Turner. Constable's letters reveal that he understood and was interested in picturesque representation to the extent that he referred to his painting, *A Boat Passing a Lock* (Pl. 16), as "an admirable instance of the picturesque." A little later, writing to Dr. Fisher, he could also say of this picture that "it is the light of nature, the mother of all that is valuable in poetry, painting, or anything else where an appeal to the soul is required."[4] Constable obviously saw nothing incongruous about admitting that a painting as spiritually vibrant as *A Boat Passing a Lock*

3   Hussey, *The Picturesque*, p. 273.
4   C. R. Leslie, *Memoirs of the Life of John Constable* (1843; rpt. London: John Lehman, 1949), p. 139.

possessed picturesque qualities. For ordinary viewers, whose souls may hold closer ties with earth than heaven, it is the picturesque details—the lock, the mossy pilings, the twisted limbs of the huge tree, the dramatic movement of the lockkeeper and the boatmen, the turbulent green water below the gate, and the landscape fading far in the distance—which first attract their attention. Indeed, they may never get beyond this stage of appreciation. And so it is, even with the greatest of Constable's art, that viewers have always a recognizable subject that is sometimes distinctly picturesque to delight their eyes and minds.

Certainly this was true of the art of less inspired landscape paint-ers of the nineteenth century. Their canvases reminded the gallery-goer of the look of things in this world. Theirs was fundamentally a representational art often differing from reality only because a choice had to be made from the bewildering array of its riches and because frequently the artist added an emotional element to create the impres-sion of either nostalgia or sentiment. The popularity of their art owed much to the fact that reason rather than imagination had predomi-nated in the act of creation. This was especially true of Victorian genre painting.

This painting of the domestic scene, often filled with picturesque detail and frequently narrative in its subject matter,[5] constituted an important genre in Victorian times as this partial list attests: Wilkie, *The Refusal*; Collins, *Rustic Civility*; Mulready, *A Sunny Day*; Leslie, *Uncle Toby and the Widow Wadman*; Landseer, *The Drover's Depar-ture*; Frith, *Derby Day*; William Holman Hunt, *Apple Gatherers in the Rhine Valley, Ragaz*; Calderon, *Broken Vows*; Orchardson, *The First Cloud*; and Solomon, *Waiting for the Verdict*.[6] With its emphasis upon detail, its interest in contemporary affairs, its tendency to point to a moral, its exploitation of the happening, and its insistence, for the viewer, on what is now taking place, this art form became a close relative of the Victorian novel which offered its readers similar ex-periences using the medium of prose rather than paint. This vogue for specific content helped put Victorian art on a course away from

5   See chapters 2 and 3, "Reading Pictures" and "The City and the Picturesque," in Peter Conrad, *The Victorian Treasure-House* (London, 1973), pp. 45-105. See also W. F. Axton, "Victorian Landscape Painting: A Change in Outlook," in U. C. Knoepflmacher and G. B. Tennyson, eds., *Nature and the Victorian Imagination* (Berkeley, 1977), pp. 305-306.

6   See also Lionel Lambourne, *An Introduction to 'Victorian' Genre Painting* (Lon-don, 1982); Norman Page, *Thomas Hardy* (London, 1977), pp. 71-77; and Joan Grundy, *Hardy and the Sister Arts* (London, 1979), pp. 30-34.

French Impressionism with its emphasis upon uninterpreted subject matter and indifference to the artist's own ideas or feelings.

The quiet course of Victorian art was not, however, without its challengers at home. The revolt staged by the Pre-Raphaelite Brotherhood (1848-53) was a reaction in part against picturesque subject painting. Brief as this revolt was, the members of the Brotherhood succeeded in creating a literary and artistic excellence which set their work apart from the much more popular genre style. They wanted to engage the viewer's attention not only aesthetically but socially as well. William Holman Hunt's *The Awakening Conscience*, for example, is an illustration of contemporary Victorian society which has been described as "a powerful chapter from a novel . . . [which] oversteps the dangerous boundary between visual art and didactic literature."[7] Using rich luminous colours to give prominence to exact detail from nature, relying upon symbolism to give depth of meaning to their art which looked to both the past and the present for its subjects, and ignoring conventional rules and taste, the Pre-Raphaelites startlingly revealed the aesthetic shallows of much popular British art of the mid-century. In these developments they were not, however, unique. Serious social issues confront the viewer, for instance, in Richard Redgrave's *The Reduced Gentleman's Daughter* (1840) and in Augustus Egg's *Past and Present* (1858); allegory in Richard Dadd's *The Passions* (1853-56); and in Samuel Palmer's best painting (1825-30), the viewer finds "the vision of the middle ages . . . a style very close to the landscape of symbols."[8]

As it turned out, despite Ruskin's championing of the Pre-Raphaelites and the transient appearance of the social realists, neither of these groups succeeded in displacing the picturesque treatment of subject matter. The Pre-Raphaelites did, however, leave their imprint in literature especially in the area of book and periodical illustration.[9] Frederic Leighton, for example, illustrated George Eliot's *Romola*. His classic designs seem oddly not well suited to the text and recall Sir Walter Scott's objection to Flaxman as an illustrator for his work. "I should fear Flaxman's genius is too classic to stoop to body forth my

---

7   T. S. R. Boase, *English Art, 1800-1870* (Oxford, 1959), p. 286. See also Meisel, *Realizations*, pp. 365-68 and illustration facing p. 367. As well, the reader should consult Meisel's chapter 14 "Prisoner's Base" in which he refers at length to "narrative configurations" in works by Sarah Setchel, W. Holman Hunt, Millais, Solomon, and Frank Hall.

8   Kenneth Clark, *Landscape into Art* (Boston, 1961), p. 72.

9   Boase, *English Art*, pp. 287-93.

Gothic Borderers. Would there not [Scott asked] be some risk of their resembling the antique of Homer's heroes?"[10]

Critics like Norman Page, Joan Grundy, and Arlene M. Jackson speak of the Pre-Raphaelite influence in Thomas Hardy's *The Return of the Native*. Norman Page states that Eustacia's description "might be applied with little change to many a Pre-Raphaelite canvas."[11] Joan Grundy agrees saying that Eustacia's "Pre-Raphaelite origins seem unmistakable."[12] Arlene Jackson would agree and sees in one of Arthur Hopkins's illustrations of Eustacia Vye his "predilection for the Pre-Raphaelite face."[13] Other examples may be offered, but these on the whole relate to the illustrations for the novels and only indirectly to the text itself. The illustrations did, however, affect many readers' interpretations of the novels.

Marianna Torgovnick's recent publication, *The Visual Arts, Pictorialism, and the Novel*, in its second chapter offers interesting objections to critical views of the place of illustration in novels. She warns us that illustrations may serve to distort and mislead more than they inform. To support her argument, she refers at length to illustrators' work in past editions of *David Copperfield* and *Tess of the D'Urbervilles*.

But another and more interesting connection between painting and fiction does exist. Although Victorian genre artists and Pre-Raphaelite painters differed greatly over the kind of subject that should be used and the treatment accorded it, both were interested in the narrative which might belong to the subject. "The evidence tells us," says Arlene Jackson, "that a special distinction of the Victorian artist, whether poet, novelist, or painter, is his predilection for relating picture and story. The relationship becomes an important and consistent part of Victorian aesthetics, and can be most clearly seen in the writings of Ruskin and Pater."[14] Here, however, the novelists

10 John Gibson Lockhart, *Memoirs of the Life of Sir Walter Scott* (Boston, 1910), I, p. 400.
11 Page, *Hardy*, p. 70.
12 Grundy, *Hardy and the Sister Arts*, p. 44.
13 Arlene M. Jackson, *Illustration and the Novels of Thomas Hardy* (London, 1981), p. 90.
14 Jackson, *Illustration and the Novels of Thomas Hardy*, p. 2. See also J. D. W. Murdoch, "Scott, Pictures, and Painting," in *The Modern Language Review* 67 (1972), p. 43: "For a generation, under Scott's influence, the border-line between story-telling and painting was almost non-existent." This idea is integral to the thinking of Martin Meisel who maintains in *Realizations*, "In the nineteenth century all three forms [novels, pictures, plays] are narrative *and* pictorial; pictures are given to storytelling and novels unfold through and with pictures," p. 3.

found genre art more helpful than Pre-Raphaelite, perhaps because the Pre-Raphaelites' marked interest in what was abstract and symbolic had less appeal for novelists in search of setting and characters that would seem credible to their mass readership. The genre art had a reality about it that both suited the authors and pleased their readers especially when the rules of picturesque viewing made the depiction seem familiar and obvious. Happily for this process, British art throughout the century remained very impervious to change. The failure of the Pre-Raphaelite group to alter the main drift of public taste, the inability of British artists to understand the importance of the French Impressionists, or to appreciate the towering achievements of their own J. M. W. Turner meant that art at home maintained its traditional patterns. A glance at J. W. North's very competent *Halsway Court, Somerset* painted about 1866, reveals the direction taken by much British art. Here is genre art enlivened by a narrative linked to rustic romance, and supported by picturesque representation of an ill-kept and named manor house, a nearby thatched shed, and an ivy-clad wall that separates the lovers while a little girl waits. *Halsway Court, Somerset* has many of the pictorial qualities we associate with Thomas Hardy's rural scenes.

About the same time that J. W. North was holidaying at Halsway Farm, the well-known artist George Arthur Fripp was commissioned by Queen Victoria to make sketches and paintings of mountain scenery in the highlands of Scotland. One of these, *Kilchurn Castle*, appeared as an engraving in *The Art-Journal* on February 1, 1858 (Pl. 17). Under the heading, "The Royal Pictures," the reviewer commented upon the associations which belonged to the locality and praised the "most picturesque character" of the castle whose circular towers projecting "on the south and east prevent the monotonous effect of a too regular line." To support various of his arguments, the reviewer referred to Sir Walter Scott, Thomas Campbell, and John Ruskin. In the last paragraph, the readers have the aesthetic qualities of the picture described for their better understanding:

> the sky is overcast with dark tempestuous clouds, except in one part, through which the sun breaks, lighting up the distant mountain and the tract of flat pasture ground immediately below. Ben Cruachan is in shadow of a deep purple grey; not so grey, however, as to conceal the silvery stream that rushes down the gorge towards the loch. The foreground, rich with the tints of the red and purple heather, diversified in strength of colour by the alternations of light and shade, is redeemed from utter solitude by a few figures judiciously scattered over it (p. 56).

As *The Art-Journal* offered many examples of such criticism, backed by full-page illustrations, it is reasonable to accord it considerable importance for maintaining the late-Victorian acceptance of picturesque vision in both painting and fiction.

Just as the mainstream of Victorian art swept by the innovations of Pre-Raphaelitism and the exciting techniques of Impressionism, it also kept clear of the idealism that informed the Romantic period in England which tended to see the individual at the centre of life and art, which exalted the imagination at the expense of reason and saw hills and clouds not just as visual experiences but as "Presences of Nature in the sky / And on the earth!"[15] The merely visual objects of the picturesque on the other hand had a practical reality quite at variance with the "huge cloudy symbols of a high romance."[16] The distinction can be readily seen in J. M. W. Turner's two renderings of *The Falls of the Clyde* (Pl. 18). The one executed in 1802 is noticeably topographical and picturesque in conception; the other (painted c. 1835) is a stunning symphony of colour that drowns out the geographical and descriptive details of place (Pl. 19).

But Turner's development as an artist from *Buttermere Lake* (1800) and the drawings for Cooke's *Picturesque Views of the Southern Coast of England* (1826) to the luminous splendours of the Petworth and Venetian paintings is not the kind which illustrates the course of Victorian taste, for Turner was at least fifty years ahead of his time. Even the staunch support of John Ruskin failed to convince the Victorians, including many of the novelists, of the merit of his best work. The luminous abstractions of his art made little impression amid the din of an industrial society committed to progress. The new forces were materialistic: matter rather than soul became the lodestar that attracted the rising middle class. Landscape art that mirrored the real world and family portraits in ornate frames won pride of place in their homes. No matter how much Ruskin talked or wrote, it was often a Bounderby whose tastes mattered most.

A Bounderby could not accept Ruskin's praise of "Turnerian mystery" for the simple reason that he could not see clearly what was going on in *The High Street, Oxford*, or even in *Rain, Steam and Speed — the Great Western Railway, 1844*, the title of which suggested

15   William Wordsworth, "The Prelude," *The Poetical Works of Wordsworth* (London, 1904), p. 639.
16   John Keats, "When I Have Fears," *The Poetical Works of John Keats* (London, 1956), p. 366.

things close to his heart. As a consequence, Bounderby and thousands of other Victorians—often more enlightened than he—relied upon picturesque art for the decoration of their expansive drawing-room walls. Much of this art was topographic and architectural, the work of artists like Samuel Prout, Augustus Charles Pugin, James Duffield Harding, and William Callow.

> It was [says Martin Hardie] for Prout and his companions to pre-
> serve and exaggerate the discomfort and decay of medieval dwell-
> ings; to present the picturesque in all its brilliant or sordid and
> forlorn aspects, so that it might hang in gilded mounts on the walls
> of formal Victorian drawing-rooms, and evoke memories of honey-
> moons and holidays which had seemed romantic adventures.
> Stately cathedrals, storied palaces, decrepit houses with timbered
> gables, high-pitched roofs and overhanging eaves, the hurly-burly
> of the street with its flutter of gay costumes, male and female
> dandies, peasants with the primitive flash of red, orange, blue or
> green, in their national dress, the market-place prismatic with the
> bright umbrellas and vividly striped awnings, the shimmering blue
> lakes and mountain scenery, gondolas gliding through Venetian
> canals, all of what the Continent means, is what Prout and his
> fellows supplied with consummate skill.[17]

And in all this—rather paradoxically—the discriminating taste of John Ruskin played an important part.

It was John Ruskin's division of the picturesque into "lower" and "higher" categories that did much to assure the Victorian public, interested in art, that the picturesque was aesthetically respectable and that "even the love for the lower picturesque ought to be culti-vated with care, wherever it exists."[18] His promotion of Samuel Prout "to be numbered among the true masters" of "the nobler pictur-esque" was further evidence of Ruskin's approval of this art form. Turner, too, he said, "admitted into his work the modern feeling of the picturesque" even though in its delight in ruin it was "the most suspicious and questionable of all the characters distinctively belong-ing to our temper, and art."[19] But despite this caveat, Ruskin sup-ported the "Turnerian picturesque," arguing that in Turner's work it was characterized by inventiveness and a largeness of sympathy for the subject, qualities lacking in the work of Clarkson Stanfield, whom

17 Martin Hardie, *Water-colour Painting in Britain*, III: *The Victorian Period* (London, 1968), p. 2.
18 *The Works of John Ruskin*, ed. by E. T. Cook and Alexander Wedderburn (London, 1904), VI, p. 22.
19 *Works of John Ruskin*, VI, p. 9.

Ruskin labelled as "the first master of the lower picturesque, among our living artists."[20]

In addition to such pronouncements, Ruskin's numerous reviews of art exhibitions, which received wide publicity in *The Art-Journal*, seldom failed to comment on landscape paintings or water colours that were significantly picturesque in composition. His admiration of Sir Walter Scott's pictorial powers as a landscape artist in prose was such that he made his readers vividly aware of Scott's descriptive ability in the Waverley novels. George Eliot's review of the third volume of *Modern Painters* in the *Westminster Review* (April 1856) offers proof that Ruskin's praise of Scott had not escaped her attention.

Although Ruskin was rightly suspicious of the picturesque's "delight in ruin" and even sensed how "heartless" the ideal of the lower picturesque could be, because it was primarily seeing without feeling, he was at the same time fair in his assessment of the sort of person who found pleasure in the work of an artist like Clarkson Stanfield, who appealed so much to Charles Dickens. Such a person, Ruskin pronounces, is *pace* Dickens:

> kind-hearted, innocent of evil, but not broad in thought; somewhat selfish, and incapable of acute sympathy with others; gifted at the same time with strong artistic instincts and capacities for the enjoyment of varied form, and light, and shade, in pursuit of which enjoyment his life is passed, as the lives of other men are for the most part, in the pursuit of what *they* also like, — be it honour, or money, or indolent pleasure.[21]

Ruskin even goes so far as to suggest that "the hunter of the picturesque" may not be altogether indifferent to the sufferings of "the victims or subjects of his picturesque fancies." His quest "will never really or seriously interfere with practical benevolence," and it may even lead "to a truer sympathy with the poor, and better understanding of the right ways of helping them."[22] Despite seeming contradictions, Ruskin's aesthetic judgments about picturesque art and the people it appealed to deserve attention for he was indeed the first really influential critic who, understanding this art form, gave it wide publicity in mid-Victorian England.

The taste of the Victorian reading public — if we can generalize so widely — was one which looked very favourably upon the survival of

20   *Works of John Ruskin*, VI, p. 16.
21   *Works of John Ruskin*, VI, p. 21.
22   *Works of John Ruskin*, VI, p. 22.

the cult of the picturesque. After all, it was a prevalent art form which they could appreciate; it was representational and, within wide limits, realistic; it was easily adaptable to all ranks of society—for the poor who crowded into theatres where they could gape at William Roxby Beverly's backdrop scenes for the pantomime, for the middle class who liked to pore over George Cattermole's sentimental engravings in *The Old Curiosity Shop*, or for the upper class who wanted to have oils and water colours by a William Callow or John Frederick Lewis as mementoes of their travels to the Continent and to the Middle East; it was, too, an art form that lent itself easily—as Jane Austen demonstrated—to conversation, for it required no very specialized terminology and certainly not much aesthetic experience.

It is reasonable then to expect that the conventions of the picturesque and the word itself should appear in nineteenth-century fiction. As early as 1822, J. L. Adolphus offered a definition of its role in fiction with illustrations from Scott's novels as substantiation: "The picturesque mode of narrative [he explained] impresses an event or situation on the fancy by a vivid representation of all the outward circumstances, as they unitedly offer themselves to the sense." Adolphus also noted how the "dramatic and picturesque are sometimes united with admirable effect."[23] His examples here could easily serve to illustrate what Scott meant by a "story told in a manner highly picturesque."

At the most obvious, the word itself was a signpost alerting the reader to special techniques of landscape description which the novelist intended to use. As such, it accomplished the same aim as did Henry Mackenzie's use of the name Salvator. Frequently, too, its appearance in fiction was evidence that novelists like Scott, Charlotte Brontë, Dickens, Thackeray, Lytton, Stevenson, Hardy, and James were themselves knowledgeable generally about art. Some of them, it should be remembered, could draw and paint, and several of them were intimate friends of artists like Wilkie, Landseer, Mulready, and Stanfield whose works were often notably picturesque. At the same time what the novelists saw of current art in public galleries, in the parlours of private homes, in illustrated travel books, and in reproductions in the popular *Art-Journal*, founded in 1838, was very much

23 [John Leycester Adolphus], *Letters to Richard Heber, Esq. M.P.* (London, 1822), pp. 141, 143. For his illustrations Adolphus quotes from the murder of Lord Menteith in *A Legend of Montrose* (chap. 23); from the account of Hatteraick's escape in *Guy Mannering* (chap. 33); and from the arrival of the mail-coach in *The Heart of Midlothian* (chap. 1).

the kind of art which simply supported what, in particular, Gilpin, Price, and Knight had said a half century earlier.

The introduction of the picturesque by the novelists into their fiction meant eventually that its meaning went well beyond a visual application. By a kind of metaphorical extension—noticeable in the hands particularly of Gilpin and Price—its range widened considerably so that the novelist and critic, too, applied it without explanation not only to the delineation of landscape but also to the appearance of characters in the novel, to their occupations, their speech, their actions, and even to the sounds they heard.

The use of the term to qualify the appearance of persons had, of course, a precedent in Gilpin's application of it to the unusual facial appearance of the elderly. His reasoning is that the "patriarchal head" is picturesque because it possesses "the *rough* touches of age,"[24] and these rough touches are analogous to the rough objects in landscape which are universally admired.[25] Gilpin makes the analogy again in his poem "On Landscape Painting" where the metaphor is extended from the aged oak to an old Briton:

> Let the oak
> Be elegant of form, that mantles o'er
> Thy shaven fore-ground: The rough forester
> Whose peel'd and wither'd boughs, and knarled trunk,
> Have stood the rage of many a winter's blast,
> Might ill such cultur'd scenes adorn. Not less
> Would an old Briton, rough with martial fears,
> And bearing stern defiance on his brow,
> Seem fitly stationed at a Gallic feast.

If propriety is to be maintained in sketches of such wild landscape, it is important, Gilpin notes, to exclude "the spade, / The plough, the patient angler with his rod" and to invite other guests "Wild as those scenes themselves, banditti fierce, / And gipsey-tribes." Likewise, he asserts that no ornament assists the woodland scene as well as an ox-team toiling up a forest glade dragging "the future keel / Of some high admiral." The aged human figure, the colourful banditti and gypsies, the waggoner with his ox-team seem more natural when they appear in a landscape that harmonizes with their activities.

On this subject Gilpin has the support of Price who widens the analogy: "Lastly," remarks Price, "among our own species, beggars, gypsies, such rough tattered figures as are merely picturesque, bear a

24   Gilpin, *Three Essays*, pp. 9-11.
25   Gilpin, *Three Essays*, p. 17.

close analogy, in all the qualities that make them so, to old hovels and mills, to the wild forest horse, and other objects of the same kind." For Price, even "more dignified characters, such as a Belisarius—a Marius in age and exile, have the same mixture of picturesqueness, and of decayed grandeur, as the venerable remains of the magnificence of past ages."[26]

It is important to realize that this picturesqueness is not always a static quality. Gilpin, as we have seen, thought that the human form was always "more picturesque in action, than at rest."[27] Such thinking may help account for how often nineteenth-century novelists thought of some occupations as being picturesque as, for example, Elizabeth Gaskell's comment on how becoming an employment spinning is:

> A woman stands at the great wool-wheel, one arm extended, the other holding the thread, her head thrown back to take in all the scope of her occupation; or if it is the lesser spinning-wheel for flax ... the pretty sound of the buzzing, whirring motion, the altitude of the spinner, foot and hand alike engaged in the business—the bunch of gay coloured ribbon that ties the bundle of flax on the rock—all make it into a picturesque piece of domestic business that may rival harp-playing any day for the amount of softness and grace which it calls out.[28]

The picturesque here attaches to a variety of details: the figure of the woman, the woman's stance, the great wool-wheel, the pretty sound of the spinning wheel, the gaily coloured ribbon, and the bundle of flax. Altogether these make "a picturesque piece of domestic business." Here the metaphor has no immediate link with landscape. The "domestic business" is picturesque because the occupation calls out "softness and grace," is unusual in the way that harp playing is unusual, and is in this novel a rural occupation in Sylvia Robson's home near Whitby and the rocks and cliffs of Yorkshire's coastline. What is picturesque about the details of the paragraph is so more by connotation than by denotation. Overall, however, these details make in the reader's mind a picture of an activity, both ancient and unusual, which would have aroused the interest of a Gilpin and a Price had they chanced to see it. It is doubtful, however, that it would have satisfied their criterion for the picturesque, for the term had acquired by 1863 (the date of the publication of *Sylvia's Lovers*) a broader

26 Price, *An Essay on the Picturesque* (1796), I, p. 76.
27 Gilpin, *Three Essays*, p. 12.
28 Elizabeth C. Gaskell, *Sylvia's Lovers* (London, 1909), p. 44.

application than it had had at the beginning of the century. They would have had to reason seriously as to whether the picture should be thought of as beautiful rather than as picturesque.

The extension of the word to apply to speech is one for which some evidence may be found in Richard Payne Knight's remarks of 1808 about the pastoral poems of Theocritus expressed in "the archaic simplicity of dialect, or with the native rusticity of imagery of Sicilian peasants."[29] Knight does not, however, say specifically that such language is picturesque. What is worth noting is his reference to "dialect" and to "the native rusticity of imagery," qualities so apparent in the speech of Thomas Hardy's rustics. But two years later Sir Uvedale Price is explicit: conversation is picturesque when its tone is witty, "full of unexpected turns, of flashes of light"; when it offered "singular, yet natural points of view"; when it struck out "such unthought-of agreements and contrasts; such combinations, so little obvious, yet never forced nor affected, that the attention cannot flag; but from the delight of what is passed, we eagerly listen for what is to come."[30] It is especially the "unexpected turns," the "unthought-of agreements and contrasts" that make us delight in Dickens's Sam Weller who, in his own language, "wos first pitched neck and crop into the world, to play at leap-frog with its troubles" (Pickwick Papers, chap. 16). Other illustrations come to mind. In 1879 Robert Louis Stevenson used the word to describe the spoken French of George Sand's companion at Lausson. "Whenever," says Stevenson, "he let slip a broad and picturesque phrase in patois, she would make him repeat it again and again till it was graven in her memory," presumably for use in her novel Le Marquis de Villemer (1860).[31] We recall, too, the German officers of the York Hussars in Hardy's The Trumpet Major (1880) "who swore the most picturesque foreign oaths" (chap. 10). Five years later in his novel, Marius the Epicurean, Walter Pater has Marius comment upon "the colloquial idiom" of Etruscan popular speech which "offered a thousand chance-tost gems of racy or picturesque expression, rejected or at least ungathered by what claimed to be classical Latin" (chap. 6). Not only were authors using the word in this sense but critics, too, applied it to speech which was vivid and dialectical as did a reviewer in Harper's New Monthly Magazine in March 1879. In The Return of the Native as in Far From

29   Knight, Analytical Enquiry, p. 190.
30   Price, Essays on the Picturesque (1810), I, pp. 341-43.
31   Robert Louis Stevenson, The Works of Robert Louis Stevenson, Tusitala Edition (London, 1924), XVII, p. 139.

the Madding Crowd, he noted that "dialect colloquies are reproduced with picturesque effect."[32]

This effect may owe as much to the pictorial quality of the dialect speech as it does to the novelty or strangeness of the diction. It is a quality which Wordsworth suggested belonged to "low and rustic life" where "the essential passions of the heart . . . speak a plainer and more emphatic language . . . and, consequently, may be . . . more forcibly communicated."[33] Certainly we are aware of the passionate force and the vividly pictorial quality of Maggie Steenson's words in *Redgauntlet* as she berates her husband Willie for his unwillingness to accept a crown from Fairford: "Ye will die," she pronounces, "the death of a cadger's powney, in a wreath of drift!" (Letter X). The application of the word "picturesque" to language seems plausible, too, when we think of Mrs. Poyser in *Adam Bede* who does not believe in restraining either her feelings or her words: "There's no pleasure i' living, if you're to be corked up for ever, and only dribble your mind out by the sly, like a leaky barrel" (chap. 32). A common characteristic of Hardy's "dialect colloquies" is that both the rustics and the readers hear and see at the same time, as happens through much of the conversation that takes place in the malthouse in *Far From the Madding Crowd*, where " 'tis blowed about from pillar to post quite common" that Gabriel Oak is a clever shepherd. Matthew Moon provides the evidence, verbally and visually (chap. 15). "We hear," Matthew remarks,

> 'that ye can make sun-dials, and prent folks' names upon their waggons almost like copper-plate, with beautiful flourishes, and great long tails. A excellent fine thing for ye to be such a clever man, shepherd. Joseph Poorgrass, used to prent to Farmer James Everdene's waggons before you came, and 'a could never mind which way to turn the J's and E's—could ye, Joseph?' Joseph shook his head to express how absolute was the fact that he couldn't. 'And so you used to do 'em the wrong way, like this, didn't ye, Joseph?' Matthew marked on the dusty floor with his whip-handle
> ꙇ A M Ǝ S .

What is picturesque belongs to the images of sun-dials, and Dorsetshire waggons with the owners' names inscribed with flourishes on their sides, and the contrast provided by the elegance of Gabriel's script compared with the "inside-out-like" look of Joseph Poorgrass's printing. "Almost like copper-plate," of course, suggests the engrav-

---

32 *Harper's New Monthly Magazine* 58 (March 1879), p. 627.
33 Wordsworth, "Preface" to *Lyrical Ballads* (1802).

ings that served as illustrations for the travel books of the time. The pictorial quality of this passage is unmistakable and certainly lends support to the reviewer's contention that Hardy's "dialect colloquies are reproduced with picturesque effect."

William Gilpin's assertions that "the human body will always be more picturesque in action, than at rest" and that an ox-train hauling a ship's keel makes a picturesque addition to a woodland scene help explain the extension of this aesthetic term to describe the action of some narratives. In 1783, and probably for years before that date, in his lectures at the University of Edinburgh, Hugh Blair advised historians to "study to render [their] narration interesting." An historian, he observed, should know when to dwell on events that are "considerable in their nature, or pregnant with consequences." It is, he went on to say, "by means of circumstances and particulars properly chosen, that a narration becomes interesting and affecting to the reader." This he described as "Historical Painting." And, in this kind of "picturesque descriptive Narration,"[34] he said, ancient historians like Livy and Tacitus excelled. Whether Sir Walter Scott had noted this observation or not, he, too, used the word "picturesque" to describe the quality of an historical narrative:

> I am highly flatterd [he wrote to Anna Seward] by your approbation of Cadyow Castle which is founded upon a fact in Scottish hist^y.—for which I referr you to the death of the Regent Murray as narrated in Robertsons history at the end of the I^st vol: where you will find the story told in a manner highly picturesque (*Letters*, I, pp. 163-64).

The story concerns the revenge which Hamilton of Bothwellhaugh took upon the Regent Murray for the death of his wife at the hands of the Regent's favourites. Waiting until the Regent was in Linlithgow in 1569, Hamilton, we read,

> took his stand in a wooden gallery, which had a window towards the street; spread a featherbed on the floor, to hinder the noise of his feet from being heard; hung up a black cloth behind him, that his shadow might not be observed from without; and after all this preparation, calmly awaited the Regent's approach, who had lodged during the night in a part of the town not far distant. Some indistinct information of the danger which threatened him had been conveyed to the Regent, and he paid so much regard to it, that he resolved to return by the same gate through which he had entered, and to fetch a compass round the town. But as the crowd

34   Hugh Blair, *Lectures on Rhetoric and Belles Lettres*, 2nd ed. (London, 1785), III, pp. 36-41.

about the gate was great, and he himself unacquainted with fear, he proceeded directly along the street; and, the throng of people obliging him to move very slowly, gave the assassin time to take so true an aim, that he shot him with a single bullet through the lower part of his belly, and killed the horse of a gentleman who rode on his other side. His followers instantly endeavoured to break into the house whence the blow had come, but they found the door strongly barricaded; and before it could be forced open, Hamilton had mounted a fleet horse, which stood ready for him at a back-passage, and was got far beyond their reach. The Regent died the same night of his wound.[35]

John Gibson Lockhart refers to this incident and says that he was with his father-in-law during the Christmas season of 1801 when the two of them visited the Hamilton estate on the banks of the Esk. Here, Lockhart tells us, the ruins of the old baronial castle inspired Sir Walter to write the ballad "Cadyow Castle," which appeared in Scott's *Minstrelsy* (February 1802). It was, Lockhart goes on to say, "especially interesting as the first in which he grapples with the world of picturesque incident unfolded in the authentic annals of Scotland."[36] Lockhart's use of the word "picturesque" in 1838 to qualify "incident" is as interesting as Scott's application of the word in 1802 to the facts surrounding the death of the Regent Murray. Both men, it should be noted, are using the word to describe a particular kind of narrative writing in which stress is upon vivid pictorial detail, exciting historical action, and the emotions of characters caught up in the rush of resulting circumstances. What is picturesque now extends well beyond the description of landscape and portrait. From its application to historical narrative, it was a fairly obvious course to fictional narrative. It was, for example, equally applicable to the adventures that befell Edward Waverley as he served by the side of the impetuous Fergus Mac-Ivor, known also as Vich Ian Vohr, or those that overtook David Balfour as he ran for his life with Alan Breck in *Kidnapped*, published more than seventy years after Scott's *Waverley*. "Picturesque incident," in fact, was an important element in fiction throughout much of the nineteenth century.

This extension of the meaning and application of the word "picturesque" was assured almost from its emergence as an aesthetic expression. In the first edition of *An Essay on the Picturesque* (1794), Uvedale Price remarked that the

35 William Robertson, *The History of Scotland During the Reigns of Queen Mary and of King James VI* (London, 1821), II, p. 204.

36 Lockhart, *Memoirs*, I, p. 318.

term (as we may judge from its etymology) is applied only to objects of sight; and that indeed in so confined a manner as to be supposed merely to have a reference to the art from which it is named. I am well convinced, however, that the name and reference only are limited and uncertain, and that the qualities which make objects picturesque are not only as distinct as those which make them beautiful or sublime, but are equally extended to all our sensations, by whatever organs they are received; and that music (though it appears like a solecism) may be as truly picturesque, according to the general principles of picturesqueness, as it may be beautiful or sublime, according to those of beauty or sublimity (pp. 39-40).

In this passage Price is extending the reference of what is picturesque not only to our sense of hearing but also to "all our sensations, by whatever organs they are received." Some support for Price's contention may be found in Hugh Blair's remarks on "figurative language" where he argues that figures "exhibit the object, on which they are employed, in a picturesque form; they can render an abstract conception, in some degree, an object of sense." Without providing evidence, Blair states that American and Indian languages are "bold, picturesque, and metaphorical; full of strong allusions to sensible qualities."[37] The tremendous popularity which Blair's *Lectures on Rhetoric and Belles Lettres* (1783) enjoyed may well account for the early extension of the meaning of "picturesque" to senses other than the purely visual. In 1794, for example, the year *An Essay on the Picturesque* appeared, Ann Radcliffe used the word to refer to a variety of sounds. When Emily St. Aubert awoke, after her first night's rest at La Voisin's cottage, she opened her casement to look outside: "The scene was filled with that cheering freshness, which seems to breathe the very spirit of health, and she heard only sweet and *picturesque* sounds, if such an expression may be allowed—the matin-bell of a distant convent, the faint murmur of the sea-waves, the song of birds, and the far-off low of cattle."[38] Ann Radcliffe's phrase "if such an expression may be allowed" suggests the novelty of this usage. But was she perhaps recalling Blair's enthusiastic response to Milton's "Il Penseroso" where "all is picturesque" including "the sound of the curfew bell heard distant"?[39] For novelists in the next century this usage, whatever its origin, was no longer a novelty, and they seldom signposted their intention. We remember Dickens's description in

37   Blair, *Lectures on Rhetoric*, I, pp. 358-63.
38   Ann Radcliffe, *The Mysteries of Udolpho* (London, 1966), p. 73.
39   Blair, *Lectures on Rhetoric*, III, p. 165.

The Old Curiosity Shop of Little Nell's "delicious journey" inside the stage-waggon:

> listening to the tinkling of the horses' bells, the occasional smack-
> ing of the carter's whip, the smooth rolling of the great broad
> wheels, the rattle of the harness, the cheery good-nights of passing
> travellers jogging past on little short-stepped horses . . . till one fell
> asleep! . . . and the slow waking up, and finding one's self staring
> out through the breezy curtain half-opened in the front, far up into
> the cold bright sky with its countless stars, and downward at the
> driver's lantern dancing on like its namesake Jack of the swamps
> and marshes, and sideways at the dark grim trees, and forward at the
> long bare road rising up, up, up, until it stopped abruptly at a sharp
> high ridge as if there were no more road, and all beyond was sky
> (chap. 46).

In a passage like this, picturesque sound, sight, action, and landscape all come together pictorially as a pleasing emotional experience ris-ing out of Dickens's immediate comprehension of the outside world, an experience which contrasts sharply with the "dense, dark, misera-ble haunts of labour," which Nell and her grandfather have just left behind.

One of the first Englishmen to understand and emphasize the importance of this sort of aesthetic feeling was Arthur Hallam[40] who saw it as the triumph of sensation over reflection. For him, "this powerful tendency of imagination to a life of immediate sympathy with the external universe, is not nearly so subject to false views of art as the opposite disposition of purely intellectual contemplation."[41] Hence Hallam praised Tennyson's *Poems, Chiefly Lyrical* (1830) for the poet's "vivid, picturesque delineation of objects, and the peculiar skill with which he holds all of them *fused* . . . in a medium of strong emotion."[42] The picturesque for Hallam meant a direct apprehension of nature through "the simple exertions of eye and ear,"[43] an emphasis upon locality, the creation of distinct and accurate images, and the bringing of variety into a harmonious whole. The music of the poet's language, he thinks, may be analogous to "the effects of Venetian colouring."[44] What Titian can do by tints, Petrarch does by tones. Alternatively, what a John Crome or a George Morland does in his

---

40 Hallam's contribution was given scholarly attention by H. M. McLuhan in an essay, "Tennyson and Picturesque Poetry," in *Essays in Criticism* 1, no. 3 (1951), pp. 262-82.

41 *The Writings of Arthur Hallam*, ed. by T. H. Vail Motter (London, 1943), p. 186.

42 *Arthur Hallam*, p. 192.

43 *Arthur Hallam*, p. 186.

44 *Arthur Hallam*, p. 195.

painting of old buildings, Tennyson does in the first stanza of "Mariana":

> With blackest moss the flower-plots
>   Were thickly crusted, one and all;
> The rusted nails fell from the knots
>   That held the pear to the gable-wall.
> The broken sheds look'd sad and strange:
>   Unlifted was the clinking latch;
>   Weeded and worn the ancient thatch
> Upon the lonely moated grange.
>   She only said, "My life is dreary,
>   He cometh not," she said;
>   She said, "I am aweary, aweary,
>   I would that I were dead!"

The picturesque details of an old cottage are here in the moss-crusted flower-plots, the knots that held the espaliered pear to the cottage wall, the ruinous sheds, the "ancient thatch," and the "lonely moated grange." But these images serve a purpose beyond what is merely visual for they represent or support the mood of weariness stressed in the last four lines. Sensation, which Hallam says marks "the highest species of poetry," and not reflection,[45] is the quality that gives meaning to "Mariana."

The importance of "visible forms" rooted in "daily life and experience" and the role Hallam gives to association in the poetic process remind us of how the poet's way and the painter's way illumine each other. The aesthetic history of this illumination requires us to give credit to the contribution made by picturesque vision which Christopher Hussey defined as "the capacity for seeing nature with a painter's eye."[46] One hundred and fifty years earlier, Richard Payne Knight described it as "the beauty of various tints and forms happily blended, without rule or symmetry, and rendered venerable by those imposing marks of antiquity."[47] It was, as we have noted, Knight's separation of the object viewed and the associations that belonged to it from its "various tints and forms" which distinguished his aesthetic from that of Price or Gilpin and led Christopher Hussey to assert that "the picturesque can . . . be seen to provide the first step in the movement towards abstract aesthetic values" because it provides "the earliest means for perceiving visual qualities in nature."[48]

45 *Arthur Hallam*, pp. 184-85.
46 Hussey, *The Picturesque*, p. 64.
47 Knight, *Analytical Enquiry*, p. 161.
48 Hussey, *The Picturesque*, p. 17.

But Knight never took a further step. It was one which had to wait in Britain until the end of the nineteenth century when the Pre-Raphaelites were accepted, the late Turners widely admired, and the Impressionists sought after by collectors. In the meantime, significantly, it was the search for what was picturesque in the world round about them that attracted so many of Britain's artists. If it was not great art, it was popular art which, despite the limits of its aesthetic, had its roots deep in the soil of the country from which it drew both its reality and its enduring favour with the people.

The novelists, therefore, found that the picturesque offered a very tempting and sensible approach whereby they could make their readers *see* and even *feel* what they wanted them to see and feel. As so many of their readers were quite familiar with the conventions of this aesthetic, really competent novelists had no need to erect "picturesque" signposts in their prose. Indeed, it was wise to use the word sparingly for the more sophisticated of their readers had laughed all too heartily at the adventures of the inept Dr. Syntax in search of picturesque parades, tombs, guideposts, ruins, and asses (Pl. 20). But despite the follies of the worthy doctor, novelists as far apart in craft and aim as Sir Walter Scott and Henry James[49] found the conventions of the picturesque very helpful as they fashioned their fictional landscapes, characters, and dramatic actions.

49 See William F. Hall, "Henry James and the Picturesque Mode," in *English Studies in Canada* 1 (Fall 1975), pp. 326-43. See also Margaret Drabble who describes James as "perhaps the most evocative of what one might call the neo-picturesque writers" in *A Writer's Britain: Landscape in Literature* (London, 1979), p. 134. Her two chapters, "The Pastoral Vision" and "Landscape as Art" make frequent reference to the picturesque.

Chapter 3

Waverley and the "Scotch Novels"[1]

> The strong contrast produced by the opposition of ancient
> manners to those which are gradually subduing them,
> affords the lights and shadows necessary to give effect to a
> fictitious narrative.
>
> Sir Walter Scott, *The Fortunes of Nigel*

From his *Journal*, letters, and novels, Sir Walter Scott provides evidence that he owed much to the theory and practice of the picturesque. Although he regretted his inability to analyse landscape as a painter could, he said that few men delighted more in the "general effect" of picturesque scenery than he did.[2] If its practice was open to the charge of superficiality, that may have been a risk that Scott was willing to assume: "Better a superficial book which brings well and strikingly together the known and acknowledged facts than a dull boring narrative."[3] As it turned out, Scott's acceptance of the picturesque provided a very natural ingredient for his narrative, blending harmoniously into place both character and incident.

In his use of it, Scott does not make the mistake—which he imputes to Mrs. Radcliffe—of fashioning characters "entirely subor-

---

1 I am indebted to the Association for Scottish Literary Studies for permission to use material in the *Waverley* section of this chapter, which was published in 1983 in *Scott and His Influence*, ed. by J. H. Alexander and David Hewitt.
2 Lockhart, *Memoirs*, I, p. 42.
3 Sir Walter Scott, *The Journal of Sir Walter Scott*, ed. by W. E. K. Anderson (Oxford, 1972), p. 45.

dinate to the scenes in which they are placed."[4] Landscape and character in poetry, as he told James Dusautoy (May 6, 1811), should be rightly proportioned: "There is [he wrote] a perspective in poetry, as well as in painting, by which I mean the art of keeping your landscape, with its attributes, in harmony with your principal figures, and reserving your force of detailed expression for what you mean shall be the most prominent in your picture."[5] That Scott had such advice ready for a correspondent years before *Waverley* appeared helps explain why this novel and other "Scotch novels," written between 1814 and 1824, make such good use of picturesque conventions and why, too, his fictional world is so readily visualized by his readers.

Scott's close acquaintance with these conventions almost certainly dates from his days at university perhaps while listening to the "striking and impressive eloquence" of Dugald Stewart, his professor of moral philosophy.[6] Philosophically, he understood the mechanism of the principles of the association of ideas which William Gilpin, Sir Uvedale Price, and Richard Payne Knight employed in elaborating their own theories of the picturesque. Something of Sir Walter's attitude to these principles is apparent when he attempts a defense of his preference for ancient hymns of the Catholic Church: "This is [he asserts], probably, all referable to the association of ideas —that is, if the 'association of ideas' continues to be the universal pick-lock of all metaphysical difficulties, as it was when I studied moral philosophy—or to any other more fashionable universal solvent which may have succeeded to it in reputation."[7] But this attitude towards "the universal pick-lock" seems to have made no difference to Sir Walter's feeling for picturesque scenery. And what he could not accomplish with a brush, he was able to do with his pen and words.

As *Waverley or 'Tis Sixty Years Since* is the first, and for many, the finest of Scott's novels, it is well to look at it in some detail for evidence as to how Scott often views his Scotland and its people "sixty years since." The best approach is through his hero, Edward Waverley.

4   Sir Walter Scott, *Miscellaneous Prose Works of Sir Walter Scott* (Edinburgh, 1848), III, pp. 359-60.
5   Sir Walter Scott, *The Letters of Sir Walter Scott, 1808-1811*, ed. by H. J. C. Grierson (London, 1932), II, p. 279. See also Marian Cusac's reference and comment on this letter in *Narrative Structure in the Novels of Sir Walter Scott* (The Hague, 1969), p. 103.
6   Lockhart, *Memoirs*, I, p. 36.
7   Lockhart, *Memoirs*, II, p. 298.

With his warm and vivid imagination, nourished so well upon the course of desultory reading that he had engaged in at his uncle's home, Edward Waverley's tastes from the beginning lean to picturesque adventure and scenery. His ideal world is one that easily encompasses both the deeds of the ancestral Crusader, Wilibert, and the "pristine and savage character" of Waverley-Chase where Edward can find "a moss-grown Gothic monument" and a long, ill-cared-for avenue that opens suddenly upon Mirkwood Mere in the midst of which stood a lonely tower on a rock, once the family refuge during the War of the Roses. Such a setting fused nicely with the "many picturesque and interesting passages [he had read] from . . . old historical chronicles" (*Waverley*, chap. 3) whose "useless imagery and emblems" (chap. 4), however, did little to prepare the young man for the real world he was about to enter.

And so it happened that, without experience in either love or war, the young Edward Waverley leaves the unreality of Waverley-Honour and Sir Everard's Jacobite leanings to accept the sudden and, for him, rather exceptional responsibilities attached to a captaincy in Gardiner's regiment of dragoons, then stationed in Dundee, where the author engages to find for him "a more picturesque and romantic country" (chap. 5). After a short period of basic training, a leave of absence frees Edward from the rather carking demands of regimental life so that he is able to visit his uncle's old friend, the Baron of Bradwardine, at Tully-Veolan on the edge of the highlands of Perthshire, whose mountains "frowned defiance over the more level country."

Well mounted on a handsome charger, Edward finds his way through the squalor of Tully-Veolan's only street, a squalor made somewhat acceptable by the pleasing forms of three or four village girls whose dress and braided hair might have met the challenge of a "lover of the picturesque" were it not for their overall need for soap. The village is depressing: idle barking dogs, half-naked children, decrepit old people with eyes "bleared with age and smoke," and miserable huts that housed starved cows and galled horses.

The village is obviously not a part of Edward's ideal world. To find that, he must pass through the gates leading into the Parks of Tully-Veolan where he sees an arch with battlements and weathered stone, an avenue of ancient chestnuts and sycamores, high walls overgrown with climbers, and a road that is little more than a footpath. Through the lower gate Edward notices, half-hidden by the trees of the avenue, the high steep roofs and narrow gables of the mansion, with lines indented into steps, and corners decorated with small turrets. One of the folding leaves of the lower gate was open, and as the sun shone full into the court behind, a long line of brilliancy was flung upon the aperture up the dark and gloomy avenue. It was one of those effects which a painter loves to represent (chap. 8).

The scene enables Edward to forget "the misery and dirt of the hamlet he had left behind."

Now his eyes rest upon the architectural oddities of the Baron's residence, the bartizans of which resembled more "a pepper-box than a Gothic watch-tower." Beyond the battlemented wall is the court with its "tun-bellied pigeon house" and a fountain displaying a huge stone bear whose counterparts of various dimensions adorned the gates and the mansion reminding the visitor constantly of the ancient family motto, "Bewar the Bar." The picturesqueness of the mansion elicits Edward's approval for it "maintained the monastic illusions of his fancy." In his portrayal of Edward Waverley, here and throughout the novel, the concrete qualities of Scott's description maintain a credible balance between the illusions that grip his hero and the reality that surrounds him. What is picturesque about character or landscape is seldom open to the objection that it is either superficial or sentimental. The Bradwardine house and garden seem as real as some of those that still exist in Scotland today.

Although the garden is laid out in terraces, these had had their formality broken by fruit trees, a "profusion of flowers," and evergreens cut into grotesque forms. The brook which forms a boundary to the garden "leapt in tumult" over a dam at the garden's end to disappear noisily into "a deep and wooded dell, from the copse of which arose a massive, but ruinous tower" (chap. 9). It is the kind of garden which Sir Uvedale Price might have found attractive despite its formal origins because, as he said, old gardens like old houses grow picturesque from neglect and from "the breaks and interruptions that arise from an irregular mixture of vegetation."[8]

Two of the inhabitants of the mansion are as picturesque as their surroundings. David Gellatley's "oddity" is noticeable at once. His face has a "wild, unsettled, irregular expression."

His gait was as singular as his gestures, for at times he hopped with great perseverance on the right foot, then exchanged that supporter

8   Price, *Essays* (1798), II, pp. 136-37.

> to advance in the same manner on the left, and then putting his feet close together, he hopped upon both at once. His attire, also, was antiquated and extravagant. It consisted in a sort of grey jerkin, with scarlet cuffs and slashed sleeves, showing a scarlet lining; the other parts of the dress corresponded in colour, not forgetting a pair of scarlet stockings, and a scarlet bonnet, proudly surmounted with a turkey's feather (chap. 9).

Except for his musical ability and general tidiness, David is an early version of Barnaby Rudge.

Equally picturesque in appearance, yet credible, is the Baron of Bradwardine. On in years, gaunt and bearded, swarthy and hollow-eyed—a kind of latter-day Don Quixote—he strides vigorously down the garden to greet Sir Everard's nephew. Constant exercise has made his every muscle "as tough as whipcord." At home he dresses carelessly "more like a Frenchman than an Englishman." But clattering along in huge jack-boots, dressed for a morning of sport and humming a French song, he becomes even more striking:

> mounted on an active and well-managed horse, and seated on a demi-pique saddle, with deep housings to agree with his livery, [he] was no bad representative of the old school. His light-coloured embroidered coat, and superbly barred waistcoat, his brigadier wig, surmounted by a small gold-laced cocked-hat, completed his personal costume (chap. 13).

His "language and habits were as heterogeneous as his external appearance." Waverley is captivated by this man whom he considered "a singular and interesting character, gifted with a memory containing a curious register of ancient and modern anecdotes" (chap. 13). Here it is interesting how, for Waverley, the implied epithet "picturesque" seems transferable from the Baron's external appearance to his character. It is an early example of how the meaning of the word began to extend beyond its purely visual application. The Baron's picturesque reality fits nicely into the world of Edward's illusions.

Although Rose Bradwardine lacks any striking qualities of appearance or character, the same cannot be said of the prospect from her Gothic balcony which extended

> down a wooded glen, where the small river was sometimes visible, sometimes hidden in copse. The eye might be delayed by a desire to rest on the rocks, which here and there rose from the dell with massive or spiry fronts, or it might dwell on the noble, though ruined tower, which was here beheld in all its dignity, frowning from a promontory over the river. To the left were seen two or three cottages, a part of the village; the brow of the hill concealed the others. The glen, or dell, was terminated by a sheet of water, called

Loch-Veolan, into which the brook discharged itself, and which now glistened in the western sun. The distant country seemed open and varied in surface, though not wooded; and there was nothing to interrupt the view until the scene was bounded by a ridge of distant and blue hills (chap. 13).

It is a scene which, save for the immediate foreground, resembles closely the outline of the print which William Gilpin used (facing page 19) in his *Three Essays* to illustrate the importance of broken lines in a landscape (Pl. 21). Scott's scene painting has its purpose because to her Gothic balcony Rose orders coffee for Edward and her father, whose mind being stimulated by the associations of the nearby crag, told stories of his family and of Scottish history, asked Rose to sing a song, and insisted she tell the story of Janet Gellatley that is so important later on to the safety of both Edward and the Baron.

Edward's penchant for romantic adventure is further whetted, some weeks later, when a tearful Rose announces news of a Highland raid and the loss of her father's milch cows. This action brings Fergus Mac-Ivor's ambassador, Evan Dhu Maccombich, to Tully-Veolan; he is the man who is to die so bravely at Carlisle for high treason. Evan is the first Highlander that Edward has seen in full costume. He is

a stout, dark, young man, of low stature, the ample folds of whose plaid added to the appearance of strength which his person exhibited. The short kilt, or petticoat, showed his sinewy and clean-made limbs; the goat-skin purse, flanked by the usual defenses, a dirk and steel-wrought pistol, hung before him; his bonnet had a short feather . . . a broadsword dangled by his side, a target hung upon his shoulder, and a long Spanish fowling-piece occupied one of his hands (chap. 16).

Evan's appearance is picturesque to Edward just as such a person was to William Gilpin who asserted that the form of the plaid in fine or wet weather made "elegant drapery" upon the Highlander especially when he was armed with his pistols and broadsword. Although Gilpin disliked the bonnet because it resembled a "beefeater's cap," he admitted that, when it was "adorned with a plume of feathers," it became "extremely picturesque."[9]

Again, it is important to stress how essential the picturesque is to the narrative. It has done much to shape Edward's romantic temperament and make him susceptible to the charm of Tully-Veolan, a kind of halfway house between Waverley-Honour and the frowning fastnesses of Perthshire. Once Edward meets the kilted Evan Dhu, his

9 Gilpin, *High-Lands of Scotland*, II, pp. 137-38.

curiosity is so aroused by his appearance and poise that he decides to return with Evan so that he can become better acquainted "with the customs and scenery of the Highlands." Setting, character, and plot become interdependent in a meaningful way largely because of Edward's curiosity and deep-seated interest in what is picturesque. It is an illustration of what Christopher Hussey meant when he said that "Walter Scott accepted the picturesque and fused it into his romances together with all their other ingredients."[10]

The narrative moves forward with Waverley and Evan as they approach Donald Bean Lean's robber hideout with its Burkean sublimities: huge dark crags, indistinct mountains, gorges, vast black bogs, its awful contrasts—"all calculated to inspire terror" and to prepare Waverley "to meet a stern, gigantic, ferocious figure, such as Salvator would have chosen to be the central object of a group of banditti" (chap. 17). The one concession to the picturesque lies in the rustic grace and gypsy-like appearance of the "little wild mountaineer," Alice, daughter of the cateran, Donald Bean Lean; she is to become an agent in the plot.

But Waverley's progress through the aesthetic subdivisions of popular eighteenth-century art is beset by awkward questions that lead to danger. The pleasures of the picturesque give way increasingly to the terrors of the sublime. Ahead lies the fatal Stewart cause exemplified by the schemes of Fergus Mac-Ivor and the illusory ideals held so tenaciously by his sister Flora, with whom Waverley falls in love. Gardiner's regiment is soon put out of mind as is the embarrassing reason for Edward's journey to Glennaquoich—the theft of the Baron's milch cows, which were probably not much less starved than the cows of his villagers.

At Glennaquoich, Edward is greatly taken by the grace and bearing of the Chief of the Mac-Ivors in tartan trews and bonnet topped by an eagle's feather, who has gathered a hundred wild Highlanders in arms and full dress for the occasion. Dinner, accompanied by shrilling bagpipes, is in a baronial-type hall that shelters the poetically extravagant family bard, Mac-Murrough. The bard's recital in Gaelic sends Waverley off to Flora Mac-Ivor for a translation of it while Vich Ian Vohr entertains his clansmen. Waverley is impressed by Flora's beauty and becomes an easy mark for the fanatic loyalty burning in her attractive bosom. Flora, like an actress, chooses the time and place for her translation of Mac-Murrough's verses with dramatic aptness.

10   Hussey, *The Picturesque*, p. 242.

Her theatricality has been often singled out as a failure on Scott's part. Here, as Maria Edgeworth complained, Scott's control of picturesque convention slipped to sentimentality: "The appearance of Flora and her harp was too much like a common heroine; she should be far above all stage effect or novelist's trick."[11] As a means, however, of captivating Edward, Flora's song, with its accompaniments of music and scenery, is a success because it makes so complete an overture to his attraction for what is picturesque. Seeing only the surface of things, Edward tends to forget the deep and dangerous political currents that swirl about him. For Edward, the Highland setting has been cunningly contrived to appeal to the sort of person he really is and to lead him ever further from Gardiner's dragoons into the Jacobite net.

Prey to Flora's beauty and charm, Edward decides to spend three weeks at Glennaquoich to be near her and also attend a great stag hunt, where again the undertones of rebellion are heard but where Edward sees only the movement of the clansmen "bound on a distant expedition" and admires the pictorial effect as they are seen

> winding up the hills, or descending the passes which led to the scene of action, the sound of their bagpipes dying upon the ear. Others made still a moving picture upon the narrow plain, forming various changeful groups, their feathers and loose plaids waving in the morning breeze, and their arms glittering in the rising sun (chap. 24).

Edward's interest in the picturesqueness of the Jacobite clans is a dangerous one in view of his ever-worsening relations with Colonel Gardiner whose letters, having been intercepted by Donald Bean Lean, eventually led to Edward's resigning his commission, a step which left him free to join the insurgents and so become a traitor.

Even Flora's rejection of his love is not enough to rouse him to his proper senses. Rather, it is news from Rose Bradwardine that convinces him to go to Edinburgh to clear his name of any charge of disloyalty. Such a decision, however, places the author in a rather awkward position with respect to some of his female readers, more interested in Edward's devotion to Flora than in the niceties of his conduct as a Hanoverian officer. To explain the effect of absence upon his hero's feelings to these readers, Scott resorts to picturesque theory:

> Distance, in truth, produces in idea the same effect as in real perspective. Objects are softened, and rounded, and rendered doubly graceful; the harsher and more ordinary points of character are

---

11 Lockhart, *Memoirs*, II, p. 538.

mellowed down, and those by which it is remembered are the more striking outlines that mark sublimity, grace, or beauty. There are mists, too, in the mental, as well as the natural horizon, to conceal what is less pleasing in distant objects, and there are happy lights, to stream in full glory upon those points which can profit by brilliant illumination (chap. 29).

This aesthetic philosophizing resembles closely that which Gilpin applied to artificial objects introduced into woodland scenery: "Distance, no doubt, hides many defects; and many an object may appear well in a remove, which brought nearer, would disgust the eye" (*Forest Scenery*, I, p. 232). Fortunately, for Waverley, travel towards Edinburgh, under the escort of Habakkuk Gilfillan, leads him into such a maze of adventure that his ill-conceived love for Flora is gradually eroded away. Edinburgh, under Jacobite siege, is picturesquely described, while Edward, like a hero in a romance, gives his allegiance to Charles Edward Stewart who, in turn, gives Edward his own "genuine Andrea Ferrara."

Throughout this succession of exciting events, Scott manages always to keep Waverley's conflicting passions[12] before his reader. Once he has renounced his allegiance to the Hanoverians, Waverley finds new difficulties in his way. He is worried by the vacillating temper and impetuousness of Fergus Mac-Ivor. Of much greater concern, however, is his growing awareness of the risks the Jacobites were incurring. He feels "damped and astonished at the daring attempt of a body not then exceeding four thousand men, and of whom not above half the number at the utmost, were armed, to change the fate, and alter the dynasty, of the British kingdoms" (chap. 44). But for a time the fortunes of war are with the Jacobites. Prestonpans gives Scott an opportunity to present a stirring account of battle, which he said he could never get from a soldier because his "mind is too much upon the *tactique* to regard the picturesque" (*Letters*, II, p. 405).

For Edward Waverley, however, the picturesqueness of the cause diminishes as he gazes on the ghastly features of Houghton, his former troop sergeant, and later fades quite away as he looks into the eyes of the dying Colonel Gardiner. The absurd concerns — antiquarian as they are — of the Baron Bradwardine for the boots of the King himself must give way before the straightforward talk of Ed-

12   In his essay "Scott's Achievement as a Novelist (1951)," David Daiches asserts that "the essence of *Waverley* is the way in which the conflicting claims of the two worlds impinge on the titular hero." In D. D. Devlin, ed., *Walter Scott, Modern Judgements* (London, 1968), p. 41.

ward's prisoner, Colonel Talbot, who, in summing up Waverley's adventures, says that he has been "trepanned into the service of this Italian knight-errant by a few civil speeches from him, and one or two of his Highland recruiting sergeants" (chap. 51).

Scott's ability to make Waverley realize gradually his true position in the midst of much that Scott himself regarded as picturesque history is an interesting illustration of his creative power. With considerable skill he undermines Waverley's Jacobite attachments and makes him recognize his own delusion. The reader follows the process: the reception of the long-delayed letters from his commanding officer; the revelations of John Hodges; the loss of his seal to the scheming cateran, John Bean Lean; the political, self-serving that motivated Fergus Mac-Ivor; the petty quarrelling within the Chevalier's court; and, in another direction, the unwillingness of Flora Mac-Ivor to reciprocate his love. Indeed, it is Flora who gives the reader the key to much that happens to Waverley in war: "High and perilous enterprise [she maintains] is not Waverley's forte. He would never have been his celebrated ancestor, Sir Nigel, but only Sir Nigel's eulogist and poet" (chap. 52).

From now on the rebellion loses its picturesque character for the hero. The Highlanders' decision at Derby to retreat is the end of "their towering hopes." Fergus's advice now to the stunned Waverley is that he should desert, take Rose Bradwardine as his wife, and give his protection to Flora. During the disastrous night attack at Clifton, Fergus and Evan Dhu Maccombich are taken prisoner, and Edward is cut off from the retreating Jacobites and forced to seek refuge in the Jopson house. It is his opportunity to desert, which he does on the grounds that it is not possible to rejoin the fleeing Highlanders. Later, to Colonel Talbot in London, he confesses that he is "heartily sick of the trade of war." And it proves easy for him consequently to retreat into the sort of person he was when he left Waverley-Honour to serve with Gardiner's dragoons.

The adventures that are left to Waverley occur after Falkirk and Culloden, as he seeks the hand of Rose Bradwardine, who is now safe at Duchran. From Edinburgh to Tully-Veolan, Waverley's view of the aftermath of war is no longer picturesque: "Broken carriages, dead horses, unroofed cottages, trees felled for palisades, and bridges destroyed, or only partially repaired—all indicated the movements of hostile armies" (chap. 63). The Bradwardine house has been sacked by the King's troops. What had been picturesque is so no longer; Scott's description of the ruined and smoke-blackened remains is effective just because it contrasts so dramatically with Edward's first view of Tully-Veolan's main residence:

> One half of the gate, entirely destroyed ... the other swung uselessly upon its loosened hinges. The battlements above the gate were broken ... and the carved Bears ... lay among the rubbish. The avenue was cruelly wasted ... the courtyard ... had been sacked ... the stables and out-houses were totally consumed. The towers and pinnacles of the main building were scorched and blackened; the pavement of the court broken and shattered; the doors torn down entirely, or hanging by a single hinge; the windows dashed in and demolished; and the court strewed with articles of furniture broken into fragments. ... The fountain was demolished. ... The whole tribe of Bears, large and small, had experienced as little favour as those at the head of the avenue; and one or two of the family pictures, which seemed to have served as targets for the soldiers, lay on the ground in tatters (chap. 63).

It is with real sadness that Waverley looks at this destruction. Rose's little balcony, from which some brief months before he had viewed the prospect, had been looted and wrecked. David Gellatley's "a dead and gane—a dead and gane" is, if not literally true, a good description of the desolation that surrounds him, to which the Baron (himself a fugitive sheltered by old Janet) adds the since so-often quoted *Fuimus Troes* that Scott's vernacular has rendered so effectively: "And there's the end of an auld sang."

These are the ruins which time has had no chance to render picturesque; these are the raw wounds of war on which the wily and realistic Baillie Macwheeble makes perhaps the most telling comment: "For my part, I never wish to see a kilt in the country again, nor a red-coat, nor a gun, for that matter, unless it were to shoot a paitrick:—they're a' tarr'd with ae stick" (chap. 66).

But this for Waverley is not yet the end of the Forty-five. For him it takes place in Carlisle, where he meets Flora once more as she makes the winding-sheet for her brother and where he hears the death penalty pronounced upon Fergus who had thrown "for life or death, a coronet or a coffin." Here in the court room he listens to the misguided but heroic Evan Dhu Maccombich make clear to his judge and his enemies how little they know of "the heart of a Hielandman, nor the honour of a gentleman." But it is to no avail. The picturesqueness of the Forty-five as an heroic adventure ends forever as Edward leaves Carlisle, where the grisly heads of Fergus and Evan remain "ower the Scotch yate, as they ca' it."

But the horrified Waverley does recover, and we have the metaphor of landscape painting to assist our understanding: "The picture which he drew for her [Rose Bradwardine's] benefit he gradually familiarized to his own mind; and his next letters were more cheerful, and referred to the prospects of peace and happiness which lay before them" (chap. 70). These prospects have eventually their picturesque side. In a miraculously short time, Waverley with his bride Rose is back at Tully-Veolan, where the Baron of Bradwardine—again the owner of the estate—is so astonished by the change that greets him that he says he can almost believe in brownies and fairies. His mansion has been quite restored to its former picturesqueness:

> excepting that the heavy stables ... were replaced by buildings of a lighter and more picturesque appearance, all seemed as much as possible restored to the state in which he had left it when he assumed arms some months before. The pigeon-house was replenished; the fountain played with its usual activity; and not only the Bear who predominated over its basin, but all the other Bears whatsoever, were replaced on their several stations ... the house itself had been thoroughly repaired, as well as the gardens, with the strictest attention to maintain the original character of both (chap. 71).

In the dining room, however, there is an addition. For here, in a "large and spirited painting," visitors see Fergus Mac-Ivor and Edward Waverley in Highland dress. In the painting, as part of the background, the visitors also see the clans descending a "wild, rocky, and mountainous pass." Beside this picturesque portrait hangs the Pretender's Andrea Ferrara and the other weapons that Waverley had borne in the cause. Tears are in the Baron's eyes as he looks at the painting that must always remind him of the glorious days of the Forty-five. At the same moment his delight becomes even more as Alexander ab Alexandro places in his hands "the celebrated cup of Saint Duthac, the Blessed Bear of Bradwardine."

Picturesqueness has been restored to the house of Tully-Veolan. From now on at its centre is a harmless nostalgia kept alive by the trappings of pictures, bits of plaid, and claymores as decorative wall pieces and, of course, the Baron's unending antiquarian observations. Waverley, the hero, is back where he began, little changed[13] despite his experiences with the loyal folk of "the old leaven." Was this why Scott once spoke of him as a "sneaking piece of imbecility" (*Letters*, III, p. 478)? Like the sound of his name, his actions bear "little of good

13   See Donald Davie's comment "Waverley (1961)," in *Walter Scott, Modern Judgements*, p. 90.

or evil" (chap. 1). His has been a superficial life. Even Evan Dhu Maccombich sheds an influence we admire beyond anything that Waverley can show. Yet Edward is on the winning side at last and will, as he
grows older, like his creator at Abbotsford, surround himself with the
picturesque and sentimental embellishments of the "auld sang." For
this opinion, we have Flora Mac-Ivor's support. Waverley, she noted,
would be most at home "in the quiet circle of domestic happiness,
lettered indolence, and elegant enjoyments" of Waverley-Honour.
Undoubtedly at Tully-Veolan he would also incorporate the same
changes and adopt the same attitudes as Flora predicts he would have
at Waverley-Honour:

> refit the old library in the most exquisite Gothic taste, and garnish
> its shelves with the rarest and most valuable volumes . . . and draw
> plans and landscapes, and write verses, and rear temples, and dig
> grottoes;—and . . . stand in a clear summer night in the colonnade
> before the hall, and gaze on the deer as they stray in the moonlight,
> or lie shadowed by the boughs of the huge old fantastic oaks;—
> and . . . repeat verses to his beautiful wife, who will hang upon his
> arm;—and . . . be a happy man (chap. 52).

For Edward Waverley, the dénouement of his active life is in one sense
a retreat from a hopeless military cause to the reality of the benefits of
the Act of Union of 1707; in another, it is a retreat from commitment to
service to the sentiment and safety of picturesque vision.

Fused as it is so closely with the narrative structure of this novel,
the picturesque element is significant. It affords Scott an effective
pictorial method whereby he can recapture the outward show of the
1745 insurrection and at the same time bring his hero by virtue of his
impractical upbringing into the rebellion which, as Scott describes it,
is a real affair of men and arms played out on a real landscape that
lends itself admirably to pictorial description. This realism tempers
considerably the romance giving it both force and credibility. As Scott
put it, "the most romantic parts of this narrative are precisely those
which have a foundation in fact" (chap. 72). *Waverley* is a fond
backward look at something which the Act of Union put an end to for
all time.

Scott's attitude to this change is admirably summed up by David
Daiches:

> in the end, with a sigh and a lingering last look, Scott withdraws
> from the picturesque. The picturesque is not enough to build a
> civilization on. That is what Scott's greatest novels are saying. He is

saying that civilization needs the picturesque, but the picturesque is not enough.[14]

Yet in *Waverley*, this withdrawal—if it is noticed at all—is a very reluctant one, for although Scott as a citizen approved the historical advance initiated by the Act of Union, he regretted very much the "lowering and grinding down" of "all those peculiarities which distinguished us as Scotsmen" (*Journal*, p. 113). For *Waverley*, in particular, it was Scott's close understanding of picturesque theory and practice which helped considerably to shape his vision of those "peculiarities." Hence, he said "the most picturesque period of history is that when the ancient rough and wild manners of a barbarous age are just becoming innovated upon." It was, he asserted, the contrast provided by "the opposition of ancient manners" to these innovations which afforded "the lights and shadows necessary to give effect to a fictitious narrative" (Introduction to *The Fortunes of Nigel*, pp. ix-x).

This illustration offers an excellent example of how Scott could adapt picturesque theory to his own fiction. We think of Gilpin's praise of the "charm of *Contrast*" which "regulates / Shape, colour, light, and shade; forms ev'ry line / By opposition just."[15] Price, too, praises the power of contrast in Rubens's landscapes: "These sudden gleams, these cataracts of light, these bold oppositions of clouds and darkness." Claude's "mild and equal sun-shine," Price thinks, ill accords "with the twisted and singular forms, and the bold and animated variety of the landscapes of Rubens."[16] It is, then, I suggest, Scott's awareness of picturesque theory which led him to the metaphor he used when speaking of "the lights and shadows necessary to give effect to fictitious narrative." It was particularly useful to him as a method of treating those "peculiarities" of Scottish life that so fascinated him. In the shaping process of creation, his own actual knowledge of Scottish topography and his actual acquaintance with those who came out in the Forty-five meant, however, that generally this picturesqueness was restrained and thereby rendered a fit instrument for the description of men and manners, of incident and landscape, and of war and peace in this very successful novel.

14   David Daiches, "David Daiches, 1965," in Allan Frazer, ed., *Sir Walter Scott, 1771-1832, an Edinburgh Keepsake* (Edinburgh, 1971), p. 143.
15   Gilpin, "On Landscape Painting, a Poem," in *Three Essays*, p. 10.
16   Price, *An Essay on the Picturesque* (1796), pp. 153-55.

As in *Waverley* so, too, in his other "Scotch novels," Scott uses
picturesque convention for the portrayal of characters and their actions and for the description of buildings, landscape, and for the
evocation of mood. The novels are rich in peasant men and women—
"originals"—whose appearance is "singular," whose manners are
"peculiar," and who "seldom fail to express [their] feelings in the
strongest and most powerful language" (*Antiquary*, "Advertise-
ment"). These men and women belong to a land that lent itself easily
to pictorial description; from time to time, like the jagger, Bruce
Snailsfoot, in *The Pirate* and Jeanie Deans in *The Heart of Midlothian*,
these characters find themselves active in a variety of moods in the
midst of stirring adventure.

Many of his plain Scottish folk have their counterparts in real life,
a fact which makes their picturesqueness the more credible, even
natural. This link with reality may explain, too, why these folk are
nearly always free of sentimentality. As Scott himself found Robert
Paterson in the ruins of Dunottar, so he describes "his appearance and
equipment . . . exactly in the Novel" (*Old Mortality*, Introduction).
Like Old Mortality, Meg Merrilies has her origin in real life in the
person of the gypsy Jean Gordon. The close relationship between that
"singular mendicant," Andrew Gemmells, and his fictional counterpart, Edie Ochiltree, may account for how realistic Edie's portrait in
the novel seems to the reader:

> He had the exterior appearance of a mendicant. A slouched hat of
> huge dimensions; a long white beard which mingled with his
> grizzled hair; an aged but strongly marked and expressive counte-
> nance, hardened, by climate and exposure, to a right brickdust
> complexion; a long blue gown, with a pewter badge on the right
> arm; two or three wallets, or bags, slung across his shoulder . . . all
> these marked at once a beggar by profession, and one of that privi-
> leged class which are called in Scotland the King's Bedesmen, or,
> vulgarly, Blue-gowns (*Antiquary*, chap. 4).

Although Caleb Balderstone in *The Bride of Lammermoor* seems
not to have been modelled from real life, our introduction to him is as
vividly pictorial as if one of Rembrandt's old faces were peering at us
through the darkened varnish of the seventeenth century:

> At length Caleb, with a trembling hand, undid the bars, opened the
> heavy door, and stood before them, exhibiting his thin grey hairs,
> bald forehead, and sharp high features, illuminated by a quivering
> lamp which he held in one hand, while he shaded and protected its
> flame with the other. The timorous courteous glance which he
> threw around him—the effect of the partial light upon his white

hair and illuminated features, might have made a good painting;
but our travellers were too impatient for security against the rising
storm, to permit them to indulge themselves in studying the picturesque (*Bride of Lammermoor*, chap. 7).

Dugald Dalgetty in *A Legend of Montrose* is not one of Scott's
plain folk, but his beginnings in life, his practical cast, and his social
garrulousness mark him as close to the lower classes. We remember,
too, Dugald's resemblance to other soldiers of fortune: Sir James
Turner and Robert Munro. Seated fully armed upon Gustavus Adolphus, Dalgetty is a copy of the scarred "weather-beaten veteran" of the
time who is prepared to serve as money and circumstances prove
enticing. Dugald was, as Scott stated in his introduction to the novel, a
favourite with his creator. Notwithstanding his unusual appearance
and his penchant for stirring adventure, Dugald's reality is like that of
many other of Scott's characters whom "he transplanted at once from
their native soil to the page which we are reading."[17] It would be naive
to regard their characterization as superficial.

Just as Sir Walter relies upon the picturesque mode to assist him
in character delineation so, too, he resorts to this sister art for help in
his description of buildings both inside and out. As he leaves Ellan-
gowan Castle, Scott has Harry Bertram turn "to take a parting look at
the stately ruins which he had just traversed. He admired the massive
and picturesque effect of the huge round towers, which, flanking the
gateway, gave a double portion of depth and majesty to the high yet
gloomy arch which it opened" (*Guy Mannering*, chap. 41). The word
"picturesque" prominently announces the effect the author wishes to
convey and brings to the reader's mind the ruined castles found in
pictures as far apart in time as those of Salvator Rosa and William
Gilpin, or Claude Lorrain and George Cattermole, or Aelbert Cuyp and
Julius Caesar Ibbetson.

The term "picturesque" is one that Scott, despite his reliance
upon its conventions, does not use frequently. Its use, however, may
be detected sometimes when he alludes to painters who relied upon
this mode of vision. In the description of the Mucklebackit cottage in
The Antiquary, the pictorial detail owes much to the "Scottish
Teniers": "In the inside of the cottage was a scene which our Wilkie
alone could have painted, with that exquisite feeling of nature that
characterizes his enchanting productions" (chap. 31). Throughout

---

17   William Hazlitt, *The Complete Works of William Hazlitt*, ed. by P. P. Howe (Lon-
     don, 1931), VI, p. 129.

the dramatic interaction of characters that takes place in this chapter, the sense of place—marked as it is—remains always subordinate to the pathos that so variously unites the activities of the funeral party. What is picturesque must be sought out: the seaside glimpse of Mussel-crag; the father's "rugged weather-beaten countenance shaded by his grizzled hair"; the old grandmother who seemed "every now and then mechanically to resume the motion of twirling her spindle; then to look towards her bosom for the distaff, although both had been laid aside"; the varied characteristics and poses of the mourners; and the picture of the sad cortège as it "moved slowly forward, preceded by the beadles, or saulies, with their batons,— miserable-looking old men, tottering as if on the edge of that grave to which they were marshalling another, and clad, according to Scottish guise, with threadbare black coats, and hunting caps decorated with rusty crape" (chap. 31). The pictorial quality of this chapter never for a moment interferes with the grief that attends Steenie's death or with the macabre utterances of the shrivelled old grandmother or even with the "creak of the screwnails" securing Steenie Mucklebackit forever from human sight. The discrete elements that make up the chapter come together under the unifying force of the tragedy that has overwhelmed the Mucklebackits so that Wilkie's way of seeing is complementary, not supplementary, to Scott's artistic purpose, a further indication of how perceptive Christopher Hussey was when he noted how Scott's use of the picturesque is "fused . . . into his romances."

On other occasions, Scott's knowledge and use of this term are more obvious than in chapter 31 of *The Antiquary*. He may refer directly to the theorists and adopt their practice openly. Willingham Rectory of *The Heart of Midlothian* was planted "in beautiful irregularity"; its front, too, was irregular, some of it being very old and showing the effect that many architectural changes made "without much regard to symmetry."

> But these incongruities of architecture were so graduated and happily mingled, that the eye, far from being displeased with the combinations of various styles, saw nothing but what was interesting in the varied and intricate pile which they displayed. Fruit-trees displayed on the southern wall, outer staircases, various places of entrance, a combination of roofs and chimneys of different ages, united to render the front, not indeed beautiful or grand, but intricate, perplexed, or, to use Mr. Price's appropriated phrase, picturesque (chap. 32).

As with buildings so, too, with scenery. Seldom does the word "picturesque" accompany the description. It is used, however, to describe the ridge of the Pentland Hills in *The Heart of Midlothian* (chap. 8); the scenery that surrounds the Earl of Menteith when he meets Dugald Dalgetty (*Legend of Montrose*, chap. 2); and the outline of Skiddaw and Glaramara (*Redgauntlet*, chap. 13). It is close to Miss Julia Mannering's heart, although the scenery of Lake Windermere with its "sounding cataracts" and "scathed hills" was for her more sublime than picturesque, and at times beautiful: "all the wildness of Salvator here—and there, the fairy scenes of Claude" (*Guy Mannering*, chap. 17). The approach, for example, to the ruins of Saint Ruth—which has its counterpart, too, in real geography—takes Lovel, and Oldbuck, and their party in *The Antiquary* round trees, "at first singly, stunted, and blighted, with locks of wool upon their trunks, and their roots hollowed out into recesses, in which the sheep love to repose themselves—a sight much more gratifying to the eye of an admirer of the picturesque than to that of a planter or a forester." This is exactly the sort of terrain that Sir Uvedale Price praises in his first essay on the picturesque.[18]

At other times it is up to the reader to identify the aesthetic mode underlying the description. Once at the top of the hill above the ruins of Saint Ruth, Jonathan Oldbuck, like Jane Austen's Henry Tilney, directs Miss Wardour—who is, unlike Catherine Morland, "an admirer of nature"—to enjoy in "full perfection" the ancient ruins and the accompaniments of the woodland scene spread out below them. The mode of description is obvious:

> They stood pretty high up on the side of the glen, which had suddenly opened into a sort of amphitheatre to give room for a pure and profound lake of a few acres extent, and a space of level ground around it. The banks then rose everywhere steeply, and in some places were varied by rocks—in others covered with the copse, which ran up, feathering their sides lightly and irregularly, and breaking the uniformity of the green pasture-ground.—Beneath, the lake discharged itself into the huddling and tumultuous brook, which had been their companion since they had entered the glen. At the point at which it entered from "its parent lake," stood the ruins ... They were not of great extent; but the singular beauty, as well as the wild and sequestered character of the spot ... gave them an interest and an importance superior to that which attaches itself to architectural remains of greater consequence, but placed

18   See Price, *An Essay on the Picturesque* (1796), I, p. 36.

near to ordinary houses, and possessing less romantic accompaniments (chap. 17).

Although Scott's description of the scene and ruin is tedious by its length, it is one that is central to the action, involving as it does the Bedesman, Edie Ochiltree, the antiquarianism of Jonathan Oldbuck, the early morning duel between Lovel and Captain M'Intyre, and Lovel's subsequent rescue by Ochiltree, the burial of the Countess of Glenallan who is linked to Elspeth Mucklebackit, and finally the unusual midnight search for treasure undertaken by Oldbuck and the charlatan Dousterswivel. Throughout the action, picturesque elements of setting, character, and incident combine rather well to enliven the tedium for readers and to introduce them to the manners of Scotland at the close of the eighteenth century—a subject very close to Scott's heart.

In referring to Sir Robert Gordon's *A Genealogical History of the Earldom of Sutherland*, Scott told the Marchioness of Stafford that it contained "for an old antiquary like me many points of great interest and curiosity. Sir Robert Gordon, no doubt, did not particularly study the picturesque, but he often gives hints which may be useful to those who do. We gather so much of the manners of old times from these genuine sources" (*Letters*, III, pp. 226-27). Scott's linking, in this passage, his antiquarian tastes with the picturesque helps explain the kind of historical event which appealed strongly to him and to theorists like William Gilpin who admired "history-painters" who emphasized old ruins and the trappings of the past: military arms, "religious utensils, and the rich furniture of banquets."[19] Gilpin, like Sir Walter, delighted in noting the stirring actions of border warfare: "On the confines of England, and Scotland, the antiquarian easily collects vestiges enough of border-feuds to fill his volume. There is scarce a bridge, or a pass, that has not been gallantly attacked, and defended—nor a house of any antiquity, that has not been plundered, or besieged."[20]

Of course, Scott's use of the term picturesque as applied to history may mean no more than Richard Payne Knight suggested in his *Principles of Taste* (1805). In speaking of how the "boundaries of the picturesque" have been enlarged, Knight remarked, "Lately, too, the word has been extended to criticism, and employed to signify that clear and vivid style of narration or description, which paints to the

19   Gilpin, *Three Essays*, p. 27.
20   Gilpin, *High-Lands of Scotland*, II, p. 99.

imagination, and shows every event or object distinctly, as if represented in a picture."[21] To support his contention, Knight refers the
reader to Hugh Blair's *Lectures on Rhetoric and Belles Lettres.*

Knight's reference to the way that the "boundaries of the picturesque" have been extended to describe a "clear and vivid style of
narration" gains in significance when put alongside Scott's letter to
Anna Seward in 1802 in which he offers the death of the Regent
Murray in Robertson's history as an example of a story told "in a
manner highly picturesque." Although Knight disapproves of the
way in which the meaning of "picturesque" seems to "comprehend,
in some degree, every thing of every kind,"[22] he nevertheless accepts
many of its extensions, saying that mankind's "restless desire for
novelty"[23] goes far towards explaining such shifts of usage. Knight
comes very close to linking the word picturesque with fiction when
he refers to the popularity of much fiction of his time: "yet known and
avowed fiction, by merely holding forth new combinations of circumstances and images, can always excite a sufficient degree of
curiosity, to procure numerous and indefatigable readers; as is abun-
dantly proved by the swarms of novels, with which the English and
French presses constantly teem."[24] The young people of his day, he
laments, are "reading merely for events, without any attention to
language, thought, or sentiment." Theirs, he continues, is a "flutter-
ing and fidgety curiosity;—that trembling irritability of habit, which
cannot stoop to the tameness of reality, or the insipidity of common
life; but is always arresting itself in the more animated and brilliant
events of fiction." No moral improvement is ever discernible for
"fiction is always treated as fiction; and considered as mere matter of
amusement."[25]

On this aspect of the picturesque, Sir Walter and Knight were far
apart. Scott was an author who wrote with the "general amusement"
of his reading public very much in mind. That reading public appreciated, as he very well knew, "animated and brilliant events"
which by their novelty could rouse readers' curiosity. These "events,"
which Knight deplored, were for Scott essential to his fiction, and
when, to use Knight's own words, they were supported by "new
combinations of circumstances and images" in a story, the ingre-

21 Knight, *Analytical Inquiry*, pp. 154-55.
22 Knight, *Analytical Inquiry*, p. 154.
23 Knight, *Analytical Inquiry*, p. 437.
24 Knight, *Analytical Inquiry*, p. 451.
25 Knight, *Analytical Inquiry*, p. 459.

dients for a reasonable definition of narrative action that is "highly picturesque" are before us.

To find examples of such narrative action from the plenitude in the "Scotch novels" is difficult only because so many and so varied instances abound. But to choose one, consider the "inexpressibly animating" quality of the scene in *Guy Mannering* (chap. 26) in which Dandie Dinmont and his friends "embarked in a crazy boat" go salmon fishing at night using the light of torches. From a high vantage point nearby, Harry Bertram observes the scene:

> Often he thought of his friend Dudley, the artist, when he observed the effect produced by the strong red glare on the romantic banks under which the boat glided. Now the light diminished to a distant star that seemed to twinkle on the waters . . . Then it advanced nearer brightening and enlarging as it again approached, till the broad flickering flame rendered bank and rock and tree visible as it passed, tinging them with its own red glare of dusky light, and resigning them gradually to darkness, or to pale moonlight, as it receded. By this light also were seen the figures in the boat, now holding high their weapons, now stooping to strike, now standing upright, bronzed, by the same red glare.

Before going back to Dandie's farmhouse, Bertram "amused himself for some time with [the] effects of light and shadow," and the actions of the fishermen: "one holding the torch, the others with their spears, ready to avail themselves of the light it affords to strike their prey." At one point in the excitement, a fisherman, not in the boat, but "up to his middle in water, jingling among broken ice" speared a fish of such size that the current made it difficult for him to land his catch. At this critical moment the torchbearer accidentally dropped his light into the water. The action continues:

> "The deil's in Gabriel!" said the spearman, as the fragments of glowing wood floated half-blazing, half-sparkling, but soon extinguished, down the stream—"the deil's in the man! I'll never master him without the light—and a braver kipper, could I but land him, never reisted abune a pair o' cleeks." Some dashed into the water to lend their assistance, and the fish, which was afterwards found to weigh nearly thirty pounds, was landed in safety.

Picturesqueness here extends beyond the effects of light and shadow and the flickering glimpses of irregular landscape to the action taking place: the movement of the boat, the men "holding high their weapons, now stooping to strike, now standing upright," the fisherman struggling in icy water with a thirty-pound salmon, the torch floating "half-blazing, half-sparkling but soon extinguished, down the stream," and the agonies of the dying fish "as they lay flapping about in the boat which they moistened with their blood"—much to Bertram's distaste. The application of the word "picturesque" to describe such an event seems reasonable enough not just because the action is unusual, or because of the "clear and vivid style of narration," but because of the pictorial quality which enables us to see the action before us. It is a scene that in Price's language may be "represented with good effect in painting" as the sketch in this edition indicates.

And this pictorial quality extends also to the language of the fisherman, as almost in despair he assesses his prize: "a braver kipper, could I but land him, never reisted abune a pair o' cleeks." Both the fisherman and the reader have a clear image of what is desirable: this splendid salmon, split and salted, hanging in the smoke of a turf fire in the chimney above the cleeks or hooks which support the iron pot over the fire. The visual power of this speech may be found elsewhere in Scott whose ordinary folk often make us see vividly as well as hear their words.

Waverley, the southerner, is puzzled, for example, by Saunders Saunderson's explanation for the absence of the Baron of Bradwardine: "His honour was with the folk who were getting doon the dark hag." It is the word "hag" with its associations with witches seen in hedges at night that makes the butler's explanation so interesting visually. "Hag" is both dialectal and archaic. Such words also appealed to Thomas Hardy, who found the substitution of a word like "greggles" for wild hyacinths "a picturesque use of dialect words" (*The Mayor of Casterbridge*, chap. 20). Scott's people, like Hardy's, offer us many examples. Lady Margaret of Tillietudlem in *Old Mortality* (chap. 7) tells old Mause that she had "rather that the rigs of Tillietudlem bare naething but windle-straes and sandy lavrocks than that they were ploughed by rebels to the king." The word "windle-straes" by both its sound and original dialect meaning (a trifling, feeble person or object) suits perfectly Lady Margaret's need to impress old Mause. Another example of this kind of word usage occurs when Mrs. Shortcake complaining of Monkbarn's objection to a written bill of account in *The Antiquary* (chap. 15) tells Mrs. Heukbane that they serve his family "wi' bread, and he settles wi' huz ilka week—only he was in an unco kippage when we sent him a book instead of the *nick-sticks*, whilk he said, were the true ancient way o' counting between tradesmen and customers." Monkbarns, like Henchard in *The Mayor of Casterbridge* (chap. 14), is attached to "the rugged picturesqueness of the old method"; each family in Fairport had its own nick-stick upon which a notch was made for each loaf of bread delivered. One more illustration may suffice. When Bailie Nicol Jarvie takes umbrage at Rob Roy's taunt about weavers and spinners, the Bailie's retort is such that the Highland reiver can easily visualize his last reel—on the gallows: "Weavers! Deil shake ye out o' the web the weaver craft made. Spinners!—ye'll spin and wind yoursell a bonny pirn" (chap. 23).

These dialect words which in their context impress the reader by their lively visual quality and their connection to what is past—be it language or myth, custom or history—may well be labelled "picturesque." The contrast offered by dialectal speech and standard English is like the effect of light and dark shadings in painting which both Gilpin and Price admired.

It is interesting, finally, that Sir Walter Scott's commitment to picturesqueness is not a mode of seeing which he reserves only for his poetry or his fiction. It was, as his letters and *Journal* reveal, an aesthetic he relied upon to fashion his home at Abbotsford and to landscape the grounds, which he was forever adding to. He must have been aware of English theories on landscaping, at least as early as 1810, when a lengthy review of Sir Uvedale Price's *Essays on the Picturesque* appeared in the November number of the *Quarterly Review*. Three years later, when writing to Lady Abercorn (March 23, 1813), he says: "I have been studying Price with all my eyes and [am] not without hopes of converting an old gravel-pit into a bower and an exhausted quarry into a bathing-house. So you see my dear Madam how deeply I am bit with the madness of the picturesque" (*Letters*, III, p. 240). It is, then, very reasonable to conclude that Scott had had a thorough grounding in the principles of landscape architecture well before the publication of *Waverley* in 1814. It was an aesthetic in which he was to acquire very considerable practical experience.

His interest in landscaping was a continuing one as letters about Abbotsford to his many friends make clear. In one to Robert Surtees (November 12, 1816) he explains that he has "the Tweed for one picturesque boundary of my little property, and a mountain lake, or tarn, at the other; both of which are tempting subjects of improvement" (*Letters*, IV, p. 286). Two years later (November 21, [1818]), he tells William Laidlaw that "we are too apt to consider plantations as a subject of the closest oeconomy whereas beauty and taste has [sic] even a marketable value after their effects come to be visible" (*Letters*, V, p. 227). And in a letter to Lady Louisa Stuart (November 14, 1816) he reveals his understanding of the technique which Humphry Repton used in his Red Books, a technique which Scott likened to a raree show (*Letters*, IV, p. 292).

Sir Walter's interest in picturesque landscape was never far removed from practice. His delight in planning and managing his Abbotsford estate even extended to work with his own hands. In April 1816, for example, he was "among my dearly beloved, peging [sic] oaks and birches" (*Letters*, IV, p. 209). Although he could not "enter into the spirit of common vulgar farming," he could work, he informed Joanna Baillie, "from morning to night" at "planting and pruning trees" (*Letters*, II, p. 402). That Sir Walter's interest was an abiding one appears over a decade later in his long review of Sir Henry Steuart's book, *The Planter's Guide*, which Scott wrote for *The Quarterly Review* in 1828.[26] Scott's knowledge of his subject in this article is both far-ranging and thorough, revealing his own special interest in planting as he declares roundly that "trees, therefore, remain the proper and most manageable material of picturesque improvement."[27] His expertise as an improver is also noticeable, for example, in *Redgauntlet*. In his seventh letter, Darsie Latimer writes at length to Alan Fairford about Joshua Geddes's grounds. In the course of his account, Darsie succeeds in giving his friend a capsule account of the history of landscape gardening and, in his description of the willow walk, further proof of the author's extensive knowledge of the art of planting for picturesque effect.

Although more than one critic has decried Scott's ability "as a judge of visual arts,"[28] it should be remembered that in the area of the picturesque Sir Walter was quite well informed.[29] He had also an extensive and sometimes intimate acquaintance with artists, many of whom—like Landseer, Leslie, de Loutherbourg, Thomson of Dudding-

---

26   See Marcia Allentuck, "Scott and the Picturesque: Afforestation and History," in Alan Bell, ed., *Scott Bicentenary Essays* (Edinburgh, 1973), pp. 188-98. Professor Allentuck's preliminary review of picturesque theory is especially valuable.

27   [Sir Walter Scott], "On Ornamental Plantations and Landscape Gardening," *The Quarterly Review* 37 (March 1828), p. 321.

28   Adèle M. Holcomb, "Scott and Turner," in *Scott Bicentenary Essays*, p. 202. See also Murdoch, "Scott, Pictures, and Painters," especially the reference to C. R. Leslie, pp. 39-40.

29   According to J. G. Cochrane's *Catalogue of the Library at Abbotsford*, Scott owned a copy of Sir Uvedale Price, *Essays on the Picturesque*, 1810 edition; a copy of Richard Payne Knight's *An Analytical Inquiry into the Principles of Taste*, 1818 edition; and a copy of Reverend William Gilpin, *The Life of Bernard Gilpin*, 2nd ed., 1753. None of Gilpin's other publications is listed.

ston, J. M. W. Turner, and Wilkie—had at one time or another relied heavily upon picturesque convention for their effects. One of these relationships, that between Turner and Scott, has recently been the subject of considerable scholarly attention.[30] Certainly Scott's acquaintance with art and artists meant that he had no difficulty appreciating the sort of dialectic which Gilpin, Price, and Knight used to show how the principles of painting applied to the art of landscape gardening.

But it is the use which Scott makes of the picturesque throughout his fiction that is important. It was Walter Bagehot in 1879 who explained the dangers which Scott recognized as the outcome of the French Revolution: the sweeping away of "prince and peasant in a common *égalité*" and setting up "a scientific rigidity for the irregular and picturesque growth of centuries," the replacing of "an abounding and genial life by a symmetrical but lifeless mechanism."[31] Later in 1892, Sir Leslie Stephen, who like Bagehot recognized Scott's weaknesses as a novelist, supported Bagehot's contention, saying that "good and far-seeing men might well look with alarm at changes whose far-reaching consequences cannot yet be estimated."[32] And in our own time the opinions of both these men have been upheld by J. H. Raleigh who is even more emphatic about what Scott saw "was being lost in the march of progress."[33]

The importance of the role of picturesque convention in this process deserves attention for its own aesthetic fitted very conveniently Sir Walter's deeply felt admiration for what was—alas—"a' dead and gane"; as well, it offered him and his readers a very acceptable method whereby they could visualize the past, seeing it in opposition to the new society struggling to be born from the social chaos of the Industrial Revolution. One does not risk much in maintaining that no author could have found a literary handmaiden any more ready, more functional, more acceptable to his audience, or even perhaps more felicitous, than the picturesque proved to be for Sir Walter Scott.

His acceptance of this mode, however, left him open to criticism. The most serious came from his fellow-countryman, Thomas Carlyle,

30   See especially Gerald Finley, *Landscapes of Memory, Turner as Illustrator to Scott* (London, 1980).
31   Walter Bagehot, *Literary Studies* (London, 1911), II, p. 140.
32   Leslie Stephen, *Hours in a Library*, new ed. (London, 1892), I, p. 165.
33   John Henry Raleigh, *Time, Place and Idea, Essays on the Novel* (Carbondale and Edwardsville, 1968), p. 121.

who deplored Scott's lack of spirituality and his proclivity to make himself "at home in a world of conventionalities." He had, said Carlyle with damning praise, "A love of picturesque, of beautiful, vigorous and graceful things; a genuine love, yet not more genuine than has dwelt in hundreds of men named minor poets: this is the highest quality to be discerned in him."[34] Since Carlyle's time much has been said and written about his indictment of Scott.[35] In pressing his attack against the tendency of the picturesque to dwell on surface characteristics and to avoid "getting near the heart," Carlyle was on firm ground. What has not perhaps been enough emphasized is his open acknowledgement of Scott's superb use of the convention. "Surely he were a blind critic," cries Carlyle, who would miss this use, and he concludes significantly, "In joyous picturesqueness and fellow-feeling, freedom of eye and heart; or to say it in a word, in general *healthiness* of mind, these Novels [*Waverley*] prove Scott to have been amongst the foremost writers."[36] Again Carlyle is on firm critical ground and fair in his judgment.

By his fiction and life, Scott bequeathed to later nineteenth-century novelists a very important inheritance, which many of them have attested to without qualification. They read his books as they appeared and lauded them extravagantly. "For fiction," cried Charlotte Brontë in 1834, "read Scott alone; all novels after his are worthless."[37] In 1839, in a letter to George Cattermole, Charles Dickens referred to *A Legend of Montrose* and *Kenilworth* which he had "just been reading with greater delight than ever."[38] To Alexander Main in 1871, George Eliot confessed that "it is a personal grief, a heart-wound to me when I hear a depreciating or slighting word about Scott."[39] And we know that as a boy Thomas Hardy read Scott and became one of his admirers. When he visited Scotland in 1881, he went to the trouble to find and talk to an old man who had known Sir Walter.[40] For

---

34   Thomas Carlyle, "Sir Walter Scott [1838]," in *Scottish and Other Miscellanies* (London, 1915), p. 65.

35   See especially "Herbert Grierson (1927)," in Allan Frazier, ed., *Sir Walter Scott, 1771-1832, an Edinburgh Keepsake* (Edinburgh, 1971), pp. 1-26.

36   Carlyle, "Sir Walter Scott," in *Scottish and Other Miscellanies*, p. 100.

37   Elizabeth Gaskell, *The Life of Charlotte Brontë* (London, 1919), p. 104.

38   Charles Dickens, *The Letters of Charles Dickens*, ed. by Madeline House and Graham Storey (Oxford, 1965-77), I, p. 576.

39   George Eliot, *The George Eliot Letters*, ed. by Gordon S. Haight (New Haven, 1955), V, p. 175.

40   Evelyn Hardy, *Thomas Hardy, a Critical Biography* (London, 1954), p. 187.

Hardy, *The Bride of Lammermoor* was "an almost perfect specimen of form."[41]

It is interesting to conjecture to what degree Sir Walter Scott's attraction for the picturesque and the use he made of it in his fiction and even in his landscaping at Abbotsford may have cast its shadow upon these four novelists who came after him. Certainly in their own fiction and, in some instances, in their own lives, the reader finds much evidence that the picturesque provided them, too, with pleasure and with a fictional technique that extended well beyond the mere delineation of landscape.

41 Thomas Hardy, *Thomas Hardy's Personal Writings, Prefaces, Literary Opinions, Reminiscences*, ed. by Harold Orel (Lawrence, 1966), p. 121.

Chapter 4

Charlotte Brontë

> If Fieldhead had few other merits as a building, it might at
> least be termed picturesque: its irregular architecture, and
> the grey and mossy colouring communicated by time,
> gave it a just claim to this epithet.
>
> Charlotte Brontë, *Shirley*

Picturesque vision in Charlotte Brontë's fiction owes very little to any
particular theorist or practitioner. Yet it is to be found in good measure as she attempts to avoid what she vaguely denotes as the "ideal"
and to write a prose that will be as "real, cool, and solid . . . as Monday
morning" (*Shirley*, chap. 1). That she fails to banish the ideal entirely
from her fiction is as apparent as her ability to write a narrative that
brings her characters and their concerns realistically before our eyes.
At the same time, however, this realism is often muted as the uncom-
promising truth is made palatable either to readers or to editors fearful
of public outcry.

Just as the picturesque landscape of the nineteenth century took
its subject matter usually from a real place and imposed upon the
details the schema of a Claude or Poussin, so, too, especially in
Charlotte Brontë's early fiction, the reader is often aware of the real
being shaped by the ideal—be it Charlotte's own youthful idealisms,
or her early reading in literature and art, or the religiosity which
infects a character like Jane Eyre. At first reading the imprint of the
picturesque may not be noticeable as attention centres on distinctions
between the ideal and the real. "Let the idealists, the dreamers about
earthly angels and human flowers," exclaims William Crimsworth,
"just look here while I open my portfolio and show them a sketch or

two, pencilled after nature" (*The Professor*, chap. 12). The three pictures from life which William offers of Aurelia Koslow, Adèle Dron-
sart, and Juanna Trista owe much to reality, to Charlotte Brontë's own
experience in the classroom in Brussels. The ideal picture is not to be
seen. Crimsworth fails to extract from his portfolio "some gentle
virgin head, circled with a halo, some sweet personification of innocence, clasping the dove of peace to her bosom" (chap. 12).

But such failure in no way diminishes the success which attends
Crimsworth's classroom performance. Teaching, as a profession in
The Professor, in *Villette*, and even in *Jane Eyre*, has an ideality about
it whether we think of the happiness that William Crimsworth and
Frances Evans found, or the three happiest years of Lucy Snowe's life,
as she develops a flourishing school, or Jane Eyre's good fortune with
her Morton scholars, some half-dozen of whom proved to be "as
decent, respectable, modest, and well-informed young women as
could be found in the ranks of the British peasantry" (*Jane Eyre*,
chap. 34). Very often, what is "real, cool, and solid" on Monday
morning in Charlotte Brontë's novels becomes passionately warm and
spiritual by Friday night.

And so, although principal characters like William Crimsworth,
Lucy Snowe, Jane Eyre, and Shirley Keeldar admonish a novelist or
painter to do his pencillings "after nature," to "cherish the plain
truth," to look "life in its iron face," or to bring the thoughts and
feelings of the heart "into the safe fold of common sense," the reader is
always cognizant of an opposing quality. Even if life at Lowood is a
kind of hell for Jane Eyre, the reader observes her feasting "on the
spectacle of ideal drawings . . . freely pencilled houses and trees,
picturesque rocks and ruins, Cuyp-like groups of cattle, sweet paintings of butterflies hovering over unblown roses, of birds picking at
ripe cherries, of wrens' nests enclosing pearl-like eggs, wreathed
about with young ivy sprays" (chap. 8). Given a choice at Lowood,
Jane, in this passage, reveals clearly her penchant for the scope of the
picturesque where the real and the ideal may both be discerned. Even
the illusory delight of hot roasted potatoes, white bread, and new milk
fades away before the "spectacle of ideal drawings." Both Gilpin and
William Henry Hunt come to mind as Jane describes what her imagination provided as the work of her own hands.

Jane's reverie here, however, should be put alongside Lucy
Snowe's comment upon the pictures she saw in the galleries in Villette. It is tempting to argue that Lucy's preferences for art which
showed at least some "fragments of truth," some recognizable repre-

sentations of nature's "power" and "glory," may have their origin in Charlotte Brontë's own visits to galleries in Brussels or London. Lucy has a "fond instinct" which inclines her to art—with certain reservations:

> It seemed to me [says Lucy] that an original and good picture was just as scarce as an original and good book; nor did I, in the end, tremble to say to myself, standing before certain *chefs-d'oeuvre* bearing great names, "These are not a whit like nature. Nature's day-light never had that colour: never was made so turbid, either by storm or cloud, as it is laid out there, under a sky of indigo: and that indigo is not ether; and those dark weeds plastered upon it are not trees" (*Villette*, chap. 19).

Lucy's dismissal of the huge canvas of Cleopatra as "an enormous piece of claptrap," her scathing reference to that "huge, dark-complexioned gypsy-queen" as "very much butcher's meat—to say nothing of bread, vegetables, and liquids" leaps past the limits of realism to naturalism. But despite Lucy's aesthetic iconoclasm and her eye for "nature's day-light," the reader suspects that her tastes in painting were probably not unlike those "ideal drawings" that appealed so much to Jane Eyre at Lowood. Tired of the "claptrap" she associates with the painting of Cleopatra, Lucy finds much satisfaction in "some exquisite little pictures of still life: wild-flowers, wild fruit, mossy wood-nests, casketing eggs that looked like pearls seen through clear green sea-water." Here Lucy's matter-of-factness goes hand in hand with the fanciful.

Always the opposition between the real and the ideal exists; it becomes apparent in the decisions that must be made by some of the characters in the novels. Reason may come forward and tell Jane "a plain, unvarnished tale" about how hopeless her passion for Rochester is, yet a "strange chill and failing at the heart" overtake her when Mrs. Fairfax reports that Rochester may have gone away for a year (chaps. 16, 17). The stuff of dreams and "the chill blue lips" of reason; what the heart whispers and the mind denies: this is the opposition. And despite her own occasional protests so obvious in the alternative assigned to Caroline Helstone—"if she has sense, she will be her own governor, and resolve to subdue and bring under guidance the disturbed realm of her emotions" (*Shirley*, chap. 7)—Charlotte Brontë finds difficulty in banishing the ideal and wedding her narrative to reality. "She seems," said Sir Leslie Stephen, "to be turning for relief alternately to different teachers, to the promptings of her own heart, to the precepts of those whom she has been taught to revere, and occasionally, though timidly and tentatively, to alien schools of thought."[1] It is this uncertainty which gives rise to a kind of ambivalence in her fiction which appeals to the taste of many modern readers. Robert Bernard Martin puts the conflict clearly and gracefully: "Fortunately, her own imperfectly mastered attraction towards the stuff that dreams are made on persists in the novel [*Jane Eyre*] in constant balance with her stern desire for a naked objectivity, and it is the eternal tension between them that gives the book such a special flavour." The result of this tension, Martin argues, "is one of the finest achievements of the romantic sensibility."[2]

Something of this feeling comes to the fore in a letter she wrote to George Smith, probably in the autumn of 1852. In speaking of *The History of Henry Esmond*, she objects to the balance of "history" and "story" which Thackeray provides: "I hold that a work of fiction ought to be a work of creation: that the *real* should be sparingly introduced in pages dedicated to the *ideal*. Plain household bread is a far more wholesome and necessary thing than cake; yet who would like to see the brown loaf placed upon the table for dessert?"[3] Here, of course, she is objecting to the intrusion of too much historical fact into a work of fiction. And yet there is the brown loaf that is so reassuringly real. If it is so much more wholesome, why should it be "sparingly introduced" in pages dedicated to the ideal? Presumably on the grounds of the incongruity of historical fact in fictional narrative.

Later, in another letter to Smith (December 6, 1852), Charlotte returns to a related subject as she worries over the reception of *Villette*. How will the public react to the realism she has felt compelled to give them in the third book of this novel? She could have done it differently and given preference to a more idealistic treatment:

> The spirit of romance would have indicated another course, far more flowery and inviting; it would have fashioned a paramount hero, kept faithfully with him, and made him supremely worshipful; he should have [been] an idol, and not a mute, unresponding idol either; but this would have been unlike real life—inconsistent with truth—at variance with probability.[4]

M. Paul is far from being "a supremely worshipful figure," and, in this, her last novel, there is no happy ending. Perhaps in *Villette* she

1   Stephen, *Hours in a Library*, III, pp. 26-27.
2   Robert Bernard Martin, *Accents of Persuasion* (London, 1966), pp. 107-108.
3   Clement Shorter, *The Brontës, Life and Letters* (London, 1908), II, pp. 284-85.
4   Shorter, *The Brontës*, II, p. 289.

was able at last to follow the promptings of her own creative taste. In the ambiguity of the novel's ending, Robert Bernard Martin finds "Miss Brontë's last refusal to bow to the dictates of romantic fiction."[5]

This ambiguity that surrounds Charlotte's attitude to romance and real life is noticeable, too, in her judgments about painting; although Miss Wooler, her teacher at Roe Head, said that she knew "much about celebrated pictures and painters,"[6] few references to great art occur in her novels. Yet, despite the limitation imposed by her determination to be realistic, she was greatly interested in painting. Perhaps it was this limitation which accounted for her interest in the picturesque. In this respect she would be a rather typical Victorian lady, but in others her interests in art marked her as atypical. Few Victorian girls of thirteen, for instance, could have possessed the knowledge of the old Italian and Flemish masters which Mrs. Gaskell said belonged to Charlotte.[7] And viewed over her lifetime, few Victorian women could have had a wider acquaintance with painting than she had.

At first, however, it was at second-hand, as she and her sisters were given art instruction at the insistence of their father. Her first exposure to the art she had seen and studied in art books and periodicals may have come when Mary Taylor, the Rose Yorke of *Shirley*, showed her father's art collection to her. In London, en route to Brussels in 1842, it is Mary Taylor who reports that Charlotte "seemed to think our business was and ought to be to see all the pictures and statues we could" and that "she knew the artists and knew where other productions of theirs were to be found."[8] In Brussels, too, Charlotte not only saw more paintings but also received art training from M. Huard, who proved to be a good drawing master.

Six years later, in 1848, she began the visits to London that attended her literary recognition. Those visits invariably included trips to the National Gallery, to private galleries like Lord Westminster's, and to exhibitions held at the Royal Academy and Somerset House. In a letter to her father (November 1849), she reported that she had seen "a beautiful exhibition of Turner's paintings."[9] As she had been reading *Modern Painters* with "much genuine pleasure" in July

5 Martin, *Accents of Persuasion*, p. 186.
6 Gaskell, *Life*, p. 80.
7 Gaskell, *Life*, p. 68.
8 Gaskell, *Life*, p. 175.
9 Shorter, *The Brontës*, II, p. 211.

1848,[10] she must have viewed the Turners with great interest. In February 1850, she wrote that "nothing charmed me more during my stay in town than the pictures I saw—one or two private collections of Turner's best water-colour drawings were indeed a treat: his later oil-paintings are strange things—things that baffle description."[11] A year later Charlotte expressed her delight at receiving in one of her Cornhill parcels some "twenty numbers of splendid engravings." It was, she said, as if "the whole Vernon Gallery had been brought to one's own fireside!"[12]

In view of the pleasure she took from art and her admiration for Ruskin's *Modern Painters* and *The Stones of Venice*,[13] it is reasonable to expect to find many apt allusions to painting in Charlotte Brontë's fiction. But this is not what happens. When she has her fictional characters refer to paintings, it is often with qualifications suggesting that she is uneasy about great art. Louis Moore, for example, thinks that Caroline Helstone is "certainly pretty: a little Raffaelle head hers; Raffaelle in feature, quite English in expression" (*Shirley*, chap. 29); Dutch paintings of madonnas provide both William Crimsworth and Lucy Snowe with useful comparisons as they describe the "solid, firm-set, sculptural style" of beauty that belonged to their pupils. They have, says Lucy, a "depth of expressionless calm, of passionless peace" that resembles "a polar snow-field" (*Villette*, chap. 20). When Lucy, too, is captivated by the realism of Vashti's acting, she cannot help thinking how Vashti's "magian power" can overwhelm all the army of Rubens's fat women.

Against this down-to-earth aesthetic is the contrast offered by Jane Eyre's desire, while she was at Lowood, to paint the kind of pictures her imagination brought to mind. What she wanted was an idealization, something spiritual, but this, she tells Rochester, she was "powerless to realize." Even so, her actual efforts cause Rochester to remark that in the act of composition she must have existed "in a kind of artist's dreamland" (chap. 13). That Jane's taste—as St. John Rivers also noted—"leans to the ideal" is apparent when she turns to classical Greek qualities to describe his face—so unlike the "irregularity" of her own—or when she extols the "perfect beauty" of Rosamond Oliver (chap. 31). In another connection, we remember how she

10   Shorter, *The Brontës*, I, p. 441.
11   Shorter, *The Brontës*, II, pp. 116-17.
12   Shorter, *The Brontës*, II, p. 225.
13   See Gaskell, *Life*, pp. 363, 386-87.

idealized Rochester, who stood almost as her hope of heaven: "an eclipse . . . between man and the broad sun" (chap. 24).

However, in her refusal to marry Rochester while he is a married man, in her recognition of St. John's marmoreal qualities, in her knowledge that Rosamond is a spoiled child, Jane reveals her common sense which makes her in the end waver about ideal standards, of either beauty or conduct. Her sketches, which she does at Morton, are representational rather than abstract: "a pencil-head of a pretty, little cherub-like girl, one of my scholars, and sundry views from Nature, taken in the Vale of Morton and on the surrounding moors" (chap. 32). She has given up the portrayal of colossal heads and icebergs piercing a polar sky (chap. 13).

If we set to one side Jane Eyre's artistic difficulties and turn more directly to Charlotte Brontë's own technique for making us see what Jane sees, for instance, as she stands in the window of Lowood School, we recognize at once how the practice of picturesque representation facilitates her description:

> There were the two wings of the building; there was the garden; there were the skirts of Lowood; there was the hilly horizon. My eye passed all other objects to rest on those most remote, the blue peaks. It was those I longed to surmount; all within their boundary of rock and heath seemed prison-ground, exile limits. I traced the white road winding round the base of one mountain and vanishing in a gorge between two. How I longed to follow it further! (chap. 10).

Visual description such as this fits the narrative admirably for, while the reader sees Jane in her exile, he can also sympathize with her in her longing for an ideal that lies beyond the blue peaks. The actual scene that Jane describes is, of course, one that the author, too, remembers. And in this connection, it is interesting to note that Charlotte Brontë herself described the Cowan's Bridge School in her time has having a "picturesque" situation.[14]

During her flight from Thornfield, Jane is precise in telling the reader what kind of landscape surrounds her. And even when she is penniless and hungry setting out from Whitcross, Charlotte Brontë has her describe what she sees as if she were looking at an early Gainsborough sketch:

> there, amongst the romantic hills . . . I saw a hamlet and a spire. All the valley at my right hand was full of pasture-fields, and corn-fields, and wood; and a glittering stream ran zig-zag through the

14   Gaskell, *Life*, p. 297.

varied shades of green, the mellowing grain, the sombre woodland, the clear and sunny lea. Recalled by the rumbling of wheels before me, I saw a heavily laden waggon labouring up the hill; and not far beyond were two cows and their drover (chap. 28).

The sketch resembles a composite one of several of Gainsborough's rural scenes, although it is very close to his *Wooded Landscape with Shepherd and Sheep and Distant Village* (ca. 1746-47).[15]

After her escape from Thornfield, when she is about to die like an animal in the cold rain, Jane sees a light and rather wonderfully gathers the strength that takes her to the Rivers's cottage, a picturesque haven, where she remains until she is fully recovered from her ordeal. As Diana and Mary Rivers loved their sequestered home, so, too, Jane becomes attached to it:

I, too, in the grey, small, antique structure, with its low roof, its latticed casements, its mouldering walls, its avenue of aged firs — all grown aslant under the stress of mountain winds; its garden, dark with yew and holly — and where no flowers but of the hardiest species would bloom — found a charm both potent and permanent. They clung to the purple moors behind and around their dwelling — to the hollow vale into which the pebbly bridle-path leading from their gate descended; and which wound between fern-banks first, and then amongst a few of the wildest little pasture-fields that ever bordered a wilderness of heath, or gave sustenance to a flock of grey moorland sheep, with their little mossy-faced lambs: they clung to this scene, I say, with a perfect enthusiasm of attachment. I could comprehend the feeling, and share both its strength and truth. I saw the fascination of the locality. I felt the consecration of its loneliness: my eye feasted on the outline of swell and sweep — on the wild colouring communicated to ridge and dell by moss, by heath-bell, by flower-sprinkled turf, by brilliant bracken and mellow granite crag. These details were just to me . . . so many pure and sweet sources of pleasure (chap. 30).

Whatever its origin, this is the kind of scene that contains many of the criteria laid down by Sir Uvedale Price for an attractive landscape. In her emphasis upon place, the view bounded by the purple moors, the muted colouring of old walls and of pasturing sheep, the presence of fern-banks and the wilderness of heath where the "eye feasted on the outline of swell and sweep . . . and mellow granite crag," and in the pleasure that these visual effects gave Jane, Charlotte Brontë proclaims her own attachment to picturesque landscape description. The attraction of this mode of seeing is that it offers her scope for the

15   See Hayes, *Gainsborough*, plate 4.

degree of realism which seemed to suit her dedication to "the study of real life"; at the same time it does not exclude the ideal: the "charm both potent and permanent."

How Caroline Helstone and Shirley Keeldar visualize their surroundings on Nunnely Common, when they look down on a nearby wood, may owe much to Gilpin, particularly to his *Forest Scenery*. In the wood, says Caroline, there is a dell, "a deep, hollow cup, lined with turf as green and short as the sod of this Common: the very oldest of the trees, gnarled mighty oaks, crowd about the brink of this dell: in the bottom lie the ruins of a nunnery" (*Shirley*, chap. 12). To this wood, Shirley proposes that they should bring their pencils and sketch-books, a move that Caroline favours for she knows of "groups of trees that ravish the eye with their perfect, picture-like effects: rude oak, delicate birch, glossy beech, clustered in contrast; and ash trees stately as Saul, standing isolated, and superannuated wood-giants clad in bright shrouds of ivy." The enthusiasm of the two young ladies for this forest scenery is such that they even agree that their appreciation of old trees and old ruins would suffer if gentlemen were to be included in their party. Caroline's appreciation of what she saw would have had the approbation of William Gilpin who maintained that "perhaps of all species of landscape, there is none, which so universally captivates mankind, as forest-scenery."[16] Her tastes resemble those of her mother, who, we are told, had a "sense of the picturesque, an appreciation of the beautiful or commonplace, a power of comparing the wild with the cultured, the grand with the tame, that gave to her discourse a graphic charm" (chap. 21).

And so has the narrator, as she describes the narrow end of the Hollow in which Caroline and her mother walk: "Here, the opposing sides of the glen approaching each other, and becoming clothed with brushwood and stunted oaks, formed a wooded ravine; at the bottom of which ran the mill-stream, in broken unquiet course, struggling with many stones, chafing against rugged banks, fretting with gnarled tree-roots, foaming, gurgling, battling as it went" (chap. 21). This is the language of the picturesque: "stunted oaks," the "broken unquiet course" of the mill stream, the "rugged banks," and the "gnarled tree-roots." The description is topographic, something that Mrs. Gaskell noted when she observed that the scenery of Charlotte Brontë's "fiction lies close around."[17]

---

16   Gilpin, *Forest Scenery*, I, p. 269.
17   Gaskell, *Life*, p. 77.

Sometimes, however, the description is less realistic, leaning to what is ideal, or as the contemporary reviewers said, "poetic." A good example is Caroline's highly imaginative account of the Faroe Islands. For the romantic Caroline the waves become "tossing banks of green light, strewed with vanishing and re-appearing wreaths of foam, whiter than lilies" (chap. 13). In spite of her admiration for Ruskin's *Modern Painters*, Charlotte Brontë's imagination seldom strays into such Turnerian extravagance. But within Ruskin's "low picturesque" she is at ease for here reality is seldom greatly distorted by high imagination. She would be more at home, we surmise, with the art, for example, of Richard Wilson, the early Gainsborough, George Morland, and John Martin than with the mature Turner. She would, for instance, admire J. M. W. Turner's sketch of *The Valley of the Wharfe, from Caley Park*, or his water colour *Patterdale*, but question the merits of *Norham Castle, Sunrise*, which in her words would "baffle description."

The distrust of the ideal or abstract may also account in her novels for much landscape description that is representational, that owes a great deal to the artistic conventions of the picturesque. Thornfield with its battlements has a "picturesque look" (*Jane Eyre*, chap. 11), and the view from its leads is attractive for the same reason. Rochester recognizes this quality in his home: "I like Thornfield [he asserts]; its antiquity; its retirement; its old crow-trees and thorn-trees; its grey façade, and lines of dark windows reflecting that metal welkin" (chap. 15). The garden at Thornfield, so important for Jane's meetings with Rochester, is picturesque in the tradition of landscape artists like Humphry Repton. In it Rochester and Jane confess their love for one another. Critically, it makes sense to argue that the splintered chestnut tree is a good example of imagery that betrays Charlotte Brontë's reliance on both Gilpin and Price. For Gilpin, the mature chestnut was extremely picturesque. "This is the tree," he explains, "which graces the landscapes of Salvator Rosa."[18] As for Price, "inequality and irregularity alone, will give to a tree a *picturesque* appearance . . . when, for instance, some of the limbs are shattered, and the broken stump remains in the void space."[19] And the imagery provided by the shattered chestnut tree carries through to the end of *Jane Eyre*, where Rochester likens himself to "the old lightning-struck chestnut tree in Thornfield orchard"; like that tree he, too, is a ruin. In her use of such

18   Gilpin, *Forest Scenery*, I, p. 58.
19   Price, *An Essay on the Picturesque* (1796), I, pp. 91-92.

imagery, the author can make the conventions of the picturesque serve her narrative well by linking setting, character, and action.

A more obvious and less imaginative use of picturesque description occurs at the close of *The Professor*. It is more obvious because of the specific way in which William Crimsworth describes his retirement home:

> a picturesque and not too spacious dwelling, with low and long windows, a trellised and leaf-veiled porch over the front door, just now, on this summer morning, looking like an arch of roses and ivy. The garden ... with herbage short and soft as moss, full of its peculiar flowers, tiny and starlike ... At the bottom of the sloping garden there is a wicket, which opens upon a lane as green as the lawn, very long, shady, and little frequented ...
>
> It terminates (the lane I mean) in a valley full of wood; which wood—chiefly oak and beech—spreads shadowy about the vicinage of a very old mansion, one of the Elizabethan structures (chap. 25).

The description here is not really fused either to character or to action. It does, however, serve as a good illustration of how the picturesque can be used to support a sentimental, happy ending for a novel. Any curious person can find the prototype for this scene in an illustration like the *View from Repton's Cottage in Essex*.[20] This picture is, of course, at odds with Charlotte Brontë's declared intention that "novelists should never allow themselves to weary of the study of real life," and that Adam's sons "should share Adam's doom."[21] The endings of both *The Professor* and *Shirley* seem tailored for the tastes of the publishers who, says Charlotte, liked "something more consonant with a highly-wrought fancy." They were, she said, men whose breasts contained remarkable stores of both "romance and sensibility" (Preface, *The Professor*).

All the same, Charlotte Brontë was aware that William Crimsworth's picturesque abode was but thirty miles away from the sullying effect of factory smoke and that Robert Moore's prophecies in *Shirley* spelled the end of unusual settings like the Hollow, whose stream provided the power for his looms. Viewed in terms of the changes that Victorian industrialism was to inflict upon the countryside, the picturesque was an ephemeral form, something which Sir Uvedale Price seemed aware of before the end of the eighteenth century:

20 Humphry Repton, *The Art of Landscape Gardening* (Boston, 1907), frontispiece.
21 Charlotte Brontë, *The Professor*, preface and chap. 19.

> Men of property [writes Price], who either from false taste, or from a
> sordid desire of gain, disfigure such scenes or buildings as painters
> admire, provoke our indignation: not so when agriculture, in its
> general progress (as is often unfortunately the case) interferes with
> picturesqueness, or beauty. The painter may indeed lament; but
> that science, which of all others most benefits mankind, has a right
> to more than his forgiveness, when wild thickets are converted into
> scenes of plenty and industry, and when gypsies and vagrants give
> way to the less picturesque figures of husbandmen, and their atten-
> dants.[22]

It may well be that the gradual disappearance of picturesque landscape before the onslaught of agriculture and industrialism (which
has brought us today's image of the "Wasteland") has done as much to
discourage the taste for the picturesque as did Wordsworth's reference to its "rules of mimic art," or the novels of Thomas Love Peacock.

But if we concede such an argument, some explanation is necessary to explain why so perceptive a person as Charlotte Brontë made
use of an aesthetic that seemed to stand so little chance of survival. At
least two reasons may be offered: the first is that perceptiveness may
not rule out a love for this particular use of one's eyes; the second may
be that picturesque scenes, characters, customs, and artifacts continued to exist long after Price's time, some being deliberately preserved. Accurate descriptions of such scenes in painting or prose
may, therefore, be both realistic and picturesque—even perhaps
truthful. And these are not limited to rural landscapes.

In *Villette*, for instance, where most of the action takes place in a
city environment, the picturesque—if less noticeable than in *Jane
Eyre* or *Shirley*—is there in surprising measure and credibly so.
Consider the ghost-haunted garden behind Madame Beck's pension-
nat, which is so important in the plot of the novel. It is a garden, says
the speaker, that "independently of romantic rubbish ... had its
charms" (chap. 12), and those charms are picturesque: the vine-
draped berceau, the gaunt skeleton of Methusaleh with its half-bared,
ivy-covered roots, the sequestered bowers nestled in vines that "ran
all along a high and grey wall, and gathered their tendrils in a knot of
beauty," the rustic seat, and the luminous haze of moonlight. Villette
itself is "full of narrow streets of picturesque, ancient, and mouldering houses" (chap. 15). At the home of the Brettons, there is a large old
Dutch kitchen that is both "picturesque and pleasant" (chap. 25) in
which Lucy Snowe and the family have "a Christmas wassail-cup,

---

22   Price, *An Essay on the Picturesque* (1796), I, p. 327.

and toast Old England." In the Basse Ville, Lucy describes M. Paul's old house with the "grey flags in front, the nodding trees behind—real trees, not shrubs—trees dark, high, and of old growth." Within the house is Père Silas, "a priest, old, bent, and grey, and a domestic—old, too, and picturesque" (chap. 35). Setting here performs a service for it enhances the narrative for the reader and brings Lucy to M. Paul's secret.

It should be observed that the picturesqueness of the settings in Brussels, for example, had a firm footing in reality. This Enid Duthie makes clear in *The Foreign Vision of Charlotte Brontë* as she connects fictional places and their geographical location in *The Professor* and in *Villette*.[23] What Charlotte did in these novels may usefully be compared with what Gilpin did in his tour books in which we have illustrations that, like the settings in Charlotte's novels, can stand by themselves without detailed reference to region and place; but for many readers, of course, such reference meant a degree of reality that was conducive to credibility. And it is interesting that Charlotte in her own writing and Gilpin in the texts for his tours both seemed anxious to achieve this illusion. In this process, Charlotte unwittingly may have freed her picturesque from its tendency to sentimentality, a quality that belongs so often to description in minor Victorian fiction and in genre art of that time.

As others did in the nineteenth century, Charlotte Brontë accepted the idea that details of a character's appearance, like the details of a landscape, could be thought of as being picturesque. William Crimsworth, for example, finds the Flemish housemaid in Brussels, with her wooden shoes and short red petticoat, not pretty or polite but "very picturesque" despite her physiognomy which is "eminently stupid." Caroline Helstone, we are told, possesses curls "in picturesque confusion," and Shirley Keeldar has a "picturesque head."

Charlotte's use of the picturesque as related to character is often more meaningful, however, than these examples indicate. Jane Eyre's first glimpse and description of Rochester, disabled and unhorsed in the moonlight, offers much more detail and raises questions:

> His figure was enveloped in a riding-cloak, fur-collared, and steel-clasped ... I traced the general points of middle height, and considerable breadth of chest. He had a dark face, with stern features and a heavy brow; his eyes and gathered eyebrows looked ireful and thwarted just now ... Had he been a handsome, heroic-looking

23 Enid Duthie, *The Foreign Vision of Charlotte Brontë* (London, 1975), pp. 79-104.

young gentleman, I should not have dared to stand thus questioning him . . . I had hardly ever seen a handsome youth; never in my life spoken to one. I had a theoretical reverence and homage for beauty, elegance, gallantry, fascination; but had I met those qualities incarnate in masculine shape, I should have known instinctively that they neither had nor could have sympathy with anything in me (chap. 12).

Jane's unwillingness to accept an ideal beauty "incarnate in masculine shape," her fear of a "handsome, heroic-looking" gentleman is in keeping with the author's own distrust of the ideal. Later in the novel, Jane's concern about whether or not Rochester is attractive—most people, she asserts, would have thought him an ugly man—recalls Sir Uvedale Price's attempt to distinguish between ugliness and deformity and his conclusion that "ugliness, like beauty, in itself is not picturesque, for it has, simply considered, no strongly marked features: but [continues Price], when the last-mentioned character is added either to beauty or to ugliness, they become more striking and varied; and . . . more strongly attract the attention."[24] By Price's definition, Rochester is striking, indeed picturesque. He is the sort of person in demand for a game of charades when the role calls for theatrical figures like an eastern emir or a captured bandit. As a fortune-telling gypsy crone, seated by a fire that throws his face in shadow and illumines Jane's, Rochester is a model for Ruskin's "low school of the surface-picturesque."

Of the three men, William Crimsworth, Robert Moore, and M. Paul, it is M. Paul whose appearance is most unusual. Charlotte shows him in the *allée défendue*, his cigar at his lips, his paletot hanging "dark and menacing," the tassel of his bonnet grec sternly shadowing his left temple, his black whiskers curling "like those of a wrathful cat" (*Villette*, chap. 15). When Lucy looks at his face on one occasion in the classroom, she sees "a close and picturesque resemblance to that of a black and sallow tiger" (chap. 28). At other times he appears less savagely picturesque. When he removes his mask, "the deep lines left his features; the very complexion seemed clearer and fresher; that swart, southern darkness which spoke his Spanish blood, became displaced by a lighter hue" (chap. 27).

In his actions M. Paul is attractive in a Napoleonic sense for he is a "waspish little despot" capable of exiling "fifty Madame de Staëls." At times his actions can be eccentric in a Dickensian way, as when he

24   Price, *An Essay on the Picturesque* (1796), II, pp. 219-20.

presides at the head of the table for the picnic breakfast in the country, or when he adorns his person with the watch-guard that Lucy made for him. It was not necessary for Charlotte Brontë to announce this sort of description for her contemporaries, because they used the term "picturesque" specifically in relation to characterization of this kind; one of the reviews of *Villette* in 1853 offers an illustration: "The men, women, and children who figure throughout it," says the reviewer, "have flesh and blood in them. All are worked out heartily, in such a way as to evince a very keen spirit of observation on the author's part, and a fine sense of the picturesque in character."[25]

M. Paul is certainly "worked out heartily," and the reviewer's application of the word "picturesque" to character rather than specifically to appearance indicates how the term had extended its meaning by mid-century. If we accept this shift of meaning, it is plausible to attach the term to the bare outline of M. Paul's whole life: his education under the Jesuit, Père Silas; his ill-fated love for the pale Justine Marie; the loss of his family's fortune; his support of the "strange, godless, loveless misanthrope," Madame Walravens; his love for the Protestant, Lucy Snowe; his three-year stay in Guadeloupe; and finally his likely death in a wild southwest storm that strewed the Atlantic with wrecks. This is the sort of picturesqueness which G. K. Chesterton may have had in mind when he spoke of Robert Louis Stevenson's "picturesque attitude and career."[26]

If Charlotte Brontë did not intend to extend the meaning this widely, she certainly felt no unease in applying it to the outward appearance of her characters or to the description of her settings where she found its mode especially useful. In her effort to avoid the ideal and to seek truth in the observation of everyday life, it also provided her with a convenient way for bypassing the unacceptable limits of the ideal and at the same time for focusing in an interesting fashion on the real world in a manner readily recognizable to her readers. Like Sir Walter Scott, she demonstrated how the *ut pictura poesis* of Horace could be accommodated within the craft of fiction in the nineteenth century.

As with Sir Walter Scott, picturesque vision for Charlotte Brontë coincides with personal experience. She herself seems to have viewed her countryside in the light of its influence, as her reaction to Sir

25 *Examiner*, February 5, 1853, pp. 84-85, quoted in Miriam Allott, ed., *The Brontës, the Critical Heritage* (London, 1974), p. 175.

26 G. K. Chesterton, *Robert Louis Stevenson* (London, [1927]), p. 25.

James Shuttleworth's seat at Gawthorpe indicates: "She took great pleasure [notes Mrs. Gaskell, as she records what Charlotte herself said] in the 'quiet drives to old ruins and old halls, situated among older hills and woods; the dialogues by the old fireside in the antique oak-panelled drawing-room, while they suited him, did not too much oppress and exhaust me. The house, too, is much to my taste; near three centuries old, grey, stately, and picturesque'" (*Life*, p. 347).

How much this Lancashire countryside meant to her appears a little later as she talks about her objections to being driven about in Sir James's carriage:

> Decidedly I find it does not agree with me to prosecute the search of the picturesque in a carriage. A waggon, a spring-cart, even a post-chaise might do; but the carriage upsets everything. I longed to slip out unseen, and to run away by myself in amongst the hills and dales. Erratic and vagrant instincts tormented me, and these I was obliged to control, or rather suppress, for fear of growing in any degree enthusiastic, and thus drawing attention to the "lioness" — the authoress (*Life*, p. 365).

This letter written to Miss Wooler (September 27, 1850) offers further evidence of how a late eighteenth-century aesthetic, based on shaky psychological and philosophical foundations, flourished well into the nineteenth century. For Charlotte Brontë, however, the picturesque was quite acceptable, all the more so because it provided a way out of a rather baffling critical problem: how, in the face of those "erratic and vagrant instincts," to be "real, cool, and solid . . . as Monday morning" and yet retain something akin to the ideal—so beloved by her Victorian reading public.

Chapter 5

Charles Dickens

> M. Daudet is fond of fiction as Dickens was fond of it,—he
> is fond of the picturesque. His taste is for oddities and
> exceptions, for touching dénouments [sic], for situations
> slightly factitious, for characters surprisingly genial.
> > Henry James, "Alphonse Daudet"

Throughout 1836-70, those who reviewed Charles Dickens's fiction continuously reminded their readers of his descriptive power. Frequently the reviewers saw in his writing qualities which they could only define by referring to the art of painting and naming, for example, Wilkie, Hogarth, Frith, Stanfield, and Maclise or Dutch painters like Ostade, Teniers, and Jan Steen. R. H. Horne not only referred to the Dutch artists but also to the Italian to account for the eye that Dickens had "for all external effects."[1] Other reviewers spoke of his "pictorial effects," his "graphic reality," his "effective strokes," and his "descriptive painting." Frequently they fell back on what Bagehot referred to as "his picturesque imagination,"[2] or David Masson as his "picturesque illustrations of criminal life,"[3] or Samuel Phillips as his "picturesqueness of detail,"[4] or R. H. Hutton as "this picturesque piece of sentiment."[5] Ruskin, however, in 1841 was critical of such descriptive technique. Dickens ought, he wrote in 1841, to

1 R. H. Horne, "A New Spirit of the Age," *Westminster Review* 44 (June 1844), p. 374.
2 Bagehot, *Literary Studies*, II, p. 172.
3 [David Masson], "Pendennis and Copperfield: Thackeray and Dickens," *North British Review* 15 (May 1851), p. 67.
4 Samuel Phillips, "David Copperfield and Arthur Pendennis," *The Times*, June 11, 1851, p. 8.
5 [R. H. Hutton], "The Genius of Dickens," *The Spectator* 43 (June 18, 1870), p. 751.

raise his mind as far as in him lies, to a far higher standard, giving up that turn for the *picturesque* which leads him into perpetual mannerism, and going into the principles out of which that picturesqueness should arise. At present he describes eccentricity much oftener than character; there is a vivid, effective touch, truthful and accurate, but on the surface only; he is in literature very much what Prout is in art.[6]

Ruskin's comment reveals his understanding of picturesque practice and its application especially to Dickens's early work. It was a practice, however, which Dickens, too, understood and appreciated well enough to be aware eventually of its aesthetic shortcomings.

Throughout his fiction, its imprint is noticeable, much more so in his early than in his later novels. It is to be found in reference to landscape in both country and city; to buildings within and without; to the appearance and speech of his characters; in one of the novels, at least, to the action of the narrative; and, in many others, to the quality of some of the sketches which he accepted for illustrations. It is not always easy to separate out these divisions, for Dickens, even more than Scott, succeeded in fusing what is picturesque with other elements in his fiction. It is well, therefore, to begin with an early work like *The Posthumous Papers of the Pickwick Club* where we find, for example, that character may not be an integral part of the landscape we are made to see.

Mr. Pickwick, for instance, has no economic, social, or historic ties with the landscape he views as he leans over the balustrades of Rochester Bridge. The picture he sees is extraneous to his own existence. It provides him merely with an "agreeable reverie." For the reader, it is interesting description in a mode he recognizes at once:

> On the left of the spectator lay the ruined wall, broken in many places, and in some, overhanging the narrow beach below in rude and heavy masses. Huge knots of sea-weed hung upon the jagged and pointed stones ... and the green ivy clung mournfully round the dark and ruined battlements. Behind it rose the ancient castle, its towers roofless, and its massive walls crumbling away, but telling us proudly of its own might and strength, as when, seven hundred years ago, it rang with the clash of arms, or resounded with the noise of feasting and revelry. On either side, the banks of the Medway, covered with corn-fields and pastures, with here and there a windmill, or a distant church, stretched away as far as the eye could see, presenting a rich and varied landscape, rendered more beautiful by the changing shadows which passed swiftly across it ... The river ... glistened and sparkled ... as the heavy

6 *Works of John Ruskin*, XXXVI, pp. 25-26.

but picturesque boats glided slowly down the stream (*The Post-humous Papers of the Pickwick Club*, chap. 5).

In its pictorial organization, its emphasis upon decay and past history, upon distant prospect enlivened by passing shadows and a glistening river, the scene which so charmed Mr. Pickwick is a picturesque one which Dickens's readers—many perhaps with minds less reflective than Mr. Pickwick's—could easily visualize. After all they had grown up amid nine editions of *The Tour of Doctor Syntax in Search of the Picturesque*, and in 1837—when *Pickwick Papers* appeared in book form—they found still another edition of *The Tour*, published by Ackerman and Tegg, with illustrations by Crowquill to delight them. For these readers, the Pickwick narrative device for describing the Medway landscape was like recognizing a not very old friend, whose peculiar talent it was to promote understanding and laughter. The act of recognition was almost immediate: there was no need for them to puzzle out what Samuel Pickwick saw from the balustrades of Rochester Bridge. So familiar was this descriptive method that readers could construe at once from the words a mental image almost as realistic as the geographical existence of Rochester itself.[7]

It would, however, be very misleading to suggest that picturesqueness is an essential quality of description in *Pickwick Papers*: it is occasional rather than pervasive. When it occurs, it is easily recognized. As Mr. Pickwick and his two friends, Winkle and Snodgrass, make their way from Rochester to Cobham, Dickens's description of the pleasure they take in what they see illustrates his reliance upon this popular mode of description: a "deep and shady wood," ivy and moss "in thick clusters over old trees," an "open park, with an ancient hall, displaying the quaint and picturesque architecture of Elizabeth's time," "long vistas of stately oaks and elm trees," herds of deer and the occasional hare that "scoured along the ground, with the speed of the shadows thrown by the light clouds which swept across a sunny landscape like a passing breath of summer" (chap. 11). But this glimpse of country is as fleeting as human joy, for once Dodson and Fogg serve the writ to begin action in the case of "Martha Bardell, widow, v. Samuel Pickwick," Mr. Pickwick must be in London where legal offices and prisons like the Fleet offer little opportunity for description of picturesque landscape.

7 J. R. Harvey, in *Victorian Novelists and Their Illustrators* (New York, 1971), sees this "picture" as a "traditional example of the picturesque," p. 65.

As most of Dickens's fiction belongs, as he did, to the urban scene, descriptions of country landscape are infrequent. When Oliver Twist is rescued by Mrs. Maylie and Rose, he is taken to the country which Dickens addresses with Wordsworthian fervour in chapter 32. The picturesque, too, is close at hand when we read about the room where Oliver was accustomed to sit:

> It was quite a cottage-room, with a lattice-window: around which were clusters of jessamine and honeysuckle, that crept over the casement, and filled the place with their delicious perfume. It looked into a garden, whence a wicket-gate opened into a small paddock; all beyond, was fine meadowland and wood. There was no other dwelling near, in that direction; and the prospect it commanded was very extensive (chap. 34).

But this rural delight is troubled by the melodrama of Oliver's family connections and almost forgotten in the events that follow: the justice that overtakes Sikes in Jacob's Island, the imprisonment of Monks in the New World, and the end of Fagin on the "black stage" by the crossbeam and rope.

Another such brief country idyll appears in *The Old Curiosity Shop*, where Nell and her grandfather, having passed through the horror of a Midland industrial city, come to the schoolmaster's village where they admire "the brown thatched roofs of cottage, barn, and homestead, peeping from among the trees; the stream that rippled by the distant watermill; the blue Welsh mountains far away." Neither of these rural scenes is as carefully arranged as a picturesque painting of them would be, but they possess all the essentials and the view or prospect is implied.

But the picturesque becomes explicit as we see what Little Nell sees when she stepped into the old churchyard at the village:

> It was a very aged, ghostly place; the church had been built many hundreds of years ago, and had once had a convent or monastery attached; for arches in ruins, remains of oriel windows, and fragments of blackened walls, were yet standing; while other portions of the old building, which had crumbled away and fallen down, were mingled with the churchyard earth and overgrown with grass, as if they too claimed a burying-place and sought to mix their ashes with the dust of men (chap. 46).

This is the scene which George Cattermole illustrated: Little Nell sitting by a grave looking towards her own final resting place which time and ruin have made picturesque. Cattermole's sketch has the same sort of ancient untidiness about it as characterizes Samuel Williams's sketch of Nell asleep in her room in the Old Curiosity

Shop, where she is surrounded by a mélange of antiquities including medieval armour. Both sketches employ the contrast provided by fictional past and present; both suggest a wide range of associations and rely upon the Gothic for effect. Even if not significant art, these illustrations possessed a strong visual appeal for many readers. In *The Athenaeum* in 1840, Thomas Hood declared that "we do not know where we have met, in fiction, with a more striking and picturesque combination of images than is presented by the simple, childish figure of Little Nelly, amidst a chaos of such obsolete, grotesque, old-world commodities as form the stock-in-trade of the Old Curiosity Shop."[8] We know that Dickens was impressed by Hood's review and admitted that his pleasure originally arose from the contrast which "heaps of fantastic things" in a "curiosity-dealer's warehouse" made with his own image of Little Nell.[9] But contrast alone, of course, is not enough to justify Hood's use of "picturesque"; its use here seems more an illustration of how wide its application was in 1840 rather than how concisely it is being applied.

The use of what is picturesque in landscape can, like the jumble of antiquities in the Old Curiosity Shop, provide startling contrast in a setting that is commonplace or in one that must accommodate the criminal and horrific. As Jonas Chuzzlewit begins his approach to Montague Tigg in chapter 47 of *Martin Chuzzlewit*, he passes into a quiet, wooded dell so picturesque that Victorian readers could reasonably expect pleasurable consequences from its description rather than foul murder.

> Vistas of silence opened everywhere, into the heart and innermost recesses of the wood; beginning with the likeness of an aisle, a cloister, or a ruin open to the sky; then tangling off into a deep green rustling mystery, through which gnarled trunks, and twisted boughs, and ivy-covered stems, and trembling leaves, and bark-stripped bodies of old trees stretched out at length, were faintly seen in beautiful confusion.

A few sentences later this wood through which the last rays of the sun made a path of golden light had become to Jonas only a "hell" serving as concealment for Tigg's blood-soaked corpse. The contrast between the expectations created by the setting and the killing of Tigg makes for effective narrative.

8   [Thomas Hood], from an unsigned review of *Master Humphrey's Clock*, I, in *The Athenaeum*, November 7, 1840, pp. 887-88, quoted in Philip Collins, ed., *Dickens, the Critical Heritage* (London, 1971), p. 96.
9   See Harvey, *Victorian Novelists and Their Illustrators*, pp. 123-24.

As early as 1839, the reader notes occasionally Dickens's uneasiness about scenery which must accommodate both poverty and the picturesque. In his mind this association, if unavoidable, is unacceptable. He cannot isolate the one from the other. Even the "ragged picturesqueness" which Henry James found attractive about the "large poverty" that belonged to Rome and Naples in 1873[10] lies outside Dickens's aesthetic sympathy. And so, as he describes the "little race-course at Hampton" in *Nicholas Nickleby*, the irony of his reference to "sentiment" and "charity" is not lost upon us:

> Every gaudy colour that fluttered in the air from carriage seat and garish tent top, shone out in its gaudiest hues. Old dingy flags grew new again, faded gilding was reburnished, stained rotten canvas looked a snowy white, the very beggars' rags were freshened up, and sentiment quite forgot its charity in its fervent admiration of poverty so picturesque (chap. 50).

That Dickens, however, found much that delighted his eye at the Hampton race-course is obvious as he details the activities quite as vividly as William Powell Frith did, who witnessed much the same scene before he painted his *Derby Day* of 1858.

At the same time Dickens knew that even a criminal could be translated into something very acceptable to sentiment: "A thief in fustian is a vulgar character, scarcely to be thought of by persons of refinement; but dress him in green velvet, with a high-crowned hat, and change the scene of his operations, from a thickly peopled city to a mountain road, and you shall find in him the very soul of poetry and adventure" (*Nicholas Nickleby*, chap. 18). But despite this knowledge of how the picturesque could be used for romantic effect, and despite his own fondness for the art form and its practitioners, like Clarkson Stanfield and George Cattermole, Dickens never lets the superficial side of this kind of art obscure his vision.

His application of the word "picturesque" in his fiction also indicates how little sympathy he had with its attraction for the romance of past ages. To Mrs. Skewton of *Dombey and Son*, the thought of an expedition to Warwick Castle is enough to draw from her "a faded little scream of rapture" and an ironic condemnation of her delight for an age renowned for its brutality:

> "Oh!" cried Mrs. Skewton... "the Castle is charming!— associations of the Middle Ages—and all that—which is so truly exquisite. Don't you doat upon the Middle Ages, Mr. Carker?"

10   Henry James, *Italian Hours* (London, 1909), p. 272.

"Very much, indeed," said Mr. Carker.

"Such charming times!" cried Cleopatra. "So full of faith! So vigorous and forcible! So picturesque! So perfectly removed from commonplace!" (chap. 27).

Mrs. Skewton's interest in the picturesque accounts for one of the few references to Switzerland in Dickens's fiction. Again the effect is comic as she inanely remarks: "Nature intended me for an Arcadian . . . Cows are my passion. What I have ever sighed for, has been to retreat to a Swiss farm, and live entirely surrounded by cows—and china" (chap. 21).

But the picturesque of Swiss scenery does make a serious appearance in *David Copperfield* briefly at the end, when David in his pilgrimage abroad finds serenity in Switzerland, not among the sublimities of the peaks, but in a village clustered in a valley "with its wooden bridge across the stream, where the stream tumbled over broken rocks, and roared away among the trees." Here he lived for three months having "almost as many friends in the valley as in Yarmouth" and saw "the quiet evening cloud grow dim, and all the colours in the valley fade, and the golden snow upon the mountain tops become a remote part of the pale night sky, yet felt that the night was passing from [his] mind, and all its shadows clearing" (chap. 58). Picturesque description in this conclusion establishes a quiet mood and settles a final harmony upon David's troubled years, a harmony that one can realize visually in John Brett's painting the *Val d'Aosta* (1858), which Angus Wilson used as an illustration for Dickens's residence in Switzerland from June until October 1846.[11]

Such interaction of nature and character does not occur in *Bleak House* published two years after *David Copperfield*. Sir Leicester Dedlock "has a general opinion that the world might get on without hills, but would be done up without Dedlocks. He would on the whole admit Nature to be a good idea (a little low, perhaps, when not enclosed with a park-fence), but an idea dependent for its execution on your great county families" (chap. 2). Dedlock Hall does, however, have a "picturesque part," called the Ghost's Walk, and Esther Summerson admires the terrace garden and the old stone balustrades and parapets "seamed by time and weather." Boythorn's place is "a picturesque old house," and much the same can be said for Bleak House and "the cheerful landscape" about which the massive tower of the

11 Angus Wilson, *The World of Charles Dickens* (Harmondsworth, Middlesex, 1972), p. 198.

old Abbey Church "threw a softer train of shadow on the view than seemed compatible with its rugged character" (chap. 8).

It was Walter Bagehot who remarked that Dickens's genius did not "stop at the city wall." He was, said Bagehot, "especially at home in the picturesque and obvious parts of country life, particularly in the comfortable and (so to say) mouldering portion of it."[12] It may be worth observing, however, in his later novels that description of both town and country is seldom representational; in at least one instance it has the appearance of a late Turner painting: "The white face of the winter day came sluggishly on, veiled in a frosty mist; and the shadowy ships in the river slowly changed to black substances; and the sun, blood-red on the eastern marshes behind dark masts and yards, seemed filled with the ruins of a forest it had set on fire" (*Our Mutual Friend*, Bk. I, chap. 6). In such description, it is feeling and mood that matter most—not the specifics of place.

But in his earlier novels, the description is more straightforward, more picturesque; no detail seems to escape his attention; irony is usually absent. The Maypole Inn in *Barnaby Rudge* serves as a good illustration; it is

> an old building, with more gable ends than a lazy man would care to count on a sunny day; huge zig-zag chimneys ... and vast stables, gloomy, ruinous, and empty.... Its windows were old diamond-pane lattices, its floors were sunken and uneven, its ceilings blackened by the hand of time, and heavy with massive beams. Over the doorway was an ancient porch, quaintly and grotesquely carved ... With its overhanging stories, drowsy little panes of glass, and front bulging out and projecting over the pathway, the old house looked as if it were nodding in its sleep. The bricks of which it was built ... had grown yellow and discoloured like an old man's skin ... and here and there the ivy, like a warm garment to comfort it in its age, wrapt its green leaves closely round the time-worn walls (chap. 1).

Such a building and Cattermole's sketch of it would serve admirably to illustrate some of the distinct characteristics of the picturesque in buildings as Sir Uvedale Price describes them: "a state of neglect," "irregularity in the shapes and heights," "variety";[13] old walls that "announce something of age, decay, and abandonment";[14] "old clustring chimnies," and "porches and trellises of various constructions,

---

12   Bagehot, *Literary Studies*, II, p. 174.
13   Price, *Essays on the Picturesque*, II, pp. 302, 303, 305.
14   Price, *Essays on the Picturesque*, II, p. 282.

often covered with vine or ivy."[15] Another effective illustration for Price on buildings is to be found in Gabriel Varden's home which is "a shy, blinking house, with a conical roof going up into a peak over its garret window of four small panes of glass, like a cocked hat on the head of an elderly gentleman with one eye. . . . [I]t was not planned, with a dull and wearisome regard to regularity, for no one window matched the other, or seemed to have the slightest reference to anything besides itself" (chap. 4). The interiors of such old houses fascinated Dickens as much as their exteriors. Mr. Snodgrass describes the kitchen of the Manor Farm for the reader with nearly as much satisfaction as he takes from his sips of cherry brandy. The kitchen is

> a large apartment, with a red brick floor and a capacious chimney; the ceiling garnished with hams, sides of bacon, and ropes of onions. The walls were decorated with several hunting-whips, two or three bridles, a saddle and an old rusty blunderbuss . . . An old eight-day clock, of solemn and sedate demeanour, ticked gravely in one corner; and a silver watch, of equal antiquity, dangled from one of the many hooks which ornamented the dresser (chap. 5).

The parlour, too, shares the sort of "antiquity" which belongs to the kitchen, and "the recollection of old times and the happiness of many years ago" are such that they bring tears to the eyes of Mrs. Wardle, as her son recalls them.

Just as the picturesque kitchens and parlours of old houses appealed to Dickens so, too, did the coach offices, the yards of coaching inns, the coaches themselves, and the old inns where the travellers ate, drank, and slept. Years later the older man looked back with nostalgia upon his coaching memories and wrote about them in the series he called *The Uncommercial Traveller*, under such titles as "Dullborough Town" and "An Old Stage-Coaching House." Of the inns he mentions, none is perhaps better known than the White Hart of *Pickwick Papers*, where Mr. Sam Weller makes his first appearance. Inns like the White Hart are, as Mr. Pickwick observed, "singular old places" (chap. 21).

> Within the yard of the White Hart, the traveller can see a double tier of bed-room galleries, with old clumsy balustrades [running] round two sides of the straggling area, and a double row of bells to correspond, sheltered from the weather by a little sloping roof, hung over the door leading to the bar and coffee-room. Two or three gigs and chaise-carts were wheeled up under different little sheds and pent-houses, and . . . a few boys in smock frocks were

15 Price, *Essays on the Picturesque*, II, pp. 376, 382.

lying asleep on heavy packages, wool-packs, and other articles that
were scattered about on heaps of straw (chap. 10).

From the yards of such inns, the traveller could also see the arrival and
departure of the stage coaches which Dickens describes so graphi-
cally in the "Story of the Bagman's Uncle" (*Pickwick Papers*,
chap. 49). The account is a nostalgic one of the "old picturesque
town" of Edinburgh and of the old-fashioned mail coaches that once
enlivened the road between the capitals of Scotland and England.
Tom Pinch's trip to London by coach also gives Dickens an opportunity in *Martin Chuzzlewit* to describe the unusual components of
coaching: the coachmen, guards, bugles, the four greys jingling, rat-
tling on over the country road towards "the immensity and uncertainty of London." Here, however, as often happens in Dickens, the
countryside whirls by so quickly that no formal picture can be given.
It is "Yoho" throughout a paragraph of proper nouns with just a
flavour of the picturesque as the reader glimpses "last year's stacks . . .
showing, in the waning light, like ruined gables, old and brown"
(chap. 36).

Less public than the White Hart but equally picturesque are Old
Sol's Instrument Shop in *Dombey and Son* and Peggotty's house in
David Copperfield. The reader has a splendid memory of both places,
inside and out, not only because of the narrative but also because of
Phiz's illustrations. The best of these are "The Wooden Midshipman
on the Look-out" and "Little Emily." In the former we have the
angularities of an Elizabethan-style street filled with Victorian activity. Within the shop was "a snug, sea-going, ship-shape concern":
"Old prints of ships . . . hung in frames upon the walls; the Tartar
Frigate under weigh, was on the plates; outlandish shells, seaweeds,
and mosses, decorated the chimney-piece; the little wainscotted back
parlour was lighted by a skylight, like a cabin" (chap. 4). In the latter
we see a lonely Emily in the foreground and a "black barge, or some
other kind of superannuated boat, not far off, high and dry on the
ground, with an iron funnel sticking out of it for a chimney and
smoking very cozily" (chap. 3). In the background sea and cloud
combine with the chiaroscuro of the whole engraving to create a note
of foreboding. The interior of Peggotty's house which was once a "real
boat" is, in David Copperfield's eyes, completely charming, an
"Aladdin's palace, roc's egg and all." As a residence it is both unusual
and natural. Its picturesqueness is obvious: without, where we see
"that ship-looking thing," and within, for example, where a little
window takes up the space that once belonged to the rudder.

Later in the novel, Dickens describes the architectural oddities and cleanliness of Mr. Wickfield's house in Canterbury where "all the angles and corners, and carvings and mouldings, and quaint little panes of glass, and quainter little windows, though as old as the hills, were as pure as any snow that ever fell upon the hills" (chap. 15). Canterbury itself "where the ivied growth of centuries crept over gabled ends and ruined walks" (chap. 39) appears very much in the visual tradition popularized by William Gilpin.

If *Hard Times* offers the reader in search of the picturesque a blank, the same cannot be said for *Little Dorrit* or *Great Expectations*, where this convention often carries ironic overtones. In his early infatuation with Estella and Satis House, Pip's imagination, for example, was such that "Miss Havisham and Estella and the strange house appeared to have something to do with everything that was picturesque" (*Great Expectations*, chap. 15). Unlike Satis House, Wemmick's Castle has a comic unreality about it, as the Aged Parent predicates: "This spot and these beautiful works upon it ought to be kept together by the nation, after my son's time, for the people's enjoyment" (chap. 25).

This ironic treatment of an architectural oddity appears again in *Little Dorrit*, especially in Blandois's observations about his desire to see through Miss Clennam's house: "An old house is a weakness with me. I have many weaknesses, but none greater. I love and study the picturesque in all its varieties. I have been called picturesque myself" (Bk. I, chap. 30); and this same treatment is noticeable also in the depiction of Covent Garden which suggests "picturesque ideas" but in fact harbours "miserable children in rags," rotting foundations, and "foul street-gutters" (Bk. I, chap. 14).

Later, as the Dorrit household, freed from the Marshalsea, moves through Switzerland, the picturesque is constantly beset by unpleasant realities: "the idiot sunning his big goitre under the eaves of the wooden chalet by the way to the waterfall"; "the thin, hard, stony wine . . . made from the grapes"; and "the searching cold" that attends the Dorrits to the Pass of the Great St. Bernard, where "blackened skeleton arms of wood by the wayside pointed upward to the convent" where rest the "dead travellers found upon the mountain." Although all that Amy Dorrit "saw was new and wonderful . . . it was not real; it seemed to her as if those visions of mountains and picturesque countries might melt away at any moment, and the carriage, turning some abrupt corner, bring up with a jolt at the old Marshalsea gate" (Bk. II, chap. 3).

In Dickens's later novels, the picturesque often serves as a premonition that all may not be well. Although Mr. Meagles's house in *Little Dorrit* has "a young picturesque, very pretty portion to represent Pet," her own life, then and later, belies this appearance even as Clennam's view of the Thames at Twickenham—which "Phiz" rendered so attractively—turns eventually to sorrow as "the flowers, pale and unreal in the moonlight floated away" (Bk. I, chap. 28). On the Roman Campagna and in Rome itself, the ruins—so dear for picturesque reasons to touring Englishmen—become, for Amy Dorrit, inextricably bound up with her life at the Marshalsea: "two ruined spheres of action and suffering" (Bk. II, chap. 15). And Dickens is seldom more delightfully ironic than when he offers Flora Finching's remark upon Amy's absence in Italy: "In Italy is she really?" said Flora, "with the grapes and figs growing everywhere and lava necklaces and bracelets too, that land of poetry with burning mountains picturesque beyond belief . . . and is she really in that favoured land with nothing but blue about her and dying gladiators and Belvederas" (Bk. II, chap. 9).

Just as the picturesque qualities of Switzerland and Italy are treated in ironic fashion so, too, the outward charm of the London scene that Dickens knew and loved so well assumes unexpected shapes and meanings. Mrs. Plornish's shop-parlour at the "crack end" of Bleeding Heart Yard is as false as the economy that warps the lives of the Bleeding Hearts themselves. The shop-parlour presents "a little fiction":

> This poetical heightening of the parlour consisted in the wall being painted to represent the exterior of a thatched cottage; the artist having introduced (in as effective a manner as he found compatible with their highly disproportioned dimensions) the real door and window. The modest sunflower and hollyhock were depicted as flourishing with great luxuriance on this rustic dwelling, while a quantity of dense smoke issuing from the chimney indicated good cheer within . . . No Poetry and no Art ever charmed the imagination more than the union of the two in this counterfeit cottage charmed Mrs. Plornish (Bk. II, chap. 13).

In this context, the picturesque has become a painted façade, a mere fiction, incongruous yet pleasing to many of the inhabitants of Bleeding Heart Yard.

Elsewhere in *Little Dorrit* and in *Great Expectations*, the quaintness of old London: its streets, buildings, river wharves, and docks become sinister and Dantesque. Pip finds Smithfield a "shameful place, being all asmear with filth and fat and blood and foam" that seemed to stick to him (*Great Expectations*, chap. 20). As Mr. Meagles and Arthur Clennam search for Tattycoram, they move towards a labyrinth of little streets near Park Lane where nothing affords pictorial pleasure:

> Wildernesses of corner houses, with barbarous old porticoes and appurtenances; horrors that came into existence under some wrong-headed person in some wrong-headed time, still demanding the blind admiration of all ensuing generations ... frowned upon the twilight. Parasite little tenements ... commanding the dung-hills in the Mews, made the evening doleful. Rickety dwellings of undoubted fashion, but of a capacity to hold nothing comfortably except a dismal smell ... seemed to be scrofulously resting upon crutches (*Little Dorrit*, Bk. I, chap. 27).

Here, as so often happens in Dickens's greatest work, the description of setting becomes grotesque to support the novelist's artistic intention. As such, the setting cannot evoke pleasurable feelings.

Only occasionally in a novel like *Our Mutual Friend* (1865) is the reader reminded of pictorial qualities that are picturesque. The Six Jolly Fellowship-Porters in its name and that of its proprietor, Miss Abbey Potterson, certainly has the right flavour as the regulars order up Purl, Flip, and Dog's Nose while they admire the knotted likenesses in the wood of the chimney piece and the old corner cupboard. But this flavour soon disappears before the mystery and the horror of the river trade in bodies. It reappears only in relation to Aaron Riah: "a picturesque grey-headed and grey-bearded old Jew, in a shovel-hat and gaberdine" (Bk. III, chap. 10), who, when he makes a little gesture as though he were about to kiss an imaginary garment, does so, humbly but "picturesquely," in a way that "was not abasing to the doer" (Bk. II, chap. 5).

Characters like Aaron Riah, of unusual appearance, with distinctive mannerisms of gesture and speech, abound throughout Dickens's fiction. The pictorial tricks of caricature make the eloquent Mr. Pickwick one of the most memorable. As he slowly mounts into the Windsor chair to address the Corresponding Society of the Pickwick Club he presents, says the author, "a study for an artist," which Robert Seymour illustrates so that we can see the inspiring Pickwick "with one hand gracefully concealed behind his coat tails, and the other waving in the air, to assist his glowing declamation." For those whose imagination needs assistance, there is the picture not only of Mr. Pickwick but also of the other club members as they give their attention to their distinguished orator. What is picturesque in both the prose and the sketch is the appearance of the individual club members. The "poetic" Snodgrass sits beside the "sporting" Winkle: "the former poetically enveloped in a mysterious blue coat with a canine-skin collar, and the latter communicating additional lustre to a new green shooting coat, plaid neckerchief, and closely-fitted drabs" (chap. 1). The talents of author and artist combine to make this club scene a memorable one.

Next to Mr. Pickwick in most readers' affection is Sam Weller, whose appearance, more than his master's, claims a degree of pictur-esqueness: "He was habited in a coarse-striped waistcoat, with black calico sleeves, and blue glass buttons; drab breeches and leggings. A bright red handkerchief was wound in a very loose and unstudied style round his neck, and an old white hat was carelessly thrown on one side of his head" (chap. 10). Sam's appearance and speech con-trast with those of Mr. Stiggins, whose white neckerchief, with its long, limp ends, "straggled over his closely-buttoned waistcoat in a very uncouth and unpicturesque fashion" (chap. 27), and whose speech is as uninteresting as his threadbare black clothing.

Sam's speech may be thought of as picturesque because he, like his creator, makes us see as well as hear. He has a rare facility for making an abstraction concrete so that we can recognize it in a sensible form. Sam's remarks are, as Hugh Blair would say, "full of strong allusions to sensible qualities." It is hardly possible that the "gentleman" who asked Sam Weller where the "what's a-name—Doctors' Commons" was will fail to find it after Sam's reply so full of what is both tangible and visible:

> Paul's Church-yard, sir; low archway on the carriage-side, bookseller's at one corner, hot-el on the other, and two porters in the middle as touts for licences."
> "Touts for licences!" said the gentleman.
> "Touts for licences," replied Sam. "Two coves in vhite aprons—touches their hats wen you walk in—'Licence, sir, licence?' Queer sort, them, and their mas'rs too, sir—Old Baily Proctors—and no mistake."

In this conversation we catch a glimpse of old London as Sam Weller sketches a section of the street known as St. Paul's Churchyard: a low archway, the front of shops, and, very much to the fore, the "two coves in vhite aprons" whose unusual appearance Sam associates with the vicissitudes his father endured getting a marriage licence from the nearby Doctors' Commons. As Sam runs on, "like a new barrow with the wheel greased," that part of London becomes very familiar to the reader who must accompany the "uncommon fat" Tony Weller:

"wery smart—top boots on—nosegay in his button-hole—broad-brimmed tile—green shawl—quite the gen'lm'n" as he walks through the archway after the touter "like a tame monkey behind a horgan." Our familiarity with Doctors' Commons is the result of the imagined dialogue which Sam furnishes as he relives his father's encounter with the lawyer:

> "What's your name, sir," says the lawyer.—"Tony Weller," says my father.—"Parish?" says the lawyer.—"Belle Savage," says my father; for he stopped there wen he drove up, and he know'd noth-ing about parishes, he didn't.—"And what's the lady's name?" says the lawyer. My father was struck all of a heap. "Blessed if I know," says he. "Not know!" says the lawyer.—"No more nor you do," says my father, "can't I put that in arterwards?"—"Impossible!" says the lawyer.—"Wery well," says my father, after he'd thought a moment, "put down Mrs. Clarke."—"What Clarke?" says the lawyer, dipping his pen in the ink.—"Susan Clarke, Mar-kis o' Granby, Dorking," says my father; "she'll have me, if I ask, I des-say—I never said nothing to her, but she'll have me, I know" (chap. 10).

And so through the medium of Sam Weller's language we are pre-sented with a picture of a London coachman, a London street, and activity in the Doctors' Commons, each of which shares qualities that are picturesque. In its own way, however, Sam's language adds much to this experience. His dialogue is a part of it for within its idiosyn-cratic nature, its distortions of syntax, grammar, and spelling we have a kind of verbal play which may be thought of as picturesque because of its novelty, its irregularity, and the contrast it makes with standard speech.

This pictorial quality of speech and street and of the appearance of characters is, of course, noticeable elsewhere in Dickens's fiction. It is obvious, for example, in the outward look of many of those who frequent the Maypole Inn in *Barnaby Rudge*: of Hugh, the half-savage ostler, and local people like Solomon Daisy, visitors like Gabriel Varden, and perhaps John Willet, the innkeeper. Of Hugh we read: "The negligence and disorder of the whole man, with something fierce and sullen in his features, gave him a picturesque appearance, that attracted the regards even of the Maypole customers who knew him well, and caused Long Parkes to say that Hugh looked more like a poaching rascal to-night than ever he had seen him yet" (chap. 11). Other characters like Solomon Daisy and his cronies, Long Parkes, Tom Cobb, and John Willet are precursors of those rustics who appear in Thomas Hardy's novels. In the particulars of his appearance, as he stands in the gloom and the light of the Maypole's chimney corner, Solomon is as striking as any. Gabriel Varden—so full of long-suffering kindness towards his wife, so genial with his friends, so natural a man with respect to taverns—is very like Mr. Samuel Pickwick, Esq.

When Nicholas Nickleby finds employment with Mr. Vincent Crummles, he meets "originals" as interesting as those of the Maypole's chimney corner. Mr. Crummles's high-flown language, the idiosyncrasies of his troopers, and their dramatic efforts, all contribute a distinctive quality to the Portsmouth Theatre rather like the peculiarities that distinguished Mr. Pickwick and his friends—the kind of picturesqueness that Henry James observed in the novels of Alphonse Daudet. Somewhat the same thing can be said, too, of the Brothers Cheeryble in London because of their "quaintness and oddity" of appearance, their genial charitableness, and their eccentricities of manner.

Always, of course, it is well to remember that the pictorialism which we imagine in our minds springs nearly always from language. In reminding us of the suggestive power of Dickens's prose, Steven Marcus notes that "the language itself seems an organ of perception, shaping the experience almost as soon as it is received."[16] Certainly we realize the seeing power of Dickens's prose when we listen to Mrs. Nickleby whose speech, like Flora Finching's, is full enough of sudden surprises, irrelevancies, and non-sequiturs to deserve the term "picturesque" even though it lacks the grammatical oddities of Sam Weller's. That Dickens himself thought of Mrs. Nickleby's brand of garrulity in this way is obvious, as he describes her reaction to Mr. Pyke's extravagant blandishments on the beauty of her daughter Kate and the ideas that subsequently enter her head:

> Mrs. Nickleby went on to entertain her guests with . . . a picturesque account of her old house in the country: comprising a full description of the different apartments, not forgetting the little store-room, and a lively recollection of how many steps you went down to get into the garden, and which way you turned when you came out at the parlour-door, and what capital fixtures there were in the kitchen. This last reflection naturally conducted her into the wash-house, where she stumbled upon the brewing utensils, among which she might have wandered for an hour, if the mere mention of those implements had not, by an association of ideas, instantly reminded Mr. Pyke that he was "amazingly thirsty" (chap. 27).

16   Steven Marcus, *Dickens from Pickwick to Dombey* (London, 1965), p. 216.

The word "picturesque" at the beginning of this quotation does not apply, as it properly should, to the description of the old house, but rather to the rambling, inconsequential direction of Mrs. Nickleby's powers of "lively recollection." The word has assumed a new meaning but closely linked to that association of ideas that played so large a part in the theorizing of Gilpin, Price, and Knight.

An even better illustration of how pictorial Dickens's language may be in the mouths of his "low" characters exists, for example, in *Martin Chuzzlewit* in Mrs. Sairey Gamp's reply to Mrs. Harris's concern for her "indiwidgle number," as Sairey thinks of her own husband's death. Here we read and see at the same time: "And as to husbands, there's a wooden leg gone likeways home to its account, which in its constancy of walkin' into wine vaults, and never comin' out again 'till fetched by force, was quite as weak as flesh, if not weaker" (chap. 40). Such play with words, such vivid irregularity of speech, such verbal pictorialism deserves, even more than Mrs. Nickleby's, the epithet "picturesque."

To find this term used more specifically than this in its customary role, we have Dickens's description of Manette at work in the chiaroscuro of his garret in *A Tale of Two Cities*. We see him with his scraps of leather at his feet, his "white beard raggedly cut," the "hollowness and thinness of his face," his dark eyebrows, his "confused white hair," the "yellow rags of shirt . . . open at the throat," and his body "withered and worn." The "rough touches of age" which attracted both Gilpin and Price belong to Manette. Dickens's portrait in words has really no need of an artist's sketch to bring him visibly before our eyes. Later, in London, Dickens shows him to us asleep, "his white hair picturesque on the untroubled pillow" (Bk. II, chap. 17). Resort to picturesque description sharpens the contrast between his Paris garret and his London habitation: "A quainter corner than the corner where the Doctor lived, was not to be found in London . . . the front windows . . . commanded a pleasant little vista of street . . . and forest-trees flourished, and wild flowers grew, and the hawthorn blossomed, in the now vanished fields" (Bk. II, chap. 6). In this setting, Carton admits to Stryver, abides "the picturesque doctor's daughter" for whom he will give his life that her husband may live. Carton's own appearance before Mr. Lorry in Paris also deserves attention. We see him as a light or shade passed from his face "as swiftly as a change will sweep over a hill-side on a bright day." What follows heightens this impression: "He wore the white riding-coat and top-boots, then in vogue, and the light of the fire touching their light surfaces made him look very pale, with his long brown hair, all untrimmed, hanging loose about him" (Bk. III, chap. 9). Equally picturesque but very different is the form of Madame Defarge, who is strikingly like one of Salvator Rosa's banditti in her rough robe which she wears with a careless gesture. On her way to confront Miss Pross,

> her dark hair looked rich under her coarse red cap. Lying hidden in her bosom, was a loaded pistol. Lying hidden at her waist, was a sharpened dagger. Thus accoutred, and walking . . . with the supple freedom of a woman who had habitually walked in her girlhood, bare-foot and bare-legged, on the brown sea-sand, Madame Defarge took her way along the streets (Bk. III, chap. 14).

What is picturesque, however, in *A Tale of Two Cities* goes well beyond this kind of surface description.

Like Sir Walter Scott, Dickens thinks of this word as proper to describe one kind of storytelling. This is obvious in the letter he wrote to John Forster (August 25, 1859) in which he tried to make clear that this novel, then running in *All the Year Round*, was to be a "*picturesque* story, rising in every chapter with characters true to nature, but whom the story should express, more than they should express themselves by dialogue." Dickens then told Forster that, in other words, what he fancied was "a story of incident" whereby the action would shape or reveal the characters. But to set aside dialogue for this purpose was, Forster thought, a hazardous experiment and one that was not "entirely successful," because the *Tale* had "so little humour and so few rememberable figures."[17] Certainly the method seemed to contradict what Dickens had once asserted about his fictional technique: characters should, he said, "work out their own purposes in dialogue and dramatic action."[18] That Dickens, however, in later years supported a departure from his usual practice appears in the preface to *A Tale of Two Cities*, where he explains that it had been one of his hopes "to add something to the popular and picturesque means of understanding that terrible time."

His intentions here seem very like those which Robert Louis Stevenson enunciated in 1882 when he wrote his "Gossip on Romance." Just as Dickens thinks that the story should pound "the characters out in its own mortar" and beat "their own interests out of them,"[19] so, too, Stevenson saw "the plastic part of literature" as the

17   John Forster, *The Life of Charles Dickens* (London, 1966), II, p. 283.

18   Charles Dickens, *The Letters of Charles Dickens, 1833-1870*, [ed. by Mamie Dickens and Georgina Hogarth] (London, 1909), p. 357.

19   Dickens, *Letters* (1909), p. 485.

art of embodying "character, thought, or emotion in some act or attitude that shall be remarkably striking to the mind's eye."[20] Both Dickens and Stevenson may be indebted to Sir Walter Scott for this technique; certainly Scott's comment about the "highly picturesque" account of the Regent Murray's death offers a good example of the kind of incident whereby the action would shape or reveal the characters.

What happens in *A Tale of Two Cities* is that a cast of characters, caught up—some of them rather accidentally—in the whirlwind of revolution, are motivated to act and in acting display, as Sidney Carton does, unexpected depths of character. And although, as John Forster has pointed out, "few rememberable figures" appear, their actions are memorable as are the blood-stained streets of Paris and the misery-worn faces and figures of the peasants who enable the Marquis St. Evrémonde to live surrounded by "the fashion of the last Louis but one." This departure from his usual fictional technique whereby, as Stevenson puts it, the characters "are lifted up by circumstances as by a breaking wave, and dashed we know not how into the future" extends the meaning of the traditional picturesque to narrative technique. What Dickens wanted to do in *A Tale of Two Cities*—and what he achieved—was the creation of a book in which the reader is carried onward irresistibly by incident which tries and shapes character. In its cumulative effect this novel does add "something to the popular and picturesque means of understanding" the revolution that so disfigured France.

An examination of Dickens's use of the picturesque throughout his fiction leaves the distinct impression that he drew rather seldom but effectively upon both its theory and practice; it was, of course, a mode current and accepted among his many acquaintances who were painters, notably Hablot K. Browne, George Cattermole, George Cruikshank, Augustus Egg, Luke Fildes, W. P. Frith, Edwin Landseer, C. R. Leslie, Daniel Maclise, William Mulready, Clarkson Stanfield, Frank Stone, David Roberts, E. M. Ward, and David Wilkie. Many of these artists were intimate friends, often with Dickens in amateur theatricals, in consultations about illustrations, in his home for dinners, or at the celebrations for the inevitable christenings; sometimes, too, as he did with Frank Stone, Augustus Egg, and Clarkson Stanfield, he included the artists as companions on travels. Few men of

20 Stevenson, "A Gossip on Romance," in *The Works of Robert Louis Stevenson*, XXIX, p. 123.

letters in the nineteenth century could have had as wide and intimate acquaintance with Victorian artists, many of whose works bear witness to the popularity of the picturesque mode. Some of their art, like that of Clarkson Stanfield, hung in Gadshill Place.[21]

In the last few years much critical attention has been given to Victorian book illustrations and to the men, for instance, who illustrated Dickens's fiction. Generally these critics demonstrate what the illustrations add to the text and in what ways they depart from the text. Sometimes, of course, they display the taste for the popular picturesque although, for the most part, the artists are more likely to reveal the influence of caricature or of the grotesque in their sketches. Nearly always, despite the close attention which Dickens gave to the work of his illustrators, they fall short of what he himself provided in his prose. This is a point which Jane R. Cohen makes in her book, *Charles Dickens and His Original Illustrators*: "Indeed, Dickens's writing became so profoundly pictorial that it was difficult for any of the illustrators of his later work to do more than represent rather than illustrate his narratives in the fullest sense."[22] The picturesque was an element of Dickens's own literary talent; he had really little need to rely upon illustrations for his readers to capture its significance.

How much it meant to him and what his objections were to it become clear in his two travel books and in some of his letters. *American Notes* (1842) is an account of his travels and experiences from January to the end of June 1842 in the United States and Canada. Like other travellers of the time he was always pleased by picturesque scenery. In the United States he applied the term to the appearance of Yale College, to the countryside around New York, to the heights above the Potomac River, and to the old houses in the French section of St. Louis; in Canada it suited the heights at Queenston and the steep streets and frowning gateways of Quebec City. His descriptions, for example, of New Haven and Quebec City parallel nicely the illustrations of these two places provided by William Henry Bartlett in *American Scenery* (1840) and *Canadian Scenery* (1842).

But not all the scenery in the New World was attractive to Dickens, who was disappointed in the visual impression made by the

21   For Dickens's acquaintance with Victorian art and artists see, for example, Forster's *Life of Charles Dickens*, II, pp. 45, 85, 132, 138, 150, 172, 211.

22   Jane R. Cohen, *Charles Dickens and His Original Illustrators* (Columbus, 1980), p. 10. See also Michael Steig, *Dickens and Phiz* (Bloomington, 1978), who argues that "from *Pickwick* through *Little Dorrit* . . . Browne's illustrations . . . complete Dickens's artistic achievement," p. 316.

western prairies and the Mississippi. Of the prairie he noted that "its very flatness and extent . . . left nothing to the imagination, tamed it down and cramped its interest" (chap. 13). At Cairo he described the Mississippi as "that intolerable river dragging its slimy length and ugly freight off towards New Orleans" (chap. 14). This impression is the one the reader gets from *Martin Chuzzlewit*, as Martin and Mark Tapley in Eden contemplate the "monotonous desolation" of their wilderness home (chap. 23).

Such scenery compares very unfavourably, for example, with a Scottish heath or even the English downs. The artistic schema that had been shaped by the picturesque landscapes and seascapes of painters like Sir Edwin Landseer and Clarkson Stanfield (Pl. 22) simply cannot accommodate the "barren monotony" of the American frontier. The prairies have no intricate prospects, no memorable ruins, and above all no historic associations. Elsewhere in *American Notes*, the serious issues of slavery and the conditions of prison life deny to the narrative the delights the tourist looks for in travel literature.

Generally, *Pictures from Italy*, an account of the author's stay in that country from July 1844 to June 1845, demonstrates that Dickens preferred the scenery in that country to that of America. From the Villa Bagnerello in Genoa he could look down "to a ruined chapel which stands upon the bold and picturesque rocks on the sea-shore" (p. 285). And the view from the Palazzo Peschiere was such that he rejoiced "in a perfect dream of happiness" as he gazed upon the city "in beautiful confusion" below him, and then on out to the broad sea and the winding road to Nice (p. 307). The city itself abounded in "the strangest contrasts; things that are picturesque, ugly, mean, magnificent, delightful, and offensive, break upon the view at every turn" (p. 291).

Elsewhere in Italy, he placed the picturesque seal of approval upon cities and towns as different as Bologna, Verona, Carrara, Siena, Capua, Rome, Tivoli, and, of course, Naples. From Genoa to Nice, Dickens admired "the beautiful towns that rise in picturesque white clusters from among the olive woods." Climbing to the upper halls of the Colosseum in Rome he looked down on "ruins, ruins, ruins" and was moved deeply by the associations they suggested. On the Appian Way "the whole wide prospect [he noted] is one field of ruin. Broken aqueducts, left in the most picturesque and beautiful clusters of arches; broken temples; broken tombs" (p. 367). While waiting to see an execution, he admired the picturesque garb and mien of those belonging to the artist colony. And while travelling to Naples, he described "the train of wine-carts," going picturesquely into Rome, "each driven by a shaggy peasant reclining beneath a little gipsy-fashioned canopy of sheepskin" (p. 409).

Even though Dickens may have his travel notes slanted in the direction of popular Victorian taste at home, his social conscience cannot accept all he sees in Italy without caveat. In the last chapter of *Pictures from Italy*, he presents the dilemma: on the one hand, art; on the other, humanity.

> But, lovers and hunters of the picturesque, let us not keep too studiously out of view the miserable depravity, degradation, and wretchedness, with which this gay Neapolitan life is inseparably associated! It is not well to find Saint Giles's so repulsive, and the Porta Capuana so attractive. A pair of naked legs and a ragged red scarf, do not make *all* the difference between what is interesting and what is coarse and odious? Painting and poetising for ever, if you will, the beauties of this most beautiful and lovely spot of earth, let us, as our duty, try to associate a new picturesque with some faint recognition of man's destiny and capabilities (p. 413).

This comment does much to explain why the term "picturesque," which obviously meant much to Dickens, appears so seldom in his novels, especially those of his later years. It is not so much its superficial qualities as its awkward association with ruined and degraded people that makes its use for him in his novels so often aesthetically impossible. The pleasure that the picturesque in theory should bring to readers seems incongruous alongside "miserable depravity, degradation, and wretchedness." Jane R. Cohen has noted how Dickens and Samuel Palmer differed in their reactions to Italy: "Palmer, interested primarily in his work, could separate his aesthetic and moral judgments; Dickens, with his overriding interest in people and their institutions, could not."[23] Her statement is both perceptive and reasonable and borne out when we scrutinize the four illustrations which Palmer did for *Pictures from Italy*. Their picturesqueness contrasts markedly with the social realism apparent in the three illustrations which Marcus Stone contributed to this same book.

It is interesting also to remember Walter Bagehot's strictures about the character of the poor and its treatment in art. Dickens, he charges, has "in various parts of his writings been led by a sort of pre-Raphaelite *cultus* of reality into an error" whereby he gives us too much about poor people and their misfortunes. Others, he alleges,

---

23   Cohen, *Charles Dickens*, p. 194.

"have fallen into an opposite mistake," and "have attributed to the poor a fancied happiness and Arcadian simplicity." The exception, for Bagehot, was Sir Walter Scott whom, he asserts, "has most felicitously avoided both these errors."[24] Bagehot's Victorian commonsense deserves attention even though it was soon to be overwhelmed by the sort of "lifelike exhibitions" which he felt should be denied a place in fiction. These had appeared in some of the genre paintings even before Bagehot wrote his essay "The Waverley Novels" in 1858. Thomas Faed's *The Mitherless Bairn* made that painter's name well known when it was hung in London in 1855;[25] Henry Wallis's *The Stonebreaker* was completed in 1857 and exhibited at the Royal Academy in 1858. A little later (1869-71), Gustave Doré's drawings of London showed the poor in all their misery. Here again the role of the artist must be reckoned with in any serious discussion of the growth of realism in the novel.[26]

But realism in either fine art or fiction did not displace the picturesque in the nineteenth century in Britain. Even for Dickens it held a place of importance, especially when offending misery and poverty were veiled from sight. Throughout his life, it remained a mode of vision which he enjoyed and appreciated. Although it was not "very picturesque ashore" at Broadstairs in 1849, it was, he wrote, "extremely so seaward; all manner of ships continually passing inshore"; in Lausanne, his letters again and again reveal his attachment to the scenery there; later, he describes Berne as "a surprisingly picturesque old Swiss town." Boulogne he finds to be "piled and jumbled about in a very picturesque manner," and "the fishing people (whose dress can have changed neither in colour nor in form for many many years), and their quarter of the town cobweb-hung with great brown nets ... are as good as Naples, every bit."[27]

Gadshill, outside Rochester, was a vicinity rich in memories for Dickens and interesting for its historical and literary associations. Here, Dickens bought Gadshill Place which became his permanent home from 1856 until his death in 1870. Although the house itself in

24 Bagehot, *Literary Studies*, II, p. 143.
25 Graham Reynolds, *Victorian Painting* (London, 1966), p. 112.
26 See Meisel, *Realizations*, chap. 18, "W. P. Frith and the Shape of Modern Life," and note the relationship, for instance, of Luke Fildes to melodrama and to *The Graphic*, p. 396. See also Howard David Rodee, "Scenes of Rural and Urban Poverty in Victorian Painting and Their Development, 1850 to 1890" (Ph.D. dissertation, Columbia University, 1975).
27 Forster, *Life of Charles Dickens*, II, p. 146.

1856 was a rather ugly, staring, old red-brick structure, Dickens, by the purchase of a large back meadow, by planting lime and chestnut trees about the property, by training ivy over the façade, and by creating a colourful English garden made the place attractive. In a letter to Cerjat in 1858 Dickens describes the changes he has made in his home: "I have added to and stuck bits upon in all manner of ways, so that it is as pleasantly irregular, and as violently opposed to all architectural ideas, as the most hopeful man could possibly desire" (*Letters*, 1909, p. 450). Certainly the addition of the Swiss chalet in 1865 made the garden distinctively attractive for the author. In the chalet, Dickens told an American friend, he could see, using mirrors, "in all kinds of ways, the leaves that are quivering at the windows, and the great fields of waving corn, and the sail-dotted river . . . and the lights and shadows of the clouds [that] come and go with the rest of the company."[28]

It is Forster who notes that here in this unusual study "the last page of *Edwin Drood* was written . . . in the afternoon of his last day of consciousness."[29] Perhaps on that fateful morning Dickens may have looked up to imagine what Pickwick saw as he leaned over the balustrade of Rochester Bridge and watched "the picturesque boats [as] they glided slowly down the stream" and to see the end that his own imagery so often shadowed forth in the rivers that made their way to "the eternal seas." Such a vision, even on this day, would come effortlessly for this creator whose imagination had pictured so vividly and so richly and in so many novels hundreds of scenes and characters to delight his readers. In this act of creation, Charles Dickens often had occasion to bring the spirit and letter of the picturesque to his side. When he did, his own moral sense restrained his enthusiasm for pleasant idealities that seemed inappropriate alongside his real sympathies for the wretchedness and suffering that blighted the lives of the poor in England in his day. At the same time his genius expanded and gave new meanings and uses to the picturesque. Few, if any, novelists had his ear for what was singular in speech, his eye for "oddities and exceptions" of appearance and conduct, his deftness in giving an ironic twist to description, or his desire to found a new picturesque more suited to "man's destiny and capabilities."

28   Forster, *Life of Charles Dickens*, II, p. 212.
29   Forster, *Life of Charles Dickens*, II, p. 367.

Chapter 6

George Eliot

Moral and picturesque ideas do not always coincide.
William Gilpin, *Observations ... Mountains
and Lakes of Cumberland and Westmoreland*

In her determination to give her readers "a faithful account of men
and things as they have mirrored themselves in [her] mind," George
Eliot tried in chapter 17 of *Adam Bede* to eliminate the picturesque
from her creed. It was, she suggested, a way "to represent things as
they never have been," a way to an "arbitrary picture," arrived at by
touching up "with a tasteful pencil." About "those old women scrap-
ing carrots," or those "heavy clowns taking holiday in a dingy pot-
house," or "those homes with their tin pans, their brown pitchers,
their rough curs, and their clusters of onions," there could be "no
picturesque sentimental wretchedness!" Real men and women, especially the majority—with mob-caps, ill-proportioned noses and lips,
roughened hands, dingy complexions and squat figures—far out-
numbered "picturesque lazzaroni" and should, therefore, be remembered and represented in art.

To what extent chapter 17 is a reliable guide to George Eliot's
practice as a novelist is a question worth asking. Certainly it supplies
an answer to her rather ironic treatment of the Rector of Broxton. But
how important, for example, are the coarse, primitive people who
appear in her novels, people like Mrs. Bede, Luke Moggs, Jem Rodney,
Monna Brigida, Tommy Trounsem, the Goffes, and the Dagleys? It is
all the more reasonable to ask this question when we recall what
George Eliot had to say about the working classes in her *Westminster
Review* article (July 1856) which bore the title, "The Natural History of

German Life." In this article she regrets the absence of the true peasant from current picture exhibitions. "What English artist," she asks, "even attempts to rival in truthfulness such studies of popular life as the pictures of Teniers or the ragged boys of Murillo?" And, remembering her reading of Ruskin, she goes on to deplore the "picturesque motley" in which social novelists of her day tended to display the working people of rural England. What she does in this review of Wilhelm Heinrich von Riehl's two books is to inform us about "the real characteristics of the working classes," and in so doing to enlist our sympathy for them. But, despite George Eliot's convictions as they appear in this review article, her fiction reveals few, if any, coarse, primitive people who deserve more than a page of critical attention for their fictional roles.

Some exceptions, however, exist, and in some instances her treatment of such characters indicates that her mind's eye is not as immune to picturesque charm as her own statements suggest. Consider Bob Jakin in his bargeman's costume, surmounted by a "low-crowned oilskin-covered hat." Two years' work on a barge and a period "tentin' the furnace" at Torry's mill have changed the ragged barefoot boy of Kennel Yard into someone Tom Tulliver scarcely recognizes as Bob stands picturesquely in the chiaroscuro of "the imperfect fire and candle light," pulling on his red hair with one hand and holding his reward money with the other. It was this money which had made a packman of Bob; as to the barge, he told Tom in language as vivid and pictorial as Sam Weller's, "I'm clean tired out wi't, for it pulls the days out till they're as long as pigs' chitterlings" (*The Mill on the Floss*, Bk. III, chap. 6).

And so in his blue plush waistcoat, seal-skin cap, his pack on his back, and accompanied by his brindled bull terrier, Mumps, Bob Jakin, like the jagger of *The Pirate*, shares many of the picturesque qualities which may be traced back at least as far as the banditti of Salvator Rosa; it is these which suggest to Mrs. Glegg's mind the possibility of her husband "being murdered in the open daylight." In the end, however, Mrs. Glegg herself succumbs to Bob's blandishments — the ingredients of which recall those in Sam Slick's rhetoric — while Bob assures her that "the moths an' the mildew was sent by Providence o' purpose to cheapen the goods a bit for the good-lookin' women as han't got much money" (Bk. V, chap. 2).

Perhaps it would be unwise to extend the application of the picturesque much further in connection with Bob Jakin, although it is true that he lived with his mother in a "queer round house" down by the river and that the windows had leaded panes and that its old wooden framework was little protection against the flood waters of the Floss; but we know little more than this about it because George Eliot avoids paragraphs of description such as Dickens delights in when describing old buildings. Still, enough has been said about Bob Jakin to indicate that his qualities go well beyond those that George Eliot associates with the common labourer. It may be, of course, that Bob is an exception because of the trade he follows. But he is not alone: Wiry Ben Cranage, renowned locally in *Adam Bede* for his musical and terpsichorean abilities, is a figure in the picturesque scene that extends back to the paintings of seventeenth-century Dutch and Flemish artists. Likewise, Tessa in *Romola* is easily recognized in this mode of description; she is "a simple contadina . . . prepared for a festa: her gown of dark-green serge, with its red girdle . . . the string of red glass beads round her neck; and her brown hair, rough from curliness . . . duly knotted up and fastened with the silver pin" (chap. 33).

But other characters, too, of more acceptable social status than Bob Jakin, or Wiry Ben, or Tessa disclose striking endowments: Caterina Sarti, Mr. Casson, Bartle Massey, Silas Marner, Tito Melema, Mr. Brooke, and Herr Klesmer are from various viewpoints picturesque, although George Eliot uses the word specifically to describe only one of them, Herr Klesmer, whose "peculiarities [she notes] were picturesque and acceptable" (*Daniel Deronda*, chap. 22). With Herr Klesmer we have almost lost sight of the simple singularity which belongs to Bob Jakin. Klesmer moves in the level of society that accommodates Daniel Deronda, Lydgate, Mrs. Grandcourt, and Mrs. Davilow.

Picturesqueness among George Eliot's characters is obviously not confined by class. Daniel Deronda's ancestry, like Caterina Sarti's in "Mr. Gilfil's Love-Story," has about it the sort of foreign strangeness which fascinated travel artists like Edward Lear and John Frederick Lewis. The home life of the Bardos in *Romola* and of the Cohens in *Daniel Deronda* is picturesque because of the customs and conventions which inform the two households. In *Middlemarch*, Lydgate comes to appreciate Mr. Farebrother for those "points of conduct" which made "his character resemble those southern landscapes which seem divided between natural grandeur and social slovenliness" (chap. 18). In *Daniel Deronda*, Mrs. Davilow "always made a quiet, picturesque figure as a chaperon" (chap. 5); and Mrs. Meyrick's son thinks that Mrs. Grandcourt is both "striking and picturesque." In the same novel we have the unusual appearance of the grandmother Cohen seated under the light of an old brass lamp; she was "arrayed in yellowish brown with a large gold chain in lieu of the necklace, and by this light her yellow face with its darkly-marked eyebrows and framing roll of grey hair looked as handsome as was necessary for picturesque effect" (chap. 34).

Throughout her life, George Eliot remained very attracted to the rural life of pre-industrial England. She would, of course, argue that her portrayal of that life in, for example, *Adam Bede*, *The Mill on the Floss*, and *Middlemarch* was realistic: "a faithful account of men and things." But perhaps because her portrayal was of a vanishing scene, her tone is often a nostalgic one, even at times idealistic, as when we listen to Adam Bede singing hymns at the end of a day's work in Jonathan Burge's workshop; or when we feel the coolness of Mrs. Poyser's dairy with its "fragrance of new-pressed cheese" and see the "soft colouring" of her red earthenware; or hear the "dreamy deafness" of Dorlcote Mill and see the waggoner feeding and watering his team of horses. In speaking of *Adam Bede* and *Silas Marner*, Henry Auster argues that "the Victorian, his interest aroused by the picturesque concreteness and regional sentiment, is made aware of the values embodied in the vanishing rural order and of the losses he has incurred in his pursuit of progress."[1] Auster's argument merits attention.

We expect concreteness in George Eliot's prose for we recall her remark that it is "the fate of poor mortals" to find that the topographical details of the external setting all too often dissolve into a "hard angular world of chairs and tables and looking-glasses" that stare at us like "naked prose" (*Letters*, I, p. 264). Such details do not, however, exemplify a concreteness that is picturesque. But that quality can be found in her fictional world, even in her "close and detailed picture of English life" in which things are named so that the author "can escape from all vagueness and inaccuracy into the daylight of distinct, vivid ideas" (*Letters*, II, p. 251). Consider the passage in *Middlemarch* in which she remarks that the "gamut of joy in landscape to midland-bred souls" lies in "little details" which give "each field a particular physiognomy, dear to the eyes that have looked on them from childhood":

> the pool in the corner where the grasses were dank and trees leaned whisperingly; the great oak shadowing a bare place in mid-pasture;

1   Henry Auster, *Local Habitations, Regionalism in the Early Novels of George Eliot* (Cambridge, 1970), p. 60.

the high bank where the ash-trees grew; the sudden slope of the old marl-pit making a red background for the burdock; the huddled roofs and ricks of the homestead without a traceable way of approach; the grey gate and fences against the depths of the bordering wood; and the stray hovel, its old, old thatch full of mossy hills and valleys with wondrous modulations of light and shadow such as we travel far to see in later life, and see larger, but not more beautiful (chap. 12).

Throughout this passage, the "little details"—the pool in the corner, the bare place in the pasture, the sudden slope of the old marl-pit, the grey gate, and the stray hovel—do not dissolve into a "hard angular world" while they remain distinct and precise.

This "pretty bit of midland landscape" offers something more than details that add up to a "particular physiognomy"; overall, the landscape has a beauty of its own which, if not of that "tempting range of relevancies called the universe" (chap. 15), certainly indicates that the "gamut of joy in landscape to midland-bred souls" goes well beyond the naming of things: perhaps Auster's term is the one that best suits—to "picturesque concreteness." Nowhere is this quality more obvious than in the reference to the old hovel: "its old, old thatch full of mossy hills and valleys with wondrous modulations of light and shadow." The whole passage is an unframed landscape painting, or rather two of them: the first, very like one of Gainsborough's wooded landscapes; the second, a close view of the sort of thatched hovel which would command Sir Uvedale Price's undivided attention. No need here to "improve the facts" or "touch [them] up with a tasteful pencil."

At the same time these descriptive details are part of the surrounding action as Fred and Rosamond Vincy ride to Stone Court where the joys of the landscape they have passed through contrast with the flinty miserliness of old Mr. Featherstone. A contemporary reviewer in 1873 noted George Eliot's "topographical power" and how "[s]he bestows upon the places the same attention she bestows upon persons ... This 'bump of locality' in her genius encircles the persons of the story with a background and scenery the colour and perspective of which double the reality of the drama."[2] Somewhat the same sort of observation can be made of Adam Bede's awareness of the picturesqueness of the tall trees of the "Fir-tree Grove" as he takes the short cut home from work that leads to his moral and physical confrontation with Arthur Donnithorne. What Adam admires—as a

2 *The Times*, March 7, 1873, p. 3.

painter would—are the "flecks and knots" and all the "curves and angles" of the great beeches, one of which he will remember for the rest of his life, for as he gazed at it his eyes caught sight of Arthur and Hetty (chap. 27). Landscape, character, and action all converge here.[3]

But picturesque treatment of landscape in George Eliot's fiction—despite the previous illustrations—is not at all habitual. When a character like Mr. Dagley of Freeman's End in *Middlemarch* appears, something seems wrong with the Midland scene. Because of the feelings that poverty gives rise to, the picturesqueness of Freeman's End is cancelled out. Authorial comment in *Adam Bede* touches upon the problem: "There are so many of us, and our lots are so different: what wonder that Nature's mood is often in harsh contrast with the great crisis of our lives?" (chap. 27). As the artist, and especially the picturesque artist, saw nature, he nearly always imaged it attractively rather than as a "pageantry of fear" or a setting for human deprivation. This distortion troubled George Eliot especially when the artist's rural scene seemed either to show contented smock-clad rustics or to leave them out entirely. And yet she told Richard Holt Hutton in 1863 that it was "the habit of [her] imagination to strive after as full a vision of the medium in which a character moves as of the character itself" (*Letters*, IV, p. 97). But, if the charm of a scene must be omitted for fear of distorting the characters within it, how is a true vision of the medium possible? Is it really true, as the author asserts, that the "softening influence of the fine arts" may make "other people's hardships picturesque" (*Middlemarch*, chap. 39)? Is art only for those not in need of social improvement? The reader is left with these questions in this chapter.

Although Brooke could have found a score of picturesque subjects about the ruinous, miserable farmhouse of Freeman's End, his awareness of the "depression of the agricultural interest" leads to "troublesome associations" which "spoiled the scene for him." For the same reason, despite the charm of the old house's architecture, its ivy, its jasmine boughs, the "mouldering garden wall with hollyhocks peeping over it," and the mossy thatch of the cow-sheds, Dorothea is unable to see anything attractive about the setting that holds the Dagleys or the neighbouring Kit Downeses in wretchedness.

---

3   In his very worthwhile book, *George Eliot and the Visual Arts* (New Haven, 1979), Hugh Witemeyer sees this as "the moment of Adam's psychic fall from innocence to experience. His innocent perception of the picturesque variegation of tree-trunks and boughs gives way to a shattering recognition of Eve with her seducer," p. 149.

George H. Ford's comment on the description of the Dagley farm-house is that "Eliot has combined two versions of the pastoral and antipastoral: Dagley's cottage is beautiful (Southey is right); it is also a human pigsty (Macaulay is right)." Ford sees these versions as an example of George Eliot's "double perspective" which he attributes to her Midlands background and the academic cast of her mind.[4]

On another social level, the most picturesque of people, the gypsies of Dunlow Common, fall so far short of Maggie Tulliver's expectations of gypsy life that she cannot imagine her role as queen of these people, whose manners and morals seemed not at all agreeable, and whose ideas of afternoon tea quite dismayed Miss Maggie. Nor has George Eliot any inclination to touch up tastefully the men who work at Dorlcote Mill or at Mr. Deane's warehouse. As in Hayslope, "the bucolic character ... was not of that entirely genial, merry, broad-grinning sort, apparently observed in most districts visited by artists" (Adam Bede, chap. 53).

Such characters were often unable to either understand or ap-preciate the aesthetic experience: "The mind of St. Ogg's did not look extensively before or after. It inherited a long past without thinking of it, and had no eyes for the spirits that walk the streets" (The Mill on the Floss, Bk. I, chap. 12). Millers, wool-staplers, farmers, book-keepers, warehousemen—"you could not live among such people; you are stifled for want of an outlet toward something beautiful, great, or noble." To introduce among these "emmet-like Dodsons and Tulli-vers" (Bk. IV, chap. 1) ideas of beauty, or sublimity, or even the pic-turesque would make for intolerable incongruity in this fictional world.

George Eliot tries to make her reader more aware of this incon-gruity when she likens the "old-fashioned family life on the banks of the Floss" to the sordid life that must have characterized those "dead-tinted, hollow-eyed, angular skeletons of villages on the Rhone." Neither the Floss nor the Rhone possesses the charm of the ruins on the "castled Rhine." Their charm and the past life associated with them, when seen side by side with the Dodson-Tulliver world, serve to make clear the latter's shortcomings which seem so oppres-sive to the author. And yet the reader wonders about the thrill she experiences as she writes about the "grand historic life" that belonged to the ruins on the Rhine. Was there not human misery to temper the

4   George H. Ford, "Felicitous Space, The Cottage Controversy," in Nature and the Victorian Imagination, p. 37.

view? Did she really believe that "those robber-barons . . . made a fine contrast in the picture with the wandering minstrel, the soft-lipped princess, the pious recluse, and the timid Israelite?" (Bk. IV, chap. 1).

This exception notwithstanding, *The Mill on the Floss* does provide other evidence to support the stand that George Eliot distrusted picturesqueness. Tom Tulliver's exposure to art lessons from Mr. Goodrich brings Tom face to face with a modish way of describing life about him:

> Tom found, to his disgust, that his new drawing-master gave him no dogs and donkeys to draw, but brooks and rustic bridges and ruins, all with a general softness of black-lead surface, indicating that nature, if anything, was rather satiny; and as Tom's feeling for the picturesque in landscape was at present quite latent, it is not surprising that Mr. Goodrich's productions seemed to him an uninteresting form of art (Bk. II, chap. 4).

It is obvious to Tom that Mr. Goodrich's satiny landscapes are out of touch with reality. George Eliot's own attitude—clothed as it is with irony here—is apparent enough: Tom, we are told, "learned to make an extremely fine point to his pencil, and to represent landscape with a 'broad generality' which, doubtless from a narrow tendency in his mind to details, he thought extremely dull." The juxtaposition of "broad generality" and "details" recalls George Eliot's own experience in 1856 when she wanted to describe the Ilfracombe lanes so as to bring out their distinctive qualities. It was not then to picturesque art that she turned for an illustration but to the meticulous exactness of the work of William Holman Hunt (*Letters*, II, p. 250). This is a quality which she admired in Ruskin: "The truth of infinite value that he teaches is *realism*—the doctrine that all truth and beauty are to be attained by a humble and faithful study of nature, and not by substituting vague forms, bred by imagination on the mists of feeling, in place of definite, substantial reality."[5]

And yet, in the face of this insistence on realism, exceptions exist, exceptions that exclude the particularities of Hunt's Pre-Raphaelitism and betray the influence of other artistic modes. Maynard Gilfil sees Foxholm Parsonage "standing snugly sheltered by beeches and chestnuts halfway down the pretty green hill which was surmounted by the church, and overlooking a village that straggled at its ease among pastures and meadows, surrounded by wild hedgerows and

---

5   George Eliot, review article of Ruskin's *Modern Painters*, III, in *The Westminster Review* 65 (April 1856), pp. 343-47.

broad shadowing trees, as yet unthreatened by improved methods of farming" ("Mr. Gilfil's Love-Story," chap. 20). Very occasionally, too, George Eliot presents panoramas of her fictional landscape to show us, for example, what the unnamed horseman in *Adam Bede* sees as he approaches the village of Hayslope,[6] or to reveal how the narrator in *The Mill on the Floss* sees the "wide plain, where the broadening Floss hurries on between its green banks to the sea," past the picturesque details of the "aged, fluted red roofs and the broad gables" of the wharves of St. Ogg's (chap. 1). To find a parallel for such picture-painting in words, one can look at some of the landscapes of David Cox (1783-1859) or of Peter de Wint (1784-1849). The paintings of Lincoln and its River Witham by Peter de Wint resemble very much the descriptions of St. Ogg's and the River Floss given by George Eliot. For another illustration of description which exposes the author's interest in large details, consider what Dorothea Brooke sees as she approaches her future home at Lowick. The manor house, we are told, had "a small park, with a fine old oak here and there, and an avenue of limes towards the south-west front, with a sunk fence between park and pleasure-ground, so that from the drawing-room windows the glance swept uninterruptedly along a slope of greensward till the limes ended in a level of corn and pastures, which often seemed to melt into a lake under the setting sun" (*Middlemarch*, chap. 9). And another example: from across a green court Gwendolyn Grandcourt in *Daniel Deronda* glimpses the west end of Sir Hugo Mallinger's stables which had been once a beautiful choir. Traces of its ancient beauty remain: finial and gargoyle, broken and fretted limestone "lending its soft grey to a powdery dark lichen." Inside, both past and present uses of the space cause the viewer to dwell "with pleasure on its piquant picturesqueness" (chap. 35).

It could, of course, be argued that these descriptive passages are realistic in the sense that things are named, that details are more apparent than generalities, and that this is how England actually appeared to George Eliot's eyes—a picturesque land. But admitting this, it is still evident that the mode of description in these quotations owes much to the conventions of Victorian artists like Stanfield, Roberts, and Creswick whose picturesque landscapes brought "a whole world of thought and bliss—'a sense of something far more

---

6 Hugh Witemeyer's remarks about the "convention of the Gilpinesque tourist-guide" and the "anonymous observer" are applicable here: *George Eliot and the Visual Arts*, p. 130.

deeply interfused' " to George Eliot as she contemplated them in 1848 (*Letters*, I, p. 248). She sees and approves very much as they do except for the Wordsworthian rider which may, as Hugh Witemeyer suggests,[7] imply a depth of feeling not usually present in Ruskin's "lower picturesque." These descriptions in her fiction are, however, limited and, in treatment, spare and precise, so that they do not attract much attention. Her Midland landscapes, for example, are as quiet and realistic as Creswick's *Landscape with Quarry*. And yet the picturesque is there, part of the "speech of the landscape" and linked to "signs of permanence":

> some of us, at least, love the scanty relics of our forests, and are thankful if a bush is left of the old hedge-row. A crumbling bit of wall where the delicate ivy-leaved toad-flax hangs its light branches, or a bit of grey thatch with patches of dark moss on its shoulder and a troop of grass-stems on its ridge, is a thing to visit. And then the tiled roof of cottage and homestead . . . the roofs that have looked out from among the elms and walnut-trees, or beside the yearly group of hay- and corn-stalks, or below the square stone steeple, gathering their grey or ochre-tinted lichens and their olive-green mosses under all ministries,—let us praise the sober harmonies they give to our landscape.

Although this account lacks a unified pictorial arrangement, all the ingredients are there for the kind of picturesque sketch that would please Morland or Crome or de Wint. And the "sober harmonies" please George Eliot, too, even though she admits that this vision of her England may be "half-visionary" because it is not linked to the sad fate of "human labour." But even so she accepts it because the "illusions . . . feed the ideal Better, and in loving them still, we strengthen the precious habit of loving something not visibly, tangibly existent, but a spiritual product of our visible tangible selves" ("Looking Backward," *The Impressions of Theophrastus Such*).

This "looking backward," it seems to me, provides an important link between George Eliot and the picturesque which, despite her protestations in *Adam Bede*, she does not succeed in exorcising from her fiction. Furthermore, these remarks from *Theophrastus Such* (1879) are not a late development of her aesthetic thought; they may, for instance, be discerned plainly in the opening paragraphs of "Amos Barton" (1857), in which she contrasts the "immense improvements" of the New Police, the Tithe Commutation Act, the penny post, and "all guarantees of human advancement" with some

---

7   Witemeyer, *George Eliot and the Visual Arts*, p. 137.

"old abuses" and "vulgar errors." By loosing her imagination, she can revel slyly "in regret that dear, old, brown, crumbling, picturesque inefficiency is everywhere giving place to spick-and-span new-painted, new-varnished efficiency, which will yield endless diagrams, plans, elevations, and sections, but alas! no picture" ("Amos Barton," chap. 1).

This backward look often appears throughout George Eliot's fiction; in its nostalgia for "dear old quaintnesses," it provides a place for the picturesque which so often looked to past monuments for its subjects. It is noticeable, for example, in the first paragraph of the introduction to *Felix Holt* in which, like Dickens, the author fondly recalls the old coach travel and tells us that "the slow old-fashioned way of getting from one end of our country to the other is the better thing to have in the memory. The tube-journey can never lend much to picture and narrative; it is as barren as an exclamatory O." Hugh Witemeyer's observation that the "sentiment of nostalgia" is noticeable in the description of Hayslope Church and of Mr. Irwine's service is also relevant here.[8]

This is the age of "Old Leisure" whose person and activities are celebrated at the end of chapter 52 in *Adam Bede*. And even though that age has gone, "gone where the spinning-wheels are gone, and the pack-horses, and the slow waggons, and the pedlars," in her mature years George Eliot often dwells fondly upon its quaint actions: the moment, for instance, "the most picturesque in the scene" when Mr. Irvine in *Adam Bede* arose to reply to the toast that Arthur Donnithorne had proposed (chap. 24); in the next chapter, the donkey race—"that sublimest of all races"; and, in *Silas Marner*, the occasion of the New Year's Eve dance at Squire Cass's when Solomon Macey, playing "Sir Roger de Coverley" vigorously on his violin, and "holding his white head on one side . . . marched forward at the head of the gay procession into the White Parlour, where the mistletoe-bough was hung, and multitudinous tallow candles made rather a brilliant effect, gleaming from among the berried holly-boughs, and reflected in the old-fashioned oval mirrors fastened in the panels of the white wainscot. A quaint procession!" (chap. 11). Another good illustration of this reconstruction of the past in picture is Mr. Brooke's electioneering speech "to the worthy electors of Middlemarch from the balcony of the White Hart, which looked out advantageously at an angle

---

8 Witemeyer, *George Eliot and the Visual Arts*, pp. 118-20. See also Margaret Drabble's reference to George Eliot—to "the landscape of her youth" which "she remembers with the clarity of regret"—in *A Writer's Britain*, p. 83.

of the market-place, commanding a large area in front and two con-
verging streets" (chap. 51). The pictorial frame, the disorder of the
speech, the raucous audience, and the appearance of the effigy are
picturesque and as richly comic as was the electioneering in the
Borough of Eatanswill in Mr. Pickwick's day.

Of all George Eliot's novels, it is only *Romola* which may be
described as picturesque throughout, a fact which owes much to the
"tumultuously picturesque and dramatic"[9] history of Florence at the
end of the fifteenth century. The exciting, unusual incidents of the
novel—the sort that Sir Walter Scott loved to record—are often obvious: the adventures of the shipwrecked stranger in chapter 1, the
meeting of Tito and Tessa in the Peasant's Fair, the "innocent, picturesque merriment" of the Carnival, many of the circumstances leading
up to the death of Tito Melema, the lurid "Burning of the Vanities,"
and finally Romola's trip by sea to the pestilence-stricken village.

But the pictorial richness of Florence goes well beyond adven-
turous incident. Throughout the novel we have memorable sketches
of Florentine streets: of the houses flanking the Arno and "making on
their northern side a length of quaint, irregularly-pierced façade, of
which the waters give a softened loving reflection" (chap. 5); of the
Mercato Vecchio, site of the old provision market; of the tumult of the
gaily attired festive crowds in the Piazza dell' Annunziata; of the
beggars, gossips, and mountebanks lounging before the Baptistery or
on the marble steps of the Duomo; and the religious procession for San
Giovanni, the patron saint of Florence. We see, too, a variety of
picturesque rooms and buildings: Bardo's library, Nello's barbershop,
where Tito sings a carnival song to his own lute accompaniment; the
candle-lit interior of San Marco, where Romola visits her dying brother, Dino; the scene in her nearly vacant home, when Romola disguises
herself as a sister belonging to the third order of St. Francis; the supper
in the Rucellai Gardens; and the culminating episode when we witness the execution of Savonarola in the great Piazza della Signoria.
These are scenes we remember and see in our mind's eye for they are
as unusual and vibrant as any rendering of Renaissance city life. But
the picturesqueness rests primarily on the author's ability to describe
pictorially the city itself so that we see and recognize its streets,
piazzas, bridges, churches, and shops.

Such ability is apparent, of course, elsewhere in her fiction when
what is picturesque becomes evident in her attention to what is old,

9   Rudolf Dircks, introduction to George Eliot's *Romola* (London, 1907), p. v.

sometimes ruinous, irregular, rough, quaint, old-fashioned, varied in outline, rural rather than urban, and often interesting to the eye because of light and shade upon the surface. Shepperton Church, as it was in the past, serves to illustrate "picturesque inefficiency": "with its outer coat of rough stucco, its red-tiled roof, its heterogeneous windows patched with desultory bits of painted glass, and its little flight of steps with their wooden rail running up the outer wall, and leading to the school-children's gallery" ("Amos Barton," chap. 1). The remains of the old abbey with its gallery above the cloisters, which adjoins Squire Donnithorne's square mansion, resembles somewhat Sir Hugo Mallinger's place which was "a picturesque architectural outgrowth from an abbey, which had still the remnants of the old monastic trunk" (*Daniel Deronda*, chap. 16). These quaint old buildings serve other uses than the merely pictorial. Squire Donnithorne's, like Sir Hugo Mallinger's, offers a setting which renders possible the net of circumstances which gradually envelops the main characters.

Other picturesque dwellings that support narrative action in George Eliot's fiction come easily to mind: Cheverel Manor in "Mr. Gilfil's Love-Story" with its new Gothic look; ancient St. Ogg's Hall, where Maggie Tulliver had her stall on the day of the bazaar, "with its open roof and carved oaken rafters . . . and light shed down from a height on the many-coloured show beneath: a very quaint place, with broad faded stripes painted on the walls, and here and there a show of heraldic animals." Like other of George Eliot's picturesque structures, St. Ogg's Hall exists for more than quaint display: "In fact, the perfect fitness of this ancient building for an admirable modern purpose, that made charity truly elegant, and led through vanity up to the supply of a deficit, was so striking that hardly a person entered the room without exchanging the remark more than once" (Bk. VI, chap. 9). Transome Court—of which John Blackwood thought that George Eliot's description had "the vivid power of an old ballad" (*Letters*, IV, p. 242)—and the rectory at Little Treby have visual characteristics that would have drawn approval from Sir Uvedale Price. The rectory, for instance, has a "great bow-window opening from the library on to the deep-turfed lawn" where are "tall trees stooping or soaring in the most picturesque variety, and a Virginian creeper turning a little rustic hut into a scarlet pavilion" (*Felix Holt*, chap. 23).

Offendene, too, in *Daniel Deronda* is interesting visually in its interior. Gwendolyn Harleth finds the drawing-room to be a "queer, quaint, picturesque room" with its organ, old embroidered chairs, garlands on the wainscot, and its pictures — with the exception of the one concealed behind the sliding panel (chap. 3). Later in the novel, the reader again sees this room as the "waning sunshine of autumn . . . came mildly through the windows in slanting bands of brightness over the old furniture" (chap. 23). Offendene's exterior in contrast is uninteresting, and the view it commands is not extensive. To remedy this shortcoming picturesquely, one "would have liked the house to have been lifted on a knoll, so as to look beyond its own little domain to the long thatched roofs of the distant villages, the church towers, the scattered homesteads, the gradual rise of surging woods, and the green breadths of undulating park which made the beautiful face of the earth in that part of Wessex" (chap. 3). This passage offers some indication of how much the author was drawn to picturesque representation. Here she comes very close to giving us description which might better be omitted, for Offendene sits in flat pasture lands and has a view on one side only of "the lofty curves of the chalk downs."

Finally, the old public house, the Cross-Keys in Pollard's End, is described lovingly despite the "fungous-featured landlord and a yellow sickly landlady, with a napkin bound round her head like a resuscitated Lazarus." Unlike other pubs of the time, the Cross-Keys "presented a high standard of pleasure" noticeable especially in the "big rambling kitchen, with an undulating brick floor; the small-paned windows threw an interesting obscurity over the far-off dresser, garnished with pewter and tin, and with large dishes that seemed to speak of better times; the two settles were half pushed under the wide-mouthed chimney; and the grate with its brick hobs, massive iron crane, and various pothooks, suggested a generous plenty" (*Felix Holt*, chap. 28). This "very old-fashioned public" was one that obviously appealed visually to the author.

Such examples as these illustrate how George Eliot made use of picturesque description despite her opposition to a way of seeing the world that would tend, in her words, "to make things seem better than they were" or would give greater prominence to a handsome "rascal in red scarf and green feathers" than to that "vulgar citizen who weighs out my sugar in a vilely-assorted cravat and waistcoat" (*Adam Bede*, chap. 17).

Some of her reluctance to accept picturesque convention comes about, of course, because its ruins, dilapidated cottages, and rock-strewn prospects are too often inhabited by miserably poor people. Like Charles Dickens, she lacks the kind of insensitivity which enabled the eighteenth-century connoisseur to overlook the human degradation to be found around a gypsy campfire. It is her sensitivity to the realities of living that stands in the way of her aesthetic appreciation. She cannot gloss over suffering by imposing upon it the necessary "aerial distance" to make it picturesque. She cannot, like Henry James, keep her morality at elbow length and merely use her eyes and, like him, see the yellow light "come filtering down through a vine-covered trellis on the red handkerchief with which a ragged contadina has bound her hair, and all the magic of Italy, to the eye, makes an aureole about the poor girl's head."[10]

It is then not really the picturesque itself which George Eliot objects to, but rather its tendency to ignore the plight of people unfortunate enough to be living within its purlieu: the Goffes, the Dagleys, and the Mosses of her fictional world. Just as it is incongruous to think of these people picturesquely so, too, this mode is artistically unacceptable for the settings that show forth middle-class characters like Bulstrode or Mr. Vincy, Mrs. Cadwallader or Dorothea Brooke, Mr. Casaubon or Mary Garth. Their solid existence is their reality. A "tasteful pencil" cannot improve this fact, this "rare, precious quality of truthfulness."

But granting these exceptions, it is still obvious that George Eliot's fiction does not preclude the picturesque. It is not, however, as prevalent as Hugh Witemeyer says it is: "Eliot's novels, from the start to the finish of her career, abound with picturesque descriptions in an eighteenth-century vein."[11] She tends rather, as Mario Praz says, to tone down her colours and to avoid overt picturesqueness.[12] But it is there, and the author's use of it detracts very little, if at all, from her avowed aim to give us "a faithful account of men and things." How the reader sees the house at Hall Farm in *Adam Bede* and how that picture is framed as we put "our eyes close to the rusty bars of the gate" illustrate how effectively this mode of vision may be used: "It is a very fine old place, of red brick, softened by a pale powdery lichen, which has dispersed itself with happy irregularity, so as to bring the red brick into terms of friendly companionship with the limestone ornaments surrounding the three gables, the windows, and the door-place" (chap. 6). The picture is realistic, but it is more than the mere naming of things: the Hall farmhouse is fine and old, its red brick suitably dulled by lichen scattered over its surface with "happy ir-

---

10 Henry James, *Italian Hours*, p. 105.
11 Witemeyer, *George Eliot and the Visual Arts*, p. 129.
12 Mario Praz, *The Hero in Eclipse in Victorian Fiction* (London, 1969), pp. 321-22.

regularity" that complements the house's ornamentation. The imprint of the picturesque is upon it. As far as it goes, this sort of description provided a perfectly natural way of introducing an old house to the mid-Victorian reader conversant with picturesque conventions.

Like Dickens, George Eliot can make very effective use of the picturesque in her narrative as an agent of contrast. *Felix Holt* offers a number of pertinent illustrations. The coachman, that "excellent travelling companion and commentator on landscape" alerts the reader—as his coach rolls past the screen of trees, the winding river, and the "finely timbered park" of the Transome estate—to the suggestion that Mrs. Transome's story may be more fittingly associated with some "dolorous enchanted forest in the underworld" than with what the passenger sees from the coach windows (author's introduction). We remember, too, Felix Holt's walk to Sproxton in chapter 11. He takes a short cut through the corner of the Debarry park, "then across a piece of common, broken here and there into red ridges below dark masses of furze; and for the rest of the way alongside the canal, where the Sunday peacefulness that seemed to rest on the bordering meadows and pastures was hardly broken if a horse pulled into sight along the towing-path, and a boat, with a little curl of blue smoke issuing from its tin chimney, came slowly gliding behind." Felix's walk ends in Sproxton in a "black landscape" of tram-roads and coal pits where men find their solace in beer at the Sugar Loaf, the Old Pits, or the Blue Cow.

To sharpen the reader's awareness of the contrasting choices facing Esther Lyon, George Eliot finds a further use for qualities associated with the picturesque. It is essential that Esther herself see her inheritance in its light, that she stand on the terrace amid the crocuses and admire the "fine view of the park and the river" and see "the dash of light on the water, and the pencilled shadows of the trees on the grassy lawn" (chap. 43). It is essential, too, that she scent "the dried rose-leaves in her corridors" and that in her day dreams she imagine "several accomplished cavaliers all at once suing for her hand" (chap. 38). All this she must recognize for what it really is if she is to come to terms with the moral emptiness of her inheritance and with Mrs. Transome, that Hecuba-like woman, whose eyes see from her window only "a chill white landscape and the far-off unheeding stars" (chap. 39). In the end, Esther's decision to resign all claim as heiress of Transome Court for the privilege of being a poor man's wife is to acknowledge that existence in Transome Court can never satisfy her needs. She is not made like Edward Waverley. For her, the picturesque is not enough.

And it was not enough for George Eliot, although a few of her letters suggest that her own interest in this mode of seeing sometimes extended to the everyday world around her. In a letter to Sara Sophia Hennell (June 29, 1856), she says that "Tenby looks insignificant in picturesqueness after Ilfracombe." With George Henry Lewes in January 1867, she sat for a half hour's "silent dreamy enjoyment" of the town of Bayonne which Lewes described as "more than half Spanish and so picturesque that it may be called a succession of Prouts" (*Letters*, IV, pp. 331-32). In a letter to Charles Lee Lewes (July 21, 1870), George Eliot announces that Whitby is "as quaintly picturesque as an old Italian town, and the scenery around it as lovely." Had she lived to enjoy it, she and John Walter Cross would have spent their declining years at 4 Cheyne Walk, Chelsea, which she characterized as "looking on a very picturesque bit of the river" (*Letters*, VII, p. 287).

Her letters also reveal that she continued to enjoy the landscape art of painters like Stanfield and Creswick and that she thought highly of Ruskin, whose third volume of *Modern Painters* she had reviewed at length (*Westminster Review*, April 1856). Referring to David Cox's *Welsh Funeral*, she told Mme. Eugène Bodichon (September 25, 1868) that there was no finer landscape at the Leeds Exhibition. To Mrs. Mark Pattison on March 3, 1876 she remarked that she "came away enriched" having seen the collection of Frederick Walker's pictures. Although such references to art are few, they suggest that her taste in landscape painting, like Dickens's, was for the representational and that here the presence of the picturesque was by no means offensive, providing the artist kept a tight rein on sentiment. Her aesthetic range, however, was limited. No one has commented on this weakness more acutely than Henry James who observed that from the beginning "perception and reflection . . . divided George Eliot's great talent between them" and that "as time went on, circumstances led the latter to develop itself at the expense of the former."[13] One is left with the feeling that the art which pleased her most was the popular art of her own time.

Her fondness for a period contemporary with her childhood made the picturesque—despite her restrictions about it—attractive to her. Like the slow, old-fashioned stage coach, the close of the eighteenth century and early nineteenth represented a time that was

13   Henry James, "George Eliot's Life," *The Atlantic Monthly* 55 (May 1885), p. 674.

past and that was pleasant. For George Eliot those years that she knew of from her parents and her own childhood offered beguiling glimpses of a rural England yet to suffer the full defacement of the Industrial Revolution. Treby Magna told the story: "Such was the old-fashioned, grazing, brewing, wool-packing, cheese-loading life of Treby Magna, until there befell new conditions ... First came the canal; next, the working of the coal-mines at Sproxton ... and thirdly, the discovery of a saline spring" (*Felix Holt*, chap. 3).

Picturesque old England attracted not only George Eliot but also many of her contemporaries appalled by "the want, the care, the sin, / The faithless coldness of the times."[14] In that old England a man's life could be "well rooted in some spot" (*Daniel Deronda*, chap. 3), free from the idle amusements of "excursion-trains, art-museums, periodical literature ... exciting novels ... [and] scientific theorizing" (*Adam Bede*, chap. 52). The Hall Farm with its seasonal round, capped by the harvest supper, offered an alternative—an escape if you will—although even here a Mr. Mills or a Mr. Craig could relay news to the field people from the outside world that required much deliberation and comment for it was "hard work to tell which is Old Harry when everybody's got boots on" (chap. 53).

This is the Old England that so many Victorian artists also portrayed: Harding, Dibdin, Creswick, Stanfield, Edward Duncan, George Cattermole, Frederick Tayler, Atkinson, Topham, Oakley, William Henry Hunt, Myles Birket Foster, and Helen Allingham who did illustrations for *Romola* after George Eliot had become dissatisfied with Leighton's work (*Letters*, VI, p. 335). This list of names is, of course, far from complete, but it does serve to remind us of how widespread was the Victorian taste for picturesque subject matter.

More specifically, to look at John William North's *Gypsy Encampment* is to see with Maggie Tulliver's eyes on Dunlow Common; substitute coal for apples in George John Pinwell's *King Pippin* and we have Eppie in the coal hole; Dibdin's *Cottage and Figures* would serve nicely to illustrate the Dagley home; and J. C. Bourne's picturesque wash drawings of railway tunnels showing "the industrious mechanic" himself at work remind us of Mr. Toodle in *Dombey and Son* "tearing through the country at from twenty-five to fifty miles an hour," and bring to mind, too, the resentment which the Frick labourers in *Middlemarch* displayed toward the coming of the railroad.

14   Tennyson, *In Memoriam*, cvi.

Paradoxically, these same drawings of railway tunnels and excavations scarring the face of the country stir our sympathy for George Eliot's tender attachment to the woodlands, pastures, the "hedge-parted corn-fields and meadows," the "bits of high common," the rivers and villages "along the old coach-roads" of Midland England ("Looking Backward," *Theophrastus Such*). Much rather the picturesqueness of a pasturage than a Sproxton, blackened with coal pits, or even a Lantern Yard transformed by the squalid factory conditions of industrial England.

But if George Eliot looks nostalgically to the past, her eyes are open to the present and what it may lead to. She accepts society around her. Change will come for the working class, but it must come slowly as a sort of organic growth out of the heritage of the past. This she makes clear in the "Address to Working Men" (1868); the scope of her mature political thought is wide enough to include the popular culture of the past which will be cherished even as it undergoes inevitable slow change: "there are the old channels, the old banks, and the old pumps, which must be used as they are until new and better have been prepared, or the structure of the old has been gradually altered."[15] That her vision extended beyond the mechanical is obvious a few pages later in the "Address," as Felix Holt explains: "I mean that treasure of knowledge, science, poetry, refinement of thought, feeling, and manners, great memories and the interpretation of great records, which is carried on from the minds of one generation to the minds of another." Such a philosophy, however, makes Felix Holt and perhaps his creator a kind of prisoner between two worlds: one already past but current; the other struggling to be born. This was a predicament which faced many Victorian thinkers, especially in the realm of art. The possibility, for instance, of giving up the picturesque that offered a fairly accurate representation of the external world for J. M. W. Turner's "haze" was for George Eliot, as late as 1878, a choice that would have been quite unacceptable to her, even though she had seen Windus's collection of Turner's water colours thirty years before (*Letters*, I, pp. 332, 347). On April 17, 1878, when she went to see the Turner drawings that were exhibited in London, she found "most of them uninteresting; more like confectionary than Nature" (*Letters*, VII, p. 21). Her intellect on this occasion ruled out the pleasure even of the "nobler picturesque."

15   George Eliot, "Address to Working Men," *Blackwood's Edinburgh Magazine* 102 (January 1868), p. 5.

Yet even this implication about her attitude to Turner's work requires some qualification when we remember in *Daniel Deronda* how Mordecai, the Jew, was "keenly alive to some poetic aspects of London," and how he liked to gaze on the Thames from Blackfriars Bridge where he could see "its long vista half hazy, half luminous" with its "grand dim masses" of buildings and feel its sounds and colours enter his mood and spirit like a fine symphony (chap. 38). Still, such Turnerian splendour[16] is rare in George Eliot's fiction. In contrast to a landscape like Turner's *Sunrise between Two Headlands*, the picturesque was recognizable and familiar, even if it framed uncultivated land and was indifferent to the lot of men condemned to make their living from it in the "sordid present." For George Eliot, this choice of landscape treatment for her fiction was one which she did not have to make and by her own philosophy did not need to make. It was easier to "submit [herself] to the great law of inheritance"[17] than it was to jettison an art form from her fiction that was so close to her own tastes, so convenient for her craft, and so acceptable to her readers as the picturesque.

And yet her submission to the picturesque was, when she recognized it, hedged by suspicion of its purpose and by reluctance to see in it the degree of truthfulness which she wanted her art to convey of the commonplace world in which her "everyday fellow-man" lived and toiled. In this view, it was as apparent to her as it was to William Gilpin that "moral and picturesque ideas do not always coincide."[18] How uneasy she was about this incompatibility of art and life appears in the ironic ambivalence of a remark meant to illustrate Mrs. Transome's role-acting in *Felix Holt*: "Even the patriarch Job, if he had been a gentleman of the modern West, would have avoided picturesque disorder and poetical laments; and the friends who called on him, though not less disposed than Bildad the Shuhite to hint that their unfortunate friend was in the wrong, would have sat on chairs and held their hats in their hands" (chap. 10). That George Eliot's fiction reveals as much reliance upon picturesque convention as it does, is, in the light of her objections to it, very remarkable and clear evidence of how tenaciously this mode of seeing held its place in Victorian fiction.

16   Witemeyer quotes Edward Dowden in this connection to support the link between Turner and Mordecai's "visionary temperament": *George Eliot and the Visual Arts*, p. 142.
17   Eliot, "Address to Working Men," p. 11.
18   Gilpin, *Mountains and Lakes of Cumberland and Westmoreland*, II, p. 44.

Chapter 7

Thomas Hardy

I don't want to see landscapes, i.e., scenic paintings of
them, because I don't want to see the original realities—
as optical effects, that is. I want to see the deeper reality
underlying the scenic, the expression of what are sometimes called abstract imaginings.
                Florence Hardy, *The Life of Thomas Hardy*

The attraction of the picturesque for Thomas Hardy related to his own
taste for painting, to his architectural training, and in the end, to the
way this mode lent itself to his needs as a novelist. It had represented,
ever since Burke's time, a kind of aesthetic middle course; committed
to no one extreme, it could meet a variety of purposes in the long
Victorian novel that incorporated so much of the human vision.
Firmly rooted in the external scene, with pleasure essentially its
purpose, it offered Hardy an easily recognized technique for organiz-
ing his Wessex scenery and passing on to his readers his own deep-
seated affection for that countryside and its people. Its use helped him
to "strike the balance between the uncommon and the ordinary":[1]
between the dynasties that pass and a man harrowing clods.

It is well to remember that Hardy's acquaintance with painting
was very extensive. As a young man in London, he frequented the
National Gallery, the Royal Academy, and the South Kensington
Museum, where he acquired a liking for and an understanding of
many of the great masters, including those of the Dutch and Flemish

---

1 Florence Emily Hardy, *The Life of Thomas Hardy, 1840-1928* (Toronto, 1962),
   p. 150.

schools,[2] whose landscapes link very easily with later English landscape painting that was so frequently picturesque. Hardy remembered this experience in the galleries when he turned his own creative
ability to writing and had to introduce his readers, for example, to
Liddy Smallbury in *Far From the Madding Crowd*: "The beauty her
features might have lacked in form was amply made up for by perfection of hue, which at this wintertime was the softened ruddiness on a
surface of high rotundity that we meet with in a Terburg or a Gerard
Douw; and, like the presentations of those great colourists, it was a
face which kept well back from the boundary between comeliness and
the ideal" (chap. 9). We imagine Liddy's features much more vividly
if we have looked closely, for example, at the face of Gerrit Dou's
Lady Playing a Clavichord in the Dulwich Gallery or, even better, if
we have seen the face of Gerard Terborch's *Woman Writing*, at The
Hague.

And just as Hardy's knowledge of painting helped him to present
portraits of his characters so, too, his training in architecture had its
effect upon his fiction. His apprentice years under John Hicks in
Dorchester served to stimulate his interest in old buildings; it was an
interest which also grew during his London years with Arthur Bloom-
field, whose concern for the Gothic Revival meant employment for his
young draftsmen on church restoration. It was work which Hardy
continued when, in 1867, he returned to Dorchester to work for John
Hicks and to carry out assignments like the one for the St. Juliot
Church. Such work gave him an intimate knowledge of ancient
monuments in decay and deepened his interest in English architecture. Like his fictional character, George Somers, he finally settled for
"his own native Gothic" and returned to "the great English-pointed
revival under Britton, Pugin, Rickman, Scott and other medievalists"
(*A Laodicean*, chap. 1).

Because of his proclivity to associate, especially what he saw in
the present with its ancient connections, Hardy must have found his
work with Gothic remains fascinating. The Gothic, of course, had
been historically of great interest to the theorists of the picturesque.
Gilpin's "picturesque eye" was "most inquisitive after the elegant
relics of ancient architecture; the ruined tower, the Gothic arch, the
remains of castles, and abbeys."[3] Richard Payne Knight praised Van-

---

2 For reference to Dutch and Flemish artists and speculation about their influence on
   Hardy, see Grundy, *Hardy and the Sister Arts*, pp. 28-30.
3 Gilpin, *Three Essays*, p. 46.

brugh[4] whose success at Blenheim drew Sir Uvedale Price's commendation for "uniting in one building, the beauty and magnificence of Grecian architecture, the picturesqueness of the Gothic, and the massive grandeur of a castle."[5] For Price, "the architect of buildings in the country should be *architetto-pittore*, for indeed he ought not only to have the mind, but the hand of a painter."[6] The picturesque was a significant influence on the Gothic Revival of the nineteenth century;[7] in fact, it is difficult sometimes to disentangle the two. Hardy accepted this connection, although for him the interest lay not so much in the surface irregularities of this architecture as in what it brought to his mind of the past. Even though he lamented that writers of his time passed over the "natural picturesqueness and singularity" of Shaston (Shaftesbury), it was really its past associations that interested him: "its castle, its three mints, its magnificent apsidal Abbey . . . its twelve churches, its shrines, chantries, hospitals . . . all now ruthlessly swept away" (*Jude the Obscure*, Pt. IV, i). But it was, of course, the singularity of the present scene that triggered off the associations whose beauty, in another context, Hardy asserts is "entirely superior to the beauty of aspect."[8]

For many readers, however, it is "the beauty of aspect" in Hardy's fiction that they prefer rather than the associations that come so readily to the author's mind and which often give his prose an undesirable density so noticeable in the opening chapter of *The Return of the Native*, where Hardy suggests that the beauty which is usually called "charming or fair" may well yield place to "a sombreness distasteful to our race" but "in keeping with the moods of the more thinking among mankind." Alastair Smart remarked of this observation that "Hardy is here questioning . . . the convention . . . of the Picturesque"[9] and prophesying the appearance of modern art which can find "beauty in ugliness." This may be so, but Smart's statement neglects that side of the picturesque which emphasized the rough and irregular and rejoiced in what appealed so much to Hardy himself— the associations that are "entirely superior to the beauty of aspect"

4 Knight, *An Analytical Inquiry*, p. 227.
5 Price, *Essays on the Picturesque* (1798), II, p. 252.
6 Price, *Essays on the Picturesque* (1798), II, p. 208.
7 See Kenneth Clark, *The Gothic Revival* (London, 1974).
8 Florence Emily Hardy, *Life of Thomas Hardy*, p. 121.
9 Alastair Smart, "Pictorial Imagery in the Novels of Thomas Hardy," *The Review of English Studies*, new series, 12 (1961), p. 274.

and may be found even in "a beloved relation's old battered tankard."[10]

It is sometimes, however, these associations which make Hardy's prose tedious for many readers. The account of "ancient British Palladour" in *Jude* is, for example, too much like a digression isolating the reader from Jude and his compelling concerns. Actually, past and present come together most effectively in this picturesque town as Jude in the Abbey gardens hears "young voices . . . in the open air" and sees "girls in white pinafores over red and blue frocks . . . dancing along the paths which the abbess, prioress, sub-prioress, and fifty nuns had demurely paced three centuries earlier" (Pt. IV, p. i). In this description, past and present, fiction and reality mingle naturally and charmingly. Palladour (Shaston) becomes as real a place as Shaftesbury.

This juxtaposition of the fictional and the real occurs, of course, throughout Hardy's novels whenever he describes a real place under the guise of a fictional name even though his portraiture sometimes "wantonly wanders from inventorial descriptions of them."[11] This kind of wanton portraiture is easily recognized in picturesque art as is the emphasis upon a real place. In the Wessex novels unusual names of real places: Nettlecombe Tout, Dogbury Hill, and Crimmercrock Lane jostle fictional ones equally unusual: Flintcomb Ash, Abbot's Cernel, Stagfoot Lane, and Sherton Abbas. This treatment, which in itself creates pictorial interest, enlivens the details of the settings of the Wessex novels.

To many of these Hardy attaches the word "picturesque": Miss Aldclyffe's house and grounds in *Desperate Remedies* (chap. 7); Endelstow House in *A Pair of Blue Eyes* (chap. 5); Casterbridge Union in *Far From the Madding Crowd* (chap. 40); Knollsea Village in *The Hand of Ethelberta* (chap. 45); Egdon Heath in *The Return of the Native* (chap. 10); the military encampment in *The Trumpet Major* (chap. 1); Stancy Castle in *A Laodicean* (chap. 13); Casterbridge in *The Mayor of Casterbridge* (chap. 36); Little Hintock House in *The Woodlanders* (chap. 8); Christminster and Shaston in *Jude the Obscure* (Pt. III, ix; Pt. IV, i); and the scenery of the Isle of Slingers in *The Well-Beloved* (Pt. II, vii, ix). Collectively these examples attest to Hardy's fondness for a particular mode of seeing landscape and

10   Florence Emily Hardy, *Life of Thomas Hardy*, p. 121.
11   Thomas Hardy, "General Preface to the Novels and Poems," in *Tess of the D'Urbervilles* (London, 1912), p. xi.

buildings and leave little doubt that he was very much interested in the "aspect" of things. What it is in the appearance of these things that interested him or that he thought would interest his reader becomes obvious on closer inspection.

Miss Aldclyffe's home in *Desperate Remedies*, framed by an avenue of trees, is made up of

> an old arched gateway, flanked by the bases of two small towers, and nearly covered with creepers, which had clambered over the eaves of the sinking roof, and up the gable to the crest of the Aldclyffe family perched on the apex. Behind this . . . came . . .an Elizabethan fragment, consisting of as much as could be contained under three gables and a cross roof behind. Against the wall could be seen ragged lines indicating the form of other destroyed gables (chap. 7).

Very like the Aldclyffe home is Endelstow House, whose ancient gateway shows the visitor a façade with windows

> long and many-mullioned; the roof lines broken up by dormer lights of the same pattern. The apex stones of these dormers, to-gether with those of the gables, were surmounted by grotesque figures in rampant, passant, and couchant variety. Tall octagonal and twisted chimneys thrust themselves high up into the sky, surpassed in height, however, by some poplars and sycamores at the back, which showed their gently rocking summits over ridge and parapet (*A Pair of Blue Eyes*, chap. 5).

Both these houses have about them that "state of neglect," that "abruptness or irregularity," those "minute and detached decorations of [the] outside," the masses of wild vegetation and climbing ivy which Sir Uvedale Price cited as characteristics of old structures.[12] We also see both these houses as a "prospect," a "scene," a "picture" within a frame whose details are arranged in a painterly fashion. Much the same can be said of Felice Charmond's home in *The Wood-landers*: "Ruthless ignorance could have done little to make [Little Hintock House] unpicturesque. It was vegetable nature's own home; a spot to inspire the painter and poet of still life" (chap. 8).

In the village of Knollsea, Ethelberta Chickerel is able through the frame of her window to see "a happy combination of grange scenery with marine." The author arranges the details so that we, like the insufferable Ladywell, become aware of the picturesque charm of Knollsea as if we were looking at a contemporary painting:

12 Price, *Essays* (1798), II, pp. 300-302.

> Upon the irregular slope between the house and the quay was an
> orchard of aged trees ... Under the trees were a few Cape sheep,
> and over them the stone chimneys of the village below: outside
> these lay the tanned sails of a ketch or smack, and the violet waters
> of the bay, seamed and creased by breezes insufficient to raise
> waves; beyond all a curved wall of cliff, terminating in a promon-
> tory, which was flanked by tall and shining obelisks of chalk rising
> sheer from the trembling blue race beneath (*The Hand of Ethel-*
> *berta*, chap. 31).

This is description for its own sake of a scene which for the reader and
Ethelberta is charming, typical of "orthodox beauty," and not at all
designed to suit the melancholy mood of "the more thinking among
mankind."

On a much wider canvas in *The Return of the Native*, Hardy
sketches the sombre limits of Egdon Heath whose "antique brown
dress," ancient barrows, shaggy recesses, bramble-sided ravines,
mists, and trees "singularly battered, rude and wild" make up part of
its picturesqueness. Diggory Venn is described seeing as William
Gilpin would: "The scene before the reddleman's eyes was a gradual
series of ascents from the level of the road backward into the heart of
the heath. It embraced hillocks, pits, ridges, acclivities, one behind
the other, till all was finished by a high hill cutting against the still
light sky" (chap. 2). The scene calls to mind the two prints Gilpin
used in his "Essay on Picturesque Beauty" to illustrate "how very
adverse the idea of *smoothness* is to the *composition* of landscape."[13]
For characters like Wildeve and Eustacia, the heath is made up of
"picturesque ravines and mists" which are of interest only to wild
birds or landscape painters; for others, like Tamsin and Clym Yeobright, the heath is "a nice place to walk in," a wide prospect that can
gladden their hearts.

Overcombe Mill and its surroundings in *The Trumpet Major* lack
altogether the malefic influence of Egdon Heath. The scene from
Anne Garland's casement window in the mill is presented pictorially
from the millpond close at hand, to the village crossroads, and on and
up to where the down "rising above the roofs, chimneys, apple-trees,
and church tower of the hamlet around her, bounded the view from
her position" (chap. 1). The landscape that Anne's eyes record is the
one we can still see in the art of Birket Foster: simple and wholesome,
but like Anne herself without much depth, a surface matter.

13   Gilpin, *Three Essays*, "Explanation of the Prints," p. i.

Unlike Overcombe Mill, which is very much a working place, Stancy Castle in *A Laodicean* is a tourist attraction written up in local county histories. Much of its attractiveness lies in its picturesqueness. A great part of it is "irregular, dilapidated, and muffled in creepers"; a square solid tower, darkened with ivy, rose over the main mass. "In spite of the habitable and more modern wing, neglect and decay had set their mark upon the outworks of the pile" (Bk. I, chap. 2). A disastrous fire at the novel's end ensures that the castle will remain "beautiful in its decay" (Bk. VI, chap. 5), a curiosity in the county history that lists it as a "picturesque and ancient structure" (Bk. I, chap. 13).

With the exception of Mixen Lane (*The Mayor of Casterbridge*, chap. 36), Hardy describes Casterbridge as a picturesque town but not primarily because of decay or ruin. Seen just before dusk from a distance and high up, this "old-fashioned place" appears

> as a mosaic-work of subdued reds, browns, greys, and crystals, held together by a rectangular frame of deep green. To the level eye of humanity it stood as an indistinct mass behind a dense stockade of limes and chestnuts, set in the midst of miles of rotund down and concave field. The mass became gradually dissected by the vision into towers, gables, chimneys, and casements, the highest glazings shining bleared and blood-shot with the coppery fire they caught from the belt of sunlit cloud in the west (chap. 4).

This is the kind of vision that Richard Payne Knight approves of: "Tints happily broken and blended, and irregular masses of light and shadow harmoniously melted into each other, are, in themselves ... more grateful to the eye, than any single tints."[14] Once Elizabeth-Jane and her mother have passed "the ancient defenses of the town," they find

> timber houses with overhanging stories, whose small-paned lattices were screened by dimity curtains on a drawing-string, and under whose barge-boards old cobwebs waved in the breeze. There were houses of brick-nogging, which derived their chief support from those adjoining. There were slate roofs patched with tiles, and tile roofs patched with slate, with occasionally a roof of thatch (chap. 4).

Here, Sir Uvedale Price would have paused to make his point:

> There is no scene where neatness and picturesqueness, where simplicity and intricacy can be so happily united as in a village ...

14 Knight, *Analytical Inquiry*, p. 151.

> Should there be a house of an old style, in which not only the forms
> were of picturesque irregularity, but the tints were of that rich
> mellow, harmonious kind, so much admired by painters—an im-
> prover who had ever studied pictures, would not suffer them to be
> destroyed by plaister or white-wash.[15]

Few, if any, of the Dorchester citizens could have studied pictures or
read Price's essay with understanding for, as Hardy points out, the
citizens had managed by 1912 to pull down most of the town's old
picturesque houses.

Both Christminster and Shaston in *Jude the Obscure* are described as being "picturesque" (Pt. III, ix; Pt. IV, i). Much of the
reason for applying this epithet to Christminster derives from the
appearance of its "ancient medieval pile[s]." Even when he is
estranged from it, Jude finds it beautiful "as the sun made vivid lights
and shades of the mullioned architecture of the façades, and drew
patterns of the crinkled battlements on the young turf of the quadrangles" (Pt. III, viii). Christminster's "picturesqueness [is] unrivalled
except by such Continental vistas as the Street of Palaces in Genoa"
(Pt. III, ix). Shaston, an ancient hill town, no longer has its rich
medieval heritage. Yet Hardy suggests that its unique position, its
historical associations, and its customs make it unusual and worth
visiting. He even notes one modern peculiarity: "It was the resting-
place and headquarters of the proprietors of wandering vans, shows,
shooting-galleries, and other itinerant concerns, whose business lay
largely at fairs and markets" (Pt. IV, i). Such itinerants were always
interesting to the traveller in search of the picturesque.

Finally, the Isle of Slingers, "this outlandish rock" in *The Well-
Beloved*, provides a narrow setting in which characters come together
on a singular peninsula where "the towering rock, the houses above
houses, one man's doorstep rising behind his neighbour's chimney,
the gardens hung up by one edge to the sky . . . [exist on] a solid and
single block of limestone four miles long" (Pt. I, i). From the grounds
of Sylvania Castle to the east "the cliffs were rugged and the
view of the opposite coast picturesque in the extreme" (Pt. II, vii).

Very often in his fiction words like "singular," "quaint," "peculiar," "singularity," "queer," "irregular," "prospect," "frame," "decay," and "ruin" are verbal signposts pointing to what may be picturesque in Hardy's description. As well, there is his marked tendency to
present scenes to his reader in a pictorial fashion so that we may the

15   Price, *Essays* (1798), II, pp. 406-407.

more easily recognize them. This pictorialism is not always a simple organization of details into foreground, middle distance, and background. As early as January 1881, Hardy was expressing some dissatisfaction with this mode of description. What he wanted to do, he said, was to see "into *the heart of a thing*" or, as he put it in 1887, "to see the deeper reality underlying the scenic."[16] At this date he still had four great novels to write, and it is true that, in these, critics have found interesting examples to show how Hardy was adapting other techniques like the Impressionist to assist him in expressing his "abstract imaginings." Alastair Smart was one of the first to draw attention to Mr. Porcomb's view of Marty South as "an impression-picture of extremest type";[17] Penelope Vigar uses the same illustration and speaks of the "illusive, kaleidoscopic quality" of *The Woodlanders*, which exhibits on a rereading "the technique of an Impressionist painter."[18] F. B. Pinion, quoting Smart, refers to Marty South as an example of Hardy's "*rapprochement* to the Impressionist vision."[19] Norman Page, it seems to me, however, offers a more rewarding study by emphasizing the influence of Victorian genre painting which he maintains, like typical Hardy description, habitually offers "the equivalent of the battered tankard—the simple object rendered poignant by its association with humanity."[20] Joan Grundy links Hardy to both Turner and the Impressionists. She, too, quotes the Marty South episode, but her investigation of the subject is more extensive and detailed than the others; she concludes that in *Jude the Obscure* "Hardy *is* the modern artist,"[21] presumably celebrating, in the author's words, "the gaunt waste in Thule."

But as illuminating as these observations and others are about Hardy's pictorialism, they do not negate or obscure the preponderant role of picturesque theory and practice discernible throughout his fiction. This role is not, of course, always announced in advance by the word "picturesque." Consider, for example, the descriptions that he offered of the Three Tranters Inn (*Desperate Remedies*); Reuben Dewey's cottage (*Under the Greenwood Tree*); the old tower of West Endelstow Church (*A Pair of Blue Eyes*); the ancient Malthouse and

16   Florence Emily Hardy, *Life of Thomas Hardy*, pp. 147, 185.
17   Smart, "Pictorial Imagery in the Novels of Thomas Hardy," p. 279.
18   Penelope Vigar, *The Novels of Thomas Hardy: Illusion and Reality* (London, 1974), p. 26.
19   F. B. Pinion, *Thomas Hardy: Art and Thought* (London, 1977), p. 22.
20   Page, *Thomas Hardy*, p. 77.
21   Grundy, *Hardy and the Sister Arts*, p. 66.

the Great Barn (*Far From the Madding Crowd*); Corvsgate Castle (*The Hand of Ethelberta*); the exterior of Captain Vye's house and that "quaint old habitation," the Yeobright home (*The Return of the Native*); Overcombe Mill (*The Trumpet Major*); the romantic old towns of Normandy (*A Laodicean*); the Three Mariners, that "ancient house of accommodation" (*The Mayor of Casterbridge*); Mr. Melbury's homestead (*The Woodlanders*); the architecture of Christminster's medieval buildings (*Jude the Obscure*); and "the quaint little Elizabethan cottage" in *The Well-Beloved*. Each one of these descriptions depends very much on a way of seeing that emphasizes, not the "deeper reality," but the "simply natural" in the familiar framework of the picturesque.

In none of these examples is the "simply natural" and the picturesque more obvious than in the representation of the shearing-barn in *Far From the Madding Crowd* (chap. 22), which "not only emulated the form of the neighbouring church of the parish, but vied with it in antiquity." We are made to see the barn as if we were looking at one of John Britton's architectural drawings:

> The vast porches at the sides, lofty enough to admit a waggon laden to its highest with corn in the sheaf, were spanned by heavy-pointed arches of stone, broadly and boldly cut, whose very simplicity was the origin of a grandeur not apparent in erections where more ornament has been attempted. The dusky, filmed, chestnut roof, braced and tied in by huge collars, curves, and diagonals, was far nobler in design, because more wealthy in material, than nine-tenths of those in our modern churches. Along each side wall was a range of striding buttresses, throwing deep shadows on the spaces between them, which were perforated by lancet openings, combining in their proportions the precise requirements both of beauty and ventilation.

But Hardy's language in this passage goes beyond what is physical in appearance to offer interpretive comment which betrays his love of a painterly scene, for a building, in Richard Payne Knight's words, "rendered venerable by ... imposing marks of antiquity."[22] He is interested not only in the huge collars and buttresses but equally in the "dusky filmed chestnut" of the roof, in the pattern of "curves and diagonals," in the deep shadows cast by the buttresses, and in the proportions of the lancet openings which offer beauty as well as ventilation.

22 Knight, *Analytical Inquiry*, p. 161.

Hardy is seeing as a Gilpin or a Price saw. Gilpin, too, remarked on a barn at Cerne in Dorsetshire, but thought it less noble than one at Choulsey in Berkshire which contained four threshing floors and bore the date 1101. Like Hardy, Gilpin was impressed by the continuing function performed by these barns. The Choulsey one, he said, "has continued doing it's [sic] offices to society, through the space of seven hundred years."[23] In Hardy's words, "For once medievalism and modernism had a common standpoint."

Hardy's interest in the picturesqueness of Bathsheba's shearing-barn becomes a painting with a restricted focus as he lets the sunlight in upon the polished black of the oak threshing floor and on the backs of a group of shearers "upon their bleached shirts, tanned arms, and the polished shears they flourished" over the panting sheep. There is absolutely no need of any illustration by Helen Paterson Allingham to help even the non-imaginative reader see the scene on the threshing floor.[24]

How much Hardy valued the qualities he associated with this mode of seeing may be noted in his observations about the Dorsetshire country labourer whose old established folkways were by 1887 being increasingly disturbed by changing agricultural practice and migration to the city. Hardy regretted that the impermanence of the labourer's residence meant he no longer took pride in his home and garden. The result was a "lack of picturesqueness" about his dwelling place.[25] Further, the labourers were "losing their peculiarities as a class." All this, said Hardy, was "the old story that progress and picturesqueness do not harmonize."[26] This was a complaint which would have elicited sympathy from Sir Walter Scott. What Hardy found very attractive was a cottage like Reuben Dewey's whose dormer windows looked out on "thick bushes of box and laurestinus," upon codlin trees once intended as espaliers, and upon ivy that clung to the walls. Reuben's cottage likely resembled Hardy's own birthplace at Upper Bockhampton.

If the exterior of many older Dorsetshire cottages appealed to Thomas Hardy, much the same can be said of the interiors. "It was," he remarked, "a satisfaction to walk into the keeper's house" (Geof-

23 Gilpin, *Forest Scenery*, II, p. 137.
24 See Jackson, *Illustration and the Novels of Thomas Hardy*, plates 3, 4, 5, 6, for examples of Helen Paterson Allingham's illustrations for *Far From the Madding Crowd*.
25 Florence Emily Hardy, *Life of Thomas Hardy*, p. 206.
26 Hardy, *Personal Writings*, pp. 180-81.

frey Day's in *Under the Greenwood Tree*). Here it was the chimney corner which was most attractive, especially one peculiarity of it:

> This peculiarity was a little window in the chimney-back, almost over the fire, around which the smoke crept caressingly when it left the perpendicular course. The window-board was curiously stamped with black circles, burnt thereon by the heated bottoms of drinking-cups which had rested there after previously standing on the hot ashes of the hearth for the purpose of warming their contents, the result giving to the ledge the look of an envelope which has passed through innumerable post-offices (Pt. II, chap. 6).

Readers are made both to see and to feel this description as if they were looking at a painting. The appeal of the prose by way of imagery goes beyond the facts of a painting when the ledge is described as having "the look of an envelope which has passed through innumerable post-offices." This is what Sir Uvedale Price would explain under the heading of association of ideas:

> All external objects affect us in two different ways; by the impression they make on the senses, and by the reflections they suggest to the mind. These two modes, though very distinct in their operations, often unite in producing one effect; the reflections of the mind, either strengthening, weakening, or giving a new direction, to the impression received by the eye.[27]

Price's emphasis upon the effect of the external object on the mind of the viewer recalls Arthur Hallam's argument in his review of Tennyson's lyrics. Tennyson's poetry, Hallam asserts, is "picturesque"; it rests upon "an immediate sympathy with the external universe"; it is "a sort of magic" producing a multiplicity of impressions by way of the interaction of the imagination and "the real appearance of Nature."[28]

Although Hallam is talking about lyric poetry, his remarks do bear upon Hardy and his mode of vision for he, too, is using the real appearance of the external world in such a way as to elicit from us an emotional response and help us, as Hallam puts it, to attain to his point of vision. He wants us to feel how satisfying it is to walk into Geoffrey Day's house and above all to sense the attractiveness and peculiarity of his chimney corner. Words like "caressingly," "curiously," and "warming" betray his intention, while the vividness of his closing postal metaphor testifies to the picturesqueness of his prose, to what Hallam refers to as "the forces of association," the "author's point of vision," and "his vivid, picturesque delineation of

27   Price, *Essays* (1798), II, pp. 282-83.
28   *Arthur Hallam*, pp. 186-87.

objects ... [held] fused ... in a medium of strong emotion." As in "Mariana"[29] so, too, in this description of Geoffrey Day's chimney corner, it is sensation rather than intellect which makes the prose so appealing. Hallam's aesthetic may, in fact, be applied with advantage to many of Hardy's pictorial passages to account for their added dimensions.

The effect upon the reader of the description of Miss Aldclyffe's home, of Endelstow House, the military encampment above Overcombe village, Stancy Castle, Casterbridge, Little Hintock House, Christminster, Shaston, and the Isle of Slingers creates something more than just credibility: the reader is made to feel their peculiarities and—for those readers who have visited the Hardy country—to share in the sort of pleasure which was Wordsworth's when he saw Tintern Abbey for the second time. Hardy's descriptions of landscape and of human habitations in it are not just a matter of authenticity, real or fictional, for he is also concerned to rouse our imaginations so that we may feel as he did when the actual scene was before him.

A good example of his technique is the description of that "starve-acre place," Flintcomb-Ash farm in *Tess of the D'Urbervilles*. At first we see its hundred odd acres of downland as details of topography and vegetation: the "bulbous, cusped, and phallic shapes" of the flints and the leafless stumps of turnips after the cattle have grubbed them off leaving the field a desolate drab colour. But even as we respond to the facts of the countryside, Hardy's imagination sweeps us on to another dimension of landscape delineation that becomes blankly emotional rather than physically detailed. The featureless drab of the swede field, notes the author, resembled the sky in all but colour; it wore a "white vacuity of countenance with the lineaments gone." And underneath that countenance Tess and Marion drudged on in the field below: "So these two upper and nether visages confronted each other all day long, the white face looking down on the brown face, and the brown face looking up at the white face, without anything standing between them but the two girls crawling over the surface of the former like flies" (chap. 43). The indifference of the white face and the brown face to the two girls stirs our sympathy for them even as it underlines our common humanity and plight in an uncaring universe.

Nature here is no longer a beauty but, as Hardy put it in 1887, "a Mystery." In going beyond the realities of a swede field and the "vivid

29   See chapter 2, pp. 43-44.

delineation of objects in it" to the question of humanity and its relationship to the universe, Hardy has moved beyond even Hallam's picturesque to a new mode of seeing external things. But despite examples such as this one, and his own assertion to the contrary, Hardy continued to use the conventions of the picturesque, although less noticeably in his later novels than in his early ones.

Throughout his novels, the landscape is always linked closely to characters whose dwellings and work mark the countryside and whose ways of life contribute a peculiar charm to the landscape. This relationship, however, may be a complex matter in which the countryside becomes only a mental picture in the character's mind. If, for example, we accept the authorial comment that the world, in Tess's imaginings, "is only a psychological phenomenon," then, of course, character is supremely important and landscape but a decorative backdrop. "Nature for Hardy," however, as J. Hillis Miller remarks, "has meaning and use only when it has been marked by man's living in it and so has become a repository of signs preserving individual and collective history."[30]

This "repository of signs" has its application to the characters themselves who are often marked as distinctively as their own dwellings, by reason of their appearance, mannerisms, language, and everyday activities. In *Under the Greenwood Tree*, so aptly subtitled "A Rural Painting of the Dutch School," a wide variety of these "signs" attests to life in Hardy's Wessex: "Going the Rounds," having "a drop of the right sort" at the Tranter's home; practising number seventy-eight, "that ancient and time-worn hymn"; meeting in front of Mr. Penny's, where "they were all brightly illuminated . . . each . . . backed up by a shadow as long as a steeple"; standing ill at ease in the vicarage; and making merry on the occasion of the Tranter's party. On Christmas morning, Hardy places them pictorially for us in the gallery of the Mellstock Church: "Old William sat in the centre of the front row, his violoncello between his knees and two singers on each hand. Behind him, on the left, came the treble singers and Dick; and on the right the tranter and the tenors. Further back was Old Mail with the altos and supernumeraries" (Pt. 1, chap. 6).

Thomas Webster's *The Village Choir*, which was exhibited in 1847, shows another arrangement and setting for a choir in Buckinghamshire and captures in pigments rather than words the quaint

---

30   See J. Hillis Miller, "Nature and the Linguistic Moment," in *Nature and the Victorian Imagination*, p. 447.

variety of such choirs some time in the early 1840s, long after the Mellstock group had given way to the organ. Norman Page thinks that Hardy must have seen Webster's painting "in what is now the Victoria and Albert Museum."[31]

Some of the picturesqueness of the Mellstock choir is to be found in the appearance and language of the members. At the Tranter's house "the older men and musicians wore thick coats, with stiff perpendicular collars, and coloured handkerchiefs wound round and round the neck till the end came to hand, over all which they just showed their ears and noses, like people looking over a wall." Collectively, the older members remain visually memorable in the simile that rounds off their description. The rest of the choir are dressed mainly in snow-white smock-frocks, embroidered upon the shoulder and breasts in ornamental forms of hearts, diamonds, and zigzags. Their language that contrasts so markedly with standard English is as striking to the ear as their dress to the eye. Old William Dewey's defense of strings, seconded by Little Jimmy, is a good illustration of this contrast and of how vividly Hardy's rustics could speak:

> 'They should ha' stuck to strings. Your brass-man is a rafting dog—well and good; your reed-man is a dab at stirring ye—well and good; your drum-man is a rare bowel-shaker—good again. But I don't care who hears me say it, nothing will spak to your heart wi' the sweetness o' the man of strings!"
> "Strings for ever!" said Little Jimmy (Pt. I, chap. 4).

The Shakespearian tricks of rhetoric, the vivid rural imagery, the occasional dialectal word, Little Jimmy's fervent advocacy of the lost cause, the conjunctive effect of "brass-man," "reed-man," "drum-man," all contribute to the picturesqueness of the Mellstock Choir on their Christmas rounds, making us see and even feel. Although such musical groups appear elsewhere in the novels—the Weatherbury band in *Far From the Madding Crowd*, the East Egdon band in *The Return of the Native*, Parson Torkingham's choir in *Two on a Tower*, or the bandsmen from Great Hintock in *The Woodlanders*—none is described with such nostalgic charm as the Mellstock one.

Another extremely effective picture of local characters is that within Warren's Malthouse in chapter 8 of *Far From the Madding Crowd*, where Gabriel Oak, Laban Tall, Henry Fray, Jan Coggan, Joseph Poorgrass, and Jacob Smallbury—characters whose names are as unusual as they themselves—group about the open kiln mouth, all

31 Page, *Thomas Hardy*, p. 68.

with a common focus upon the warming "God-forgive-me" and later upon Gabriel Oak as he strikes up "Jockey to the Fair" on his flute. Of these characters it is the Malster who is, by his calling and appearance, the most picturesque. Red-eyed and bleary, we see this aged man sitting opposite his fire, "his frosty white hair and beard overgrowing his gnarled figure like the grey moss and lichen upon a leafless apple tree."

The Malthouse itself is a fitting habitation for the old man: "enclosed by an old wall inwrapped with ivy . . . the character and purposes of the building were clearly enough shown by its outline upon the sky" which revealed "an over-hanging thatched roof sloped up to a point in the centre, upon which rose a small wooden lantern, fitted with louvre-boards on all the four sides, and from these openings a mist was dimly perceived to be escaping into the night air" (chap. 8). The care which Hardy takes to bring the Malthouse vividly before us has a purpose beyond pictorial effect. The vivid delineation of characters and building serves first to rouse our curiosity and then to provide a credible means whereby we can learn about Gabriel, Bathsheba Everdene, and the disappearance of Fanny Robin. Throughout the chapter, picturesqueness of character and setting accompanies in a natural way story elements that are richly comic but moving toward concern for what Joseph Poorgrass describes as "a night of horrors!"

In *The Return of the Native*, the somewhat Mephistophelean appearance of the interior of the Malthouse has its counterpart, especially by night, in the abode and person of Diggory Venn. Gypsy-like in his wanderings and home, Diggory is another character to whom the term picturesque properly belongs. He was, says Hardy, "an instance of the pleasing being wasted to form the ground-work of the singular" (Bk. I, chap. 9). Without the dye of his trade, he would have appeared as a rather handsome man, but the author obviously likes him as he is, "a curious, interesting, and nearly perished link between obsolete forms of life and those which generally prevail" (Bk. I, chap. 2).

Diggory's van with its tilt, little stove, and chimney, its stock of reddle—the whole drawn by two heath-croppers—provides an oddly suitable home for him within the brambly dells of Egdon Heath, as attractive visually as gypsy encampments were to Price and Knight. In addition, the van's site places Diggory very conveniently with respect to the action of the narrative. The scene, for instance, in which, by the light of thirteen glowworms, Diggory wins the last of the sovereigns from Wildeve is not more than two hundred yards from his van. The scene's subject and its limits, so narrowly circumscribed by the candle's light and the heads of the curious heath-croppers, would have appealed to any artist fond of the picturesque in the same way as the "parley with the cardsharpers" in *The Old Curiosity Shop* may have appealed to Hablot Browne.[32] Throughout most of *The Return of the Native*, the special qualities and activities which attach to Diggory Venn, his van, and his trade give him very considerable importance in the action that courses through "the wild and picturesque vale[s]" of Egdon Heath (chap. 10).

Other Hardy characters possess picturesqueness to varying degrees: Mr. Springrove and his smock-frocked cider makers in *Desperate Remedies* form a Wilkie-like picture under the wide-spreading elm trees of the Three Tranters Inn, as Hardy recalls the days when this inn was part of "the romantic and genial experience of stage-coach travelling" (chap. 8); Ethelberta Petherwin's unusual appearance before the ladies and gentlemen of the Imperial Archaeological Society provides for them a whimsical happening, "the picturesque form of acquaintance" (*The Hand of Ethelberta*, chap. 31); "removed to some half-known century, [Captain de Stancy's] deeds would have won a picturesqueness of light and shade that might have made him a fascinating subject for some gallery of illustrious historical personages" (*A Laodicean*, Bk. III, chap. 4); Michael Henchard in *The Mayor of Casterbridge*, like Rochester in *Jane Eyre*, "had a rich complexion, which verged on swarthiness, a flashing black eye, and dark, bushy brows and hair"—upon which "time, the magician," also plays its tricks (chap. 5); Giles Winterbourne, looking and smelling "like Autumn's very brother" (*The Woodlanders*, chap. 28) is a singular figure as he walks beside his apple-mill; "to almost everybody [Tess of the D'Urbervilles] was a fine and picturesque country girl, and no more" (Phase I, chap. 2); and Alfred Somers in *The Well-Beloved* is as "picturesque as his own paintings" (Pt. III, iv).

When Hardy in *The Mayor of Casterbridge* refers to Elizabeth Newson's "occasional pretty and picturesque use of dialect words" like *bide, dumbledores, greggles, hag-rid*, and *fay* (chap. 20), he clearly associates the word "picturesque" with language that is unusual because of its deviation from what is standard. That same language, of course, can become vividly pictorial when it is linked with suitable imagery. Consider Timothy Fairway's comment in *The Return of the Native* about Humphrey's father's illiteracy:

---

32   Arlene M. Jackson, in *Illustration and the Novels of Thomas Hardy*, rightly objects
      to the weakness of Arthur Hopkins's illustration of this scene, p. 93 and plate 31.

"Ah, Humph, well I can mind when I was married how I zid thy father's mark staring me in the face as I went to put down my name. He and your mother were the couple married just afore we were, and there stood thy father's cross with arms stretched out like a great banging scarecrow" (Bk. I, chap. 3).

Timothy's closing simile, meant to ensure that Humph will see as well as understand, is one of the truly memorable images of illiteracy and an excellent illustration of how Hardy, throughout his fiction, made the speech of his rural folk picturesque. It is tempting to quote more, but the aptness of Reuben Dewey's observation about women also applies to such quotations: "they be all alike in the groundwork; 'tis only in the flourishes there's a difference" (Pt. II, chap. 8).

As it is with their appearance and language, so it is with many of the age-old customs of the Wessex folk: hiving bees, sheep shearing, thatching, bark ripping, cider making, cutting furze, shrouding trees, and the transport of timber which are often described pictorially with all the care that a painter devotes to a picture. One remembers particularly such scenes as Tess gleaning in the harvest field, Gabriel Oak thatching a rick in a storm, or John Upjohn ripping bark from oak trees. Although the processes of the barking season are explained in *The Woodlanders* so that readers can visualize the workers dipping into the cider pail or observe them, gathered about the hut fire, listening to Melbury tell "ancient timber-stories," Hardy's picturesque treatment has an imaginative dimension that goes beyond fact and scenic organization, that touches readers' emotions so that they feel not only for the captive Marty South, but also for the trees, the victims of her ripping tool:

Marty South was an adept at peeling the upper parts; and there she stood encaged amid the mass of twigs and buds like a great bird, running her ripping-tool into the smallest branches . . . branches which, in their lifetime, had swayed high above the bulk of the wood, and caught the earliest rays of the sun and moon while the lower part of the forest was still in darkness (chap. 19).

This again is Hallam's picturesque in which Marty South and her unusual rural occupation come together to elicit an emotional response from readers.[33]

At other times this emotional element may be absent as Hardy mentions rural activities and customs which still existed in his own day. In these he often found what was visually interesting and un-

33   See chapter 2, pp. 43-44, and chapter 8, pp. 161-62.

common and to which he did not hesitate to attach the word "picturesque." And so he chronicles "rare old market town activities of
Casterbridge" taking his readers into Henchard's hay barns, showing
them the "wooden granaries on stone staddles," and even introducing them to "the rugged picturesqueness of the old method" of book-
keeping (chap. 14). In the midst of these rural occupations, Henchard
and Farfrae, Giles and Marty live out strenuous lives but in such a way
that their work possesses visual charm and very often emotional
significance as well.

It is not too fanciful to suggest, especially in *The Return of the
Native*, that picturesqueness may attach to the sounds of the heath
somewhat as Hardy thought that emotions may "attach themselves to
scenes that are simultaneous" (*Desperate Remedies*, chap. 1). The
best illustration of "the linguistic peculiarity of the heath" is the
description of the action of the night wind upon the dried heath bells
which, we are told, "bore a great resemblance to the ruins of human
song which remain to the throat of fourscore and ten" (Bk. I, chap. 6).
In this passage, the author is being much more than simply descriptive. He is intent on creating within the reader an emotion to match
the "shrivelled and intermittent recitative" of the heath bells and to
accompany the visual impression of the peculiarities of the landscape
with its pits and prominences, brilliant lights and shadows, lonely
barrows and furzy distances picturesquely cast in an "antique, brown
dress." It is an emotion extending back in time to associations with
Roman and pre-Roman Britain. But the pictorial quality of this landscape goes beyond the limits established by eighteenth-century
theorists when Hardy assigns a spiritual content to the sound from the
trumpets of the heath bells:

> 'The spirit moved them'. A meaning of the phrase forced itself
> upon the attention; and an emotional listener's fetichistic mood
> might have ended in one of more advanced quality. It was not, after
> all, that the left-hand expanse of old blooms spoke, or the right-
> hand, or those of the slope in front; but it was the single person of
> something else speaking through each at once (Bk. I, chap. 6).

The mood created is one that resembles closely Eustacia's so that her
sigh and the worn whisper of the heath bells become the "same
discourse." Hardy's imaginative range, as he sets this scene, a kind of
prologue to the meeting of Eustacia and Wildeve, reveals clearly how
he varies his use of the picturesque and of how, as Sir Uvedale Price
thought, the picturesque may be "equally extended to all our sensations, by whatever organs they are received." Readers' imaginations

enable them to see the "mummied heath-bells . . . originally tender and purple . . . washed colourless by Michaelmas rains, and dried to dead skins by October rains." By their sense of touch, they can imagine the "dry and papery" texture of the flowers; and by their hearing they can also imagine the scouring effect of the wind in hundreds of the tiny trumpets, so suggestive of ruin and decay. This extension of the meaning of the picturesque beyond the simply visual to the senses of touch and hearing, and the inclusion of an emotional mood of consequence to both Eustacia and the readers, is a remarkable literary achievement.[34]

In moving from *The Return of the Native* (1874) to *Tess of the D'Urbervilles* (1891), readers become aware of less emphasis upon the picturesque treatment of landscape and character. It is as if such viewing no longer interested the author, as if, as he said, he were seeking "the deeper reality underlying the scenic, the expression of what are sometimes called abstract imaginings."[35] Such a direction is away from, not toward, the vision of a Gilpin or a Price. And yet, even in *Tess*, Hardy cannot entirely throw off a mode of seeing which he had cultivated—perhaps unknowingly—since his early days of gallery viewing in London. So that readers can get a "bird's eye perspective" of the Valley of the Great Dairies, Hardy places Tess on a summit overlooking the valley and then describes how the lower Froom landscape differed from that of Blackmoor Vale:

> The world was drawn to a larger pattern here. The enclosures numbered fifty acres instead of ten, the farmsteads were more extended, the groups of cattle formed tribes hereabout; there only families. These myriads of cows stretching under her eyes from the far east to the far west outnumbered any she had ever seen at one glance before. The green lea was speckled as thickly with them as a canvas by Van Alsloot or Sallaert with burghers. The ripe hue of the red and dun kine absorbed the evening sunlight, which the white-coated animals returned to the eye in rays almost dazzling, even at the distant elevation on which she stood (chap. 16).

Even so this description lacks the kind of topographical reference and organization we associate with picturesque landscapes. In fact, what we see is not a landscape at all but enclosures and cattle which, by process of a simile, are likened to canvases by the little-known Flemish artists, Van Alsloot and Sallaert. The concluding sentence de-

---

34   See also Evelyn Hardy, *Thomas Hardy*, p. 166.
35   Florence Emily Hardy, *Life of Thomas Hardy*, p. 185.

pends for its effect upon impressionistic rather than picturesque qualities. But in its overall technique, this paragraph is rather neatly summed up in Richard Payne Knight's words as "the habit . . . of spontaneously mixing associated ideas with organic perceptions in contemplating objects of vision."[36] The organic perceptions in this paragraph belong to "the simply natural" rather than the "deeper reality underlying the scenic" and for this reason do have affinity with the picturesque.

This word occurs just once in this novel, when it is used to describe Tess: "to almost everybody she was a fine and picturesque country girl, and no more" (chap. 2). The particular adjective may fit because what "almost everybody" sees on looking at Tess is her "bouncing handsome womanliness" and her "pouted-up deep red mouth" whose sounds betray the local dialect. On this surface assessment, Tess is like Liddy Smallbury or Maryann Money of *Far From the Madding Crowd* (chaps. 9, 22), but Tess's picturesqueness soon gives way before the brutal facts of life: childbirth, suckling Sorrow in the midst of the harvest workers, the death of "that bastard gift of shameless Nature," the change "from simple girl to complex woman." Then, after a brief spell of happiness in the pleasant bucolic atmosphere of Dairyman Crick's farm, Tess's attractiveness dulls in outline and colour until near Flintcomb-Ash she becomes "a fieldwoman pure and simple, in winter guise; a gray serge cape, a red woollen cravat, a stuff skirt covered by a whitey-brown rough wrapper, and buff-leather gloves. Every thread of that old attire has become faded and thin under the stroke of raindrops, the burn of sunbeams, and the stress of winds" (chap. 42). And finally at Stonehenge, she becomes a tired woman asleep on an oblong slab of stone. The picturesqueness of the Valley of the Great Dairies is but a brief interlude in the course of her tragic pilgrimage.

Stonehenge is merely "solemn and lonely" in contrast with the "great happiness" which Tess had known at Dairyman Crick's. The singularity of Stonehenge, its pagan history, its winds playing a "booming tune" amid its stone columns become for Tess only a convenient and necessary place of rest. The divorce of emotion and landscape, so noticeable finally in *Jude*, is apparent here. The disjunction of human feeling from the external world eliminates the possibility of picturesque treatment. In *Jude* this separation is foreshadowed even at the beginning of the novel.

36 Knight, *Analytical Inquiry*, p. 95.

Jude as a bakery boy, on his "quaint and singular vehicle" drawn by "an aged horse with a hanging head," studying "the dusty volumes called the classics," is too nearly a youthful portrait of Dr. Syntax for the reader to miss. Later, however, Jude leaves Marygreen to move to Christminster where, at first, the picturesqueness of this medieval city makes a compelling appeal to him as he rambles "under the walls and doorways, feeling with his fingers the contours of their mouldings and carving" (Pt. II, i). But in the stonemason's yard, Jude becomes aware of how the results of the foreman's work differed from the old: "They were marked by precision, mathematical straightness, smoothness, exactitude: there in the old walls were the broken lines of the original idea; jagged curves, disdain of precision, irregularity, disarray" (Pt. II, ii). The old had picturesque qualities preferable to the new, but what Jude did not see then was "that medievalism was as dead as a fern-leaf in a lump of coal"; that "other developments were shaping in the world around him, in which Gothic architecture and its associations had no place" (Pt. II, ii).

Gradually, with his realization of how futile it is for him to be enrolled in one of Christminster's ancient institutions, Jude sees "what a curious and cunning glamour the neighbourhood of the place had exercised over him." The "spires, halls, gables, streets, chapels, gardens, quadrangles" of picturesque Christminster are not for him whose destiny lies "among the manual toilers in the shabby purlieu which he himself occupied" (Pt. II, vi). Sue, even more than Jude, senses that the medieval aspects of Christminster are "played out"; Old Grove Place in Shaston is "so antique and dismal" that it depressed her dreadfully. Aware of how hopeless their relationship is, Sue and Jude become "so absorbed in their own situation that their surroundings were little in their consciousness" (Pt. V, i). The "ache of modernism" that Tess experienced is upon them, and the ancient glories of a Christminster or a Shaston can only serve as a painted back-cloth to their cheerless stage that becomes in the end for Jude a deathbed, for Sue an empty existence. The alienation that they experience isolates them from the external world and renders inoperative an aesthetic theory that postulated pleasure for viewers of that world.

If the cold pulses of the stars do indeed beat "amid the black hollows above, in serene dissociation from . . . wisps of human life" (*Tess of the D'Urbervilles*, chap. 4), it is hardly possible to view them, and presumably other nearer objects of the physical world, picturesquely, for the picturesque always requires a rational connection between the perceiver and the thing perceived. Furthermore, if, as Hardy asserts in *Tess*, "the world is only a psychological phenomenon," we become of concern only to ourselves and the process of alienation is set in motion. The novel must retreat from a meaningless universe and equally meaningless social relationships to a position in our mind alone.

But even though he hints at such a possibility, Hardy's fictional creed does not really encompass such a pessimistic view of humanity or fiction. The fields of Wessex and the constellations which Gabriel Oak observe wheeling eastward over Norcombe Hill are as real in their externality to Gabriel as they are to Hardy; likewise, Gabriel's relationships with Farmer Boldwood and Bathsheba Everdene seem meaningful for us and must have been so to Hardy. In his insistence that "a story *must be worth the telling*,"[37] that "romanticism will exist in human nature as long as human nature itself exists,"[38] Hardy, in effect, is confirming his own belief in the reality of human relations in a universe that is fascinating despite its seeming indifference to human endeavour.

And this confirmation may go far to explain why the aesthetic of the picturesque so generally meets Hardy's fictional requirements. In his hands it strikes a recognizable "balance between the uncommon and the ordinary." Its use means that for his readers, past and present, Wessex becomes a familiar countryside, one they can visualize with enjoyment. Little that is symbolic or fuzzily impressionistic restrains them from seeing this landscape, its people, and their artifacts. Such a visual process is important if the readers are to see the Wessex that envelops the fictional characters, and this process Hardy achieves with splendid success. That he was himself dissatisfied with these "original realities" is a critical matter of importance but of limited application to his novels as a whole.

His desire in 1887 to get at the "deeper reality" beneath the surface of the ordinary is a clear indication, however, of his dissatisfaction with picturesque representation. Although we can applaud this desire, it may be worth noting that his intention would be dismissed as meaningless by most of his rural characters to whom the notes of "Jockey to the Fair" would bring more consolation than the knowledge that an abstract President of the Immortals meted out justice to suffering shepherds. But to Hardy himself in 1887 it was, as

---

37 Florence Emily Hardy, *Life of Thomas Hardy*, p. 362.
38 Florence Emily Hardy, *Life of Thomas Hardy*, p. 147.

he described it, the "mad, late-Turner rendering" that appealed rather than the earlier picturesque Turner of the coastal scenes of England. It was the mystery rather than the appearance of nature which mattered. How possible it is for writers to achieve by their words what a Turner could eventually by his oils is an aesthetic question that cannot be argued here. That both Hardy and Turner had to see the "simply natural" before they could sound its mysteries must, however, be acknowledged; that both of them at first saw it picturesquely is also evident. Furthermore, that Hardy, like Turner, was able to free himself from what Ruskin called the "lower picturesque" and move imaginatively to view the external world and the humans caught in its mysteries with great sympathy and understanding is a literary commonplace, nowhere better summed up than by Virginia Woolf: "There is, in the first place, that sense of the physical world which Hardy more than any novelist can bring before us; the sense that the little prospect of man's existence is ringed by a landscape which, while it exists apart, yet confers a deep and solemn beauty upon his drama."[39] Taking what early picturesque theory and example had to offer him, Thomas Hardy—like Wordsworth, Turner, and Tennyson—had moved on to the "nobler picturesque" with its power to touch not only the mind but also the emotions.

39   Virginia Woolf, "The Novels of Thomas Hardy," *The Common Reader*, 2nd series (London, 1959), p. 248.

Chapter 8

The Inheritance

> Let us hold painting by the hand a moment longer, for
> though they must part in the end, painting and writing
> have much to tell each other; they have much in common.
> Virginia Woolf, *Walter Sickert, a Conversation*

Looking back over the fiction that links Thomas Hardy with Sir Walter
Scott, it is difficult to understand why Christopher Hussey thought
that, with the exception of Thomas Love Peacock, "only second-rate
writers continued, after *Waverley*, to be conscious of the picturesque."[1] This is not a judgment that accords with the findings of this
study. Charlotte Brontë, Dickens, George Eliot, and Hardy were, like
Scott, all conscious of and in varying degrees indebted to picturesque
theory and practice which helped them to picture for us their landscape, the people in it, and their habitations. That they were also
prepared to use this visual mode more widely and even to give it new
meaning is apparent, too, in their use of the term to describe speech,
movements, and sounds. As well, it may refer to narrative action and
to mood arising, for example, from the nostalgia attendant upon what
was ruinous or simply old-fashioned. "A ragged Ruin" remained, to
use the language of Polyphon in Gilpin's *Dialogue*, "vastly picturesque" to many Victorians, and very competent artists like Peter de
Wint on occasion catered to this taste (Pl. 23).

Nineteenth-century novelists—even the greatest of them—had,
like the artists, good reason to retain the conventions of the picturesque. It was a way of seeing which complemented the literalness of

---

1 Hussey, *The Picturesque*, p. 242.

their fiction which so often—like the landscape painting of the century—made use of topographical details of real places and regions. Likewise, in character portraiture, the novelists made certain that their readers had the sort of particulars which made it possible for them to visualize the appearance of their characters. Both Gilpin and Price had given them the necessary advice and examples for this kind of "singular" portraiture in words. And it is possible, too, that in the theories of Gilpin, Price, and especially Richard Payne Knight, we can find a popular source for the function in fiction of what Henry James referred to as the "infinite magic" of the association of ideas.[2]

For novelists interested in placing their characters in a recognizable setting, the picturesque was a pictorial method they could use that would at once be realized and perceived as credible by the majority of their readers. It was a method with which they were very familiar. They—and their parents—had accepted and assimilated its conventions in the galleries of the stately homes of England, in the engravings of popular art which appeared in many journals of the time, and in nearly all travel books where it took the place of the non-existent photograph. It was a convention which required some suspension of disbelief, some assurance of human goodness, some confidence in form. These requirements the Victorians accepted happily, perhaps because they offered some solace, some assurance that weighed against the disturbing social and moral currents of their day. This assurance was supported by the way in which other art forms accepted and adapted the picturesque to their own needs.

Well before Victoria's reign, the picturesque had been clearly defined and adapted to the practice of fiction. As distinguished a man of letters as William Hazlitt had accepted its aesthetic. His essay, "On the Picturesque and the Ideal,"[3] illuminates its position with respect both to "the natural in visible objects" and to the ideal "which answers to the preconceived imagination and appetite in the mind for love and beauty." Hazlitt's placing the picturesque intermediately between the "natural" and the "ideal" is interesting especially in relation to Charlotte Brontë's experience. Of great importance is Hazlitt's succinct description of the picturesque as opposed to the ideal: "The picturesque depends chiefly on the principle of discrimination or contrast; the *ideal* on harmony and continuity of effect: the one

2   Henry James, *The Art of the Novel* (New York, 1934), p. 125.
3   Hazlitt, *The Complete Works of William Hazlitt*, VIII, pp. 317-21. See also Jean H. Hagstrum's comment in *The Sister Arts* (Chicago, 1958), pp. 157-58.

surprises, the other satisfies the mind; the one starts off from a given point, the other reposes on itself; the one is determined by an excess of form, the other by a concentration of feeling." To illustrate his description, Hazlitt turns to painting. Van Dyck, he observes, "was at once the least picturesque and least *ideal* of all the great painters. He was purely natural." In contrast, Rubens is picturesque and Claude ideal. For Hazlitt, the ideal is "the height of the pleasing, that which satisfies and accords with the inmost longing of the soul," whereas "the picturesque is merely a sharper and bolder impression of reality." The first of these, he says, is "truth"; the second is "good." The picturesque "appeals to the sense and understanding"; the ideal to the "will and the affections."

It would be difficult to find a more reasonable and discerning statement than Hazlitt's on this subject. For novelists who wanted to gain their readers' attention by avoiding the tedium of the ordinary and the perfection of the ideal, the picturesque offered much. Its emphasis on contrast, surprise, form, its appeal to "sense and understanding" suited many of the requirements of Victorian fiction. Furthermore, Victorian novelists had a distinct advantage in that they had before them the example of the Waverley novels, in which time and again Scott demonstrated how to make settings not only visual and memorable, but also essential to narrative and characterization. In the process he seldom hesitated to enlist the conventions of the picturesque.

It was very likely his example that encouraged admirers like Charlotte Brontë, Dickens, George Eliot, and Hardy to rely from time to time upon the same visual process, although with differing degrees of emphasis and — particularly with Dickens and George Eliot — with suspicions as deep as Ruskin's about an aesthetic whose practitioners delighted in disorder and ruin, not seeing at the same time the human deprivation and suffering that so often belonged to the scene that occasioned the pleasure. But despite such suspicions — more closely linked to the subject than to the form — both Dickens and George Eliot admit the picturesque to their fiction. As a visual aid, it was too useful a technique to discard entirely. Even in Bleeding Heart Yard, it had a role to play in the lives of Mr. and Mrs. Plornish.

In the fiction, however, of both Charlotte Brontë and Thomas Hardy, readers are very seldom, if ever, aware of social incongruities that render picturesque description suspect. Charlotte Brontë's acceptance of this aesthetic in her fiction was as unquestioned as her acceptance of it in her own short, sad life. For Hardy, the Wessex landscape, its architecture, and unusual rural people were, to begin with, picturesque, and he described them as such in his fiction. By 1887, however, his vision had deepened; in his dissatisfaction with "scenic paintings" and the representation of "optical effects," Hardy was serving notice that the days of picturesque description had to give way to the much more allusive and metaphorical methods of the twentieth century. But, with possible exceptions in *Tess* and *Jude*, Hardy's fictional descriptions were those of the nineteenth century, not the twentieth. His readers needed only what they already had—their inheritance of picturesque vision—to see and appreciate the word pictures of the Wessex novels. So long as sentiment was reined in and "heartlessness" curbed, the presentation was an acceptable one—especially for readers who wanted to see and to understand. To Victorian readers, it seemed good sense to find the external world as well as human passions not only mirrored but also intertwined in the pages of the fiction they enjoyed.

Many people still appreciate this Victorian taste in fiction. But today's conventions, both of painting and fiction, confine readers very closely to abstractions in oil or water colour and to internal consciousness in fiction. The authoritative narrator of the nineteenth century has had to stand aside so that today's fictional characters, often uncertain, irresolute, and alienated can speak and choose for themselves. Where these characters live in the external world and how they appear to the sight are questions of little concern to contemporary novelists, preoccupied as they are with "psychological landscape." Human feeling and the external world have become distinct and separate entities. It is not the artist or novelist in our time but the scientist who has reminded us of the significance of the natural world so that we are beginning again to look at nature—almost to revere it—as we are made to realize our fatal dependence upon it, not only for survival but for our own hearts' ease as well.[4] In this return to a commonsense view of the unity of the natural world, the picturesque may regain something of its past importance.

What the picturesque preserved throughout the nineteenth century was a rich sense of place and individuality so nearly lost in the placelessness of our large cities and, even to a considerable degree, of our countryside, where technological advances have brought city living to the villages and farmhouses of the people. It is doubtful,

---

4   See Jay Appleton, *The Experience of Landscape* (Chichester, 1975), pp. 171-77, for a geographer's comment on the "basic predicament of man in nature."

indeed, if Sir Uvedale Price could be as tolerant of agricultural improvement today as he was in 1796.

There is, as Asa Briggs has said, "relentless pressure to consider questions of contemporary environment exclusively in functional and quantitative terms." And this pressure, he goes on to say, has been such that "to most writers it is a *fait accompli*"; to others, it is merely "a source of melancholy and nostalgia,"[5] an extension of the very same feeling which George Eliot experienced at the beginning of our brave, new industrial world when she looked backward to the days of "fine old Leisure."

As we read many nineteenth-century novels, little doubt remains that some of the pleasure we enjoy owes much to the novelists' creation of settings, distinctive and real, and to the creation of characters deeply rooted and bound by tradition to these same places and regions. When this sense of identity is heightened so that place or person or both become singular and pictorial, we are close to the picturesque—especially if the overall effect is one of pleasure arising often from authors' attempts to compromise between an idealization of the individual or nature and the reality as it faces them in the external world.

Any careful consideration of the role of picturesque theory and practice in either nineteenth-century art or fiction will provide many reasons for excluding apology or pejorative comment. Like the artists, the novelists consciously used the conventions and effectively incorporated them into the body of their fiction. Critical comment since 1951, when H. M. McLuhan's essay on "Tennyson and Picturesque Poetry" appeared, has shown renewed interest in exploring the application of this theory and practice.

How much of this interest was generated by McLuhan's remarkable critical insights it is difficult to say, but certainly much credit must go to him for realizing the implications of Arthur Hallam's aesthetic theory: its emphasis upon immediate sensation or experience as opposed to logical relationships in poetry and his belief that the poetry of Shelley and Keats should be called picturesque rather than descriptive. "As in Wordsworth's 'Solitary Reaper' or Tennyson's 'Mariana,' the picturesque poet," according to McLuhan and Hallam, "is consciously manipulating a magical formula. The external situation is employed as a magical device for eliciting a precise mental state in the

5   Asa Briggs, "The Sense of Place," in *The Quality of Man's Environment*, Voice of America Forum Lectures (Washington, 1968), pp. 81, 85.

reader."[6] Accepting Christopher Hussey's statement that the comple-
tion of Thomson's *Seasons* in 1730 marks "the first step to Picturesque
vision,"[7] McLuhan finds its "plenary realization in Rimbaud's
metaphysical landscapes — *Les Illuminations*,"[8] published in 1886. It
is a bold critical leap from Thomson to Rimbaud and one in which
McLuhan enlists the support of Ruskin, of T. S. Eliot's "objective
correlative," and includes not only the poetry of the French Symbolists but also works like *Ulysses* and *Finnegan's Wake*, the *Four
Quartets*, and *The Wasteland*. Left a century behind, Arthur Hallam's
aesthetic theories serve eventually only as a catalyst for McLuhan's
thought process:

> There is in all these works [of Joyce and Eliot] a vision of the
> community of men and creatures which is not so much ethical as
> metaphysical. And it had been, in poetry, due to the technical
> innovations of Baudelaire, Laforgue and Rimbaud that it was possi-
> ble to render this vision immediately in verse without the ex-
> traneous aids of rhetoric or logical reflection and statement. The
> principal innovation was that of *le paysage intérieur* or the
> psychological landscape. This landscape, by means of discon-
> tinuity, which was first developed in picturesque painting, effected
> the apposition of widely diverse objects as a means of establishing
> what Mr. Eliot has called "an objective correlative" for a state of
> mind.[9]

The attribution of the word "picturesque" in its "plenary realization"
to the work of the Symbolists is one that demands an effort of belief
which the early theorists of the mode would surely have balked at
despite the connection between McLuhan's word "discontinuity"
and those "broken lines," irregularities," and "rough surfaces" so
beloved by Gilpin, Price, and Knight. This is not to deny McLuhan's
argument but rather to suggest that his use of "picturesque" has taken
the word a very long way from its origins.

But the word is one that McLuhan returned to in his essay "The
Aesthetic Moment in Landscape Poetry" (1952), emphasizing its "features of discontinuity," and arguing that the "art of Fielding, like that
of Scott and Dickens, is strictly 'picturesque' in achieving social
inclusiveness by means of discontinuous perspectives. Social panoramas, if they are to include more than one level of society, must

---

6   H. M. McLuhan, Introduction, in H. M. McLuhan, ed., *Alfred Lord Tennyson,
    Selected Poetry* (New York, 1956), p. xv. See also *Arthur Hallam*, pp. 186-87.
7   Hussey, *The Picturesque*, p. 31.
8   H. M. McLuhan, "Tennyson and Picturesque Poetry," *Essays in Criticism* 1, no. 3
    (1951), p. 264.
9   McLuhan, "Tennyson and Picturesque Poetry," pp. 270-71.

exploit techniques of juxtaposition or discontinuity."[10] Such an extension of meaning for this word would certainly have dismayed Richard Payne Knight who, in 1805, thought its semantic boundaries already in need of definition and containment.

Although in his book *Rococo to Cubism in Art and Literature* (1961), Wylie Sypher makes no reference to Marshall McLuhan, his thinking, especially in Part II, "Picturesque, Romanticism, Symbolism," seems to owe a great deal to him. What Sypher does, however, is add weight or example to McLuhan's critical discernment, and in fairness, interesting observations of his own. The picturesque was, he maintains, an art that was "usually saturated with a mood," noticeable, for example, in Gainsborough's *Cottage Door*.[11] It is, he says, "reminiscent imagining"[12] which owes much to the power of association. Unlike McLuhan, Sypher makes no mention of Hallam, but like McLuhan, he draws upon Ruskin for support and thinks of symbolism as "an extension of picturesque,"[13] and like him, too, he sees Wordsworth as "a great artist of the picturesque who was transitional between the earlier picturesque of the eighteenth century and the nineteenth-century development of the picturesque toward symbolist art."[14]

Sypher falls back interestingly upon Wordsworth's poetry to illustrate what he calls the psychological picturesque:

> In sum, "Tintern Abbey," identifying a "sad perplexity" with the Wye Valley, is in a tradition of picturesque art that arose with Milton's "Il Penseroso," developed through the landscape poets of the eighteenth century, and reached transcendental intimations in Wordsworth, these intimations later inspiring Mallarmé's flight to the azure of the Absolute. Wordsworth's verse is the highest achievement of the picturesque in literature, which, in Alison's sense, is a way of seeing the world emotively, a means of associating a mood with objects until the contour of a landscape becomes the image of one's consciousness.[15]

Sypher's statement is another indication of how both the meaning of the word "picturesque" and its application to art and literature have

---

10 H. M. McLuhan, "The Aesthetic Moment in Landscape Poetry," in Alan S. Downer, ed., *English Institute Essays, 1951* (New York, 1952), p. 159.
11 Wylie Sypher, *Rococo to Cubism in Art and Literature* (New York, 1960), p. 86.
12 Sypher, *Rococo to Cubism*, p. 96.
13 Sypher, *Rococo to Cubism*, p. 81.
14 Sypher, *Rococo to Cubism*, p. 89. See also McLuhan, "Tennyson and Picturesque Poetry," p. 280.
15 Sypher, *Rococo to Cubism*, p. 101.

changed since the eighteenth century. His statement deserves attention, too, because it encourages us to look beyond Wordsworth's
dismissal of the picturesque as "meagre novelties"[16] to see it not just
as a "cult" or a superficial impression of the external world washed in
sentiment but, in Sypher's words, as a significant "technique" which
developed eventually "into symbolism in poetry and painting."[17] It
should perhaps be observed, too, in passing that Sypher's rather too
sweeping reference to the picturesqueness of Wordsworth's poetry
gains some support from John Barrell who noted how close Wordsworth was in "Michael" to "the picturesque travellers whom he
despised."[18]

In an essay included in *From Sensibility to Romanticism* (1965),
Martin Price argues that the picturesque persists because it is a "new
sensibility" that serves to link classic and romantic art: the formal and
the informal, the sublime and the beautiful, Addison and Blake, wit
and imagination, Ruskin and Proust, Vanbrugh and Eero Saarinem.
"The picturesque remains a living concern [Price asserts] so long as
we are interested in planning variety, fostering the lucky accident,
preserving the significant ruin . . . or the local character of a town."[19]
Throughout his essay, Price makes a variety of stimulating observations about the picturesque, both its past and its present functions. He
is especially interested in what he refers to as its "witty complexity
and playfulness." In his analysis of Wordsworth's dismissal of the
term, he is more cautious than Wylie Sypher for, although he admits
that Wordsworth underestimated its influence on his poetry, he does
make clear, in his conclusion, how Wordsworth's greatest poetry
transcends the picturesque as "the usual beauties dissolve into sublime mysteries."

Viola Hopkins Winner accepts a more traditional approach than
Marshall McLuhan or Wylie Sypher or Martin Price. In her book
Henry James and the Visual Arts (1970), she draws attention in her
third chapter to Wölfflin's analysis of picturesque theory and to a
"curious dualism" in James's criticism of art:

> on the one hand, he valued monumentality, symmetry, proportion,
> and clearly defined contours and lines . . . . On the other hand, he

16   Wordsworth, "The Prelude," Bk. XII, 117.
17   Sypher, *Rococo to Cubism*, p. 79.
18   John Barrell, *The Idea of Landscape and the Sense of Place* (Cambridge, 1972),
     p. 183.
19   Martin Price, "The Picturesque Moment," in F. W. Hilles and Harold Bloom, eds.,
     From Sensibility to Romanticism (New York, 1965), p. 261.

keenly enjoyed the picturesque in art and in scenery: shifting colour, light, and tone; the crooked and irregular; the moss covered and angle softened; spectacle and movement; views and perspectives—all visual qualities detached from objects themselves.[20]

The contrast which Winner provides here is informative and a reminder of the essential nature of the picturesque.

Both Martin Price and Winner refer to qualities that can be applied to buildings and even to towns. The application of the picturesque to architecture in our time has been stressed frequently by Nikolaus Pevsner. In 1954, in one of his articles, "Twentieth Century Picturesque," Pevsner asserted that "the Picturesque movement . . . [was] far the greatest contribution England has made to aesthetic theory." It was, he went on to say, for the town planner "the life-line by which he can defeat chaos."[21] Two years later he advised English urban planners to turn back to "the writings of the improvers from Pope to Uvedale Price and Payne Knight."[22] Like Price, Pevsner cites Sir Joshua Reynolds's emphasis upon "accident," "variety," and "intricacy" in architecture.[23] A more recent work dealing with the picturesque in architecture is *The English Vision* (1982). Here, in his last chapter, David Watkin sketches the architectural course of this convention from Sir Uvedale Price to John Nash, P. F. Robinson, Sir Charles Barry, Clough Williams-Ellis, Nikolaus Pevsner, and others. Watkin's reference to postwar reconstruction and the interest which architects like John Summerson and painters like John Piper took in wartime ruins offers a further illustration of how the twentieth century has found a practical use for the picturesque.[24]

One more reference must conclude this brief survey of how our inheritance of picturesque theory and practice has spilled over from one century to another. In his article "Henry James and the Picturesque Mode" (1975), William F. Hall maintains that the "picturesque" is a more useful concept with which to approach James's fiction than either "romance" or "realism." Hall's exposition—difficult and elusive—links the picturesque with "three major techniques peculiar to it, caricature, melodrama, and mythic reference

20 Viola Hopkins Winner, *Henry James and the Visual Arts* (Charlotteville, 1970), pp. 31-32.
21 Nikolaus Pevsner, "Twentieth Century Picturesque," *The Architectural Review* 115 (April 1954), p. 229.
22 Nikolaus Pevsner, *The Englishness of English Art* (London, 1956), p. 168.
23 See Joshua Reynolds, *Discourses on Art* (Indianapolis, 1965), p. 206.
24 David Watkin, *The English Vision* (London, 1982), pp. 181-200.

and allusion."[25] Using this framework, Hall goes on to advance reasons for appreciating the subtleties of the use of the picturesque mode in the fiction of Hawthorne and Henry James. Throughout the essay, the conventions examined lead to such tenuous complexities that the interrelation of the "three major techniques" with picturesque art seems remote, even speculative.

Henry James did, however, understand and appreciate how the picturesque could be made to serve the requirements of his fiction. As well as using it in the allusive manner that William F. Hall suggests, he also made it serve in many ways that Scott, Charlotte Brontë, Dickens, George Eliot, and Hardy found so effective. If, as James said, "The only reason for the existence of a novel is that it does attempt to represent life,"[26] and if we accept, as I think we must, his assertion in 1884 that the descriptive technique of the novelist resembles closely that of the artist, then we can understand why James says that the novelist must compete with the artist "in *his* attempt to render the look of things, the look that conveys their meaning, to catch the colour, the relief, the expression, the surface, the substance of the human spectacle."[27] In this competition, Victorian novelists found the picturesque particularly useful. For if it was short on significance and given, on occasion, to sentiment that altered expression disturbingly, it could render admirably "the colour, the relief, the surface," in short, "the look of things." And at its best, it appealed to "feeling hearts and imaginative tempers."[28] Too often, however, its critics — in the heavy swell of William Wordsworth's wake—laboured over its aesthetic insensible "to the moods / Of time and season, to the moral power, / The affections and the spirit of the place";[29] too seldom did they recognize its real merits and place, particularly in the fiction of the nineteenth century. The picturesque and fiction of that age were in several distinct ways closely related; both had "much to tell each other"; both had "much in common."

25   Hall, "Henry James and the Picturesque Mode," p. 326.
26   Henry James, "The Art of Fiction," in *Partial Portraits* (Ann Arbor, 1970), p. 378.
27   James, "The Art of Fiction," p. 390.
28   *Arthur Hallam*, p. 198.
29   Wordsworth, "The Prelude," Bk. XII, 118-20.

Bibliography

Addison, Joseph. "The Pleasures of the Imagination." *The Spectator*, June 21-July 4, September 6, 1712.

[Adolphus, John Leycester]. *Letters to Richard Heber, Esq. M.P.* 2nd ed. London, 1822.

Allentuck, Marcia, "Scott and the Picturesque: Afforestation and History." In Alan Bell, ed., *Scott Bicentenary Essays*. Edinburgh: Scottish Academic Press, 1973, pp. 188-98.

Allott, Miriam, ed. *The Brontës, the Critical Heritage*. London: Routledge & Kegan Paul, 1974.

Appleton, Jay. *The Experience of Landscape*. Chichester: John Wiley, 1975.

Auster, Henry. *Local Habitations, Regionalism in the Early Novels of George Eliot*. Cambridge: Harvard Univ. Press, 1970.

Bagehot, Walter. *Literary Studies*. 2 vols. London: Dent, 1911.

Baker, William, ed. *Critics on George Eliot*. London: George Allen and Unwin, 1973.

Barbier, Carl Paul. *William Gilpin, His Drawings, Teaching, and Theory of the Picturesque*. Oxford: Clarendon, 1963.

Barrell, John. *The Idea of Landscape and the Sense of Place*. Cambridge: Cambridge Univ. Press, 1972.

————— . *The Dark Side of the Landscape, the Rural Poor in English Painting, 1730-1840*. Cambridge: Cambridge Univ. Press, 1983.

Beauty, Horror and Immensity, Picturesque Landscape in Britain 1750-1850. Cambridge: Cambridge Univ. Press, 1981.

Bell, Alan, ed. *Selected Papers Read at the Sir Walter Scott Bicentenary Conference*. Edinburgh: Scottish Academic Press, 1973.

Blair, Hugh. *Lectures on Rhetoric and Belles Lettres*. 3 vols. 2nd ed. London, 1785.

Boase, T. S. R. *English Art, 1800-1870*. Oxford: Clarendon, 1959.

Briggs, Asa. "The Sense of Place." In *The Quality of Man's Environment*. Voice of America Forum Lectures. Washington, D.C., 1968.

Brontë, Charlotte. *Novels of the Sisters Brontë*. 12 vols. Thornton Edition. Edinburgh: John Grant, 1905.

Burke, Edmund. *A Philosophical Enquiry into the Origin of Our Ideas of the Sublime and Beautiful*. Edited by James T. Boulton. London: Routledge & Kegan Paul, 1958.

Carlyle, Thomas. *Scottish and Other Miscellanies*. London: Dent, 1915.

Chesterton, Gilbert Keith. *Robert Louis Stevenson*. London: Hodder & Stoughton, [1927].

Clark, Kenneth. *The Gothic Revival, an Essay in the History of Taste*. 3rd ed. London: John Murray, 1962.

_____ . *Landscape into Art*. Boston: Beacon Press, 1961.

Clarke, Michael. *The Tempting Prospect, a Social History of English Watercolours*. London: British Museum Publications, 1981.

Cohen, Jane R. *Charles Dickens and His Original Illustrators*. Columbus: Ohio State Univ. Press, 1980.

Collins, Philip, ed. *Dickens, the Critical Heritage*. London: Routledge & Kegan Paul, 1971.

[Combe, William]. *The Tour of Doctor Syntax in Search of the Picturesque*. 9th ed. London, 1819.

Conrad, Peter. *The Victorian Treasure-House*. London: Collins, 1973.

Craik, W. A. *The Brontë Novels*. London: Methuen, 1968.

Cusac, Marian H. *Narrative Structure in the Novels of Sir Walter Scott*. The Hague: Mouton, 1969.

Daiches, David. "Scott's Achievement as a Novelist, 1951." In D. D. Devlin, ed., *Walter Scott, Modern Judgements*. London: Macmillan, 1968, pp. 33-62.

Davie, Donald. "*Waverley, 1961*." In D. D. Devlin, ed., *Walter Scott, Modern Judgements*. London: Macmillan, 1968, pp. 84-97.

Devlin, D. D. *The Author of Waverley, a Critical Study of Walter Scott*. London: Macmillan, 1971.

_____ , ed. *Walter Scott, Modern Judgements*. London: Macmillan, 1968.

Dickens, Charles. *The Letters of Charles Dickens*. Edited by Madeline House, Graham Storey, and Kathleen Tillotson. 4 vols. Pilgrim Edition. Oxford: Clarendon, 1965-77.

_____ . *The Letters of Charles Dickens*. Edited by [Mamie Dickens and Georgina Hogarth]. London: Macmillan, 1909.

_____ . *The Oxford Illustrated Dickens*. 21 vols. London: Oxford Univ. Press, 1947-56.

Drabble, Margaret. *A Writer's Britain, Landscapes in Literature*. London: Thames and Hudson, 1979.

Duthie, Enid. *The Foreign Vision of Charlotte Brontë*. London: Macmillan, 1975.

Eliot, George. "Address to Working Men." *Blackwood's Edinburgh Magazine* 102 (January 1868), pp. 1-11.

_____ . *The George Eliot Letters*. Edited by Gordon S. Haight. 7 vols. New Haven: Yale Univ. Press, 1954-55.

_____ . "The Natural History of German Life." *Westminster Review* 66 (July 1856), pp. 51-79.

_____ . *The Works of George Eliot*. 20 vols. Cabinet Edition. Edinburgh: Blackwood, 1877-80.

Fernando, Lloyd. "Thomas Hardy's Rhetoric of Painting." *A Review of English Literature* 6 (October 1965), pp. 62-73.

Finley, Gerald. *Landscapes of Memory: Turner as Illustrator to Scott*. London: Scolar Press, 1980.

Forster, John. *The Life of Charles Dickens*. 2 vols. London: Dent, 1966.

Frazer, Allan, ed. *Sir Walter Scott, 1771-1832, an Edinburgh Keepsake*. Edinburgh: Edinburgh Univ. Press, 1971.

Garside, P. D. "*Waverley's* Pictures of the Past." *ELH* 44 (1977), pp. 659-82.

Gaskell, Elizabeth. *The Life of Charlotte Brontë*. London: Oxford Univ. Press, 1919.

——————. *Sylvia's Lovers*. London: Oxford Univ. Press, 1909.

[Gilpin, William]. *A Dialogue Upon the Gardens of the Right Honourable The Lord Viscount Cobham at Stow in Buckinghamshire*. 1748; rpt. Los Angeles: The Augustan Reprint Society, 1976.

[Gilpin, William]. *An Essay Upon Prints: Containing Remarks Upon the Principles of Picturesque Beauty; the Different Kinds of Prints; and the Characters of the Most Noted Masters*. 2nd ed. London, 1768.

Gilpin, William. *Observations, Relative Chiefly to Picturesque Beauty, Made in the Year 1772, on Several Parts of England; Particularly the Mountains, and Lakes of Cumberland and Westmoreland*. London, 1786.

——————. *Observations, Relative Chiefly to Picturesque Beauty, Made in the Year 1776, on Several Parts of Great Britain; Particularly the High-Lands of Scotland*. 2 vols. London, 1789.

——————. *Observations on the River Wye, and Several Parts of South Wales, etc. Relative Chiefly to Picturesque Beauty: Made in the Summer of the Year 1770*. 5th ed. London, 1800.

——————. *Observations on the Western Parts of England, Relative Chiefly to Picturesque Beauty; to Which Are Added a Few Remarks on the Picturesque Beauties of the Isle of Wight*. 2nd ed. London, 1808.

——————. *Remarks on Forest Scenery and Other Woodland Views (Relative Chiefly to Picturesque Beauty)*. 2 vols. London, 1791.

——————. *Three Essays: on Picturesque Beauty; on Picturesque Travel; and on Sketching Landscape: to Which Is Added a Poem, on Landscape Painting*. London, 1792.

——————. *Three Essays: on Picturesque Beauty; on Picturesque Travel; and on Sketching Landscape: With a Poem on Landscape Painting. To These Are Now Added Two Essays, Giving an Account of the Principles and Mode in Which the Author Executed His Own Drawings*. 3rd ed. London, 1808.

Goldberg, Norman L. *Landscapes of the Norwich School, an American Début*. Jacksonville: Cumner Gallery of Art, 1967.

Gombrich, E. H. *Art and Illusion, a Study in the Psychology of Pictorial Representation*. London: Phaidon, 1968.

Grierson, Sir Herbert, et al. *Sir Walter Scott Lectures, 1940-1948*. Introduction by W. L. Renwick. Edinburgh: Edinburgh Univ. Press, 1950.

Grundy, Joan. *Hardy and the Sister Arts*. London: Macmillan, 1979.

Hagstrum, Jean H. *The Sister Arts, the Tradition of Literary Pictorialism and English Poetry from Dryden to Gray*. Chicago: Univ. of Chicago Press, 1958.

Haight, Gordon S. *George Eliot, a Biography*. Oxford: Oxford Univ. Press, 1978.

Hall, William F. "Henry James and the Picturesque Mode." *English Studies in Canada* 1 (Fall 1975), 326-43.

Hallam, Arthur. *The Writings of Arthur Hallam*. Edited by T. A. Vail Motter. New York: Modern Language Association of America, 1943.

Hamilton, Harlan W. *Doctor Syntax, a Silhouette of William Combe, Esq. (1742-1823)*. London: Chatto and Windus, 1969.

Hardie, Martin. *Water-colour Painting in Britain*. I: *The Eighteenth Century*. 2nd ed. London: Batsford, 1967.

———. *Water-colour Painting in Britain*. II: *The Romantic Period*. London: Batsford, 1967.

———. *Water-colour Painting in Britain*. III: *The Victorian Period*. London: Batsford, 1968.

Hardy, Evelyn. *Thomas Hardy, a Critical Biography*. London: Hogarth Press, 1954.

Hardy, Florence Emily. *The Life of Thomas Hardy, 1840-1928*. Toronto: Macmillan, 1962.

Hardy, Thomas. *Thomas Hardy's Personal Writings, Prefaces, Literary Opinions, Reminiscences*. Edited by Harold Orel. Lawrence: Univ. of Kansas Press, 1966.

———. *The Works of Thomas Hardy in Prose and Verse*. 23 vols. Wessex Edition. London: Macmillan, 1912-14.

Harvey, John Robert. *Victorian Novelists and Their Illustrators*. New York: New York Univ. Press, 1971.

Hayden, John O., ed. *Scott, the Critical Heritage*. London: Routledge & Kegan Paul, 1970.

Hayes, John. *Gainsborough, Paintings and Drawings*. London: Phaidon, 1975.

Hazlitt, William. *The Complete Works of William Hazlitt*. Edited by P. P. Howe. 33 vols. London: Dent, 1930-34.

Hermann, Luke. *British Landscape Painting of the Eighteenth Century*. London: Faber and Faber, 1973.

Hipple, Walter John, Jr. *The Beautiful, the Sublime, and the Picturesque in Eighteenth-Century British Aesthetic Theory*. Carbondale: Southern Illinois Univ. Press, 1957.

Holcomb, Adele M. "Scott and Turner." In Alan Bell, ed., *Scott Bicentenary Essays*. Edinburgh: Scottish Academic Press, 1973, pp. 188-212.

Holmstrom, John, and Lawrence Lerner, eds. *George Eliot and Her Readers*. London: Bodley Head, 1966.

Hussey, Christopher. *The Picturesque, Studies in a Point of View*. London: Frank Cass, 1967.

Hyams, Edward. *Capability Brown and Humphry Repton*. London: Dent, 1971.

———. *The English Garden*. London: Thames and Hudson, 1966.

Irwin, Michael. *Picturing: Description and Illusion in the Nineteenth-Century Novel*. London: Allen and Unwin, 1979.

Jackson, Arlene. *Illustration and the Novels of Thomas Hardy*. London: Macmillan, 1981.

James, Henry. "Alphonse Daudet." *The Atlantic Monthly* 49 (June 1882), pp. 846-51.

———. *The Art of the Novel, Critical Prefaces*. Introduction by Richard P. Blackmur. New York: Scribner's, 1934.

————. "George Eliot's Life." *The Atlantic Monthly* 55 (April 1856), pp. 668-78.

————. *Italian Hours*. London: Heinemann, 1909.

————. *Partial Portraits*. Ann Arbor: Univ. of Michigan Press, 1970.

Johnson, Edgar. *Sir Walter Scott, the Great Unknown*. 2 vols. London: Hamish Hamilton, 1970.

Keats, John. *The Poetical Works of John Keats*. London: Oxford Univ. Press, 1956.

Klingender, Francis D. *Art and the Industrial Revolution*. Edited and revised by Arthur Elton. New York: Kelley, 1968.

Knight, Richard Payne. *An Analytical Inquiry into the Principles of Taste*. 4th ed. 1808; rpt. Westmead, Farnborough: Gregg International, 1972.

————. *The Landscape, a Didactic Poem Addressed to Uvedale Price, Esq.* 2nd ed. London, 1795.

Knoepflmacher, U. C., and G. B. Tennyson, eds. *Nature and the Victorian Imagination*. Berkeley: Univ. of California Press, 1977.

Kroeber, Karl. *Romantic Landscape Vision, Constable and Wordsworth*. Madison: Univ. of Wisconsin Press, 1975.

Lambourne, Lionel. *An Introduction to 'Victorian' Genre Painting*. London: Her Majesty's Stationery Office, 1982.

Lee, Rensselaer W. *Ut Pictura Poesis, the Humanistic Theory of Painting*. New York: Norton, 1967.

Leslie, Charles Robert. *Memoirs of the Life of John Constable*. 1843; rpt. London: John Lehman, 1949.

Lockhart, John Gibson. *Memoirs of the Life of Sir Walter Scott*. 5 vols. Boston: Houghton Mifflin, 1910.

McEwen, Fred Bates. "Techniques of Description in Eight Selected Novels of Sir Walter Scott." Dissertation, University of Pittsburgh, 1961.

Mackenzie, Henry. *The Man of Feeling*. New York: Norton, 1958.

MacLaren, E. Ann. "The Picturesque in Thomas Hardy's Fiction." Thesis, University of Guelph, 1969.

McLuhan, H. M. "The Aesthetic Moment in Landscape Poetry." In Alan S. Downer, ed., *English Institute Essays, 1951*. New York: Columbia Univ. Press, 1952.

————. "Introduction." In H. M. McLuhan, ed., *Alfred Lord Tennyson, Selected Poetry*. New York: Holt, Rinehart and Winston, 1956.

————. "Tennyson and Picturesque Poetry." *Essays in Criticism* 1, no. 3 (1951), pp. 262-82.

Malins, Edward. *English Landscaping and Literature, 1660-1840*. London: Oxford Univ. Press, 1966.

Manwaring, Elizabeth Wheeler. *Italian Landscape in Eighteenth Century England*. London: Frank Cass, 1925.

Marcus, Stephen. *Dickens: From Pickwick to Dombey*. London: Chatto and Windus, 1965.

Martin, Robert Bernard. *The Accents of Persuasion, Charlotte Brontë's Novels*. London: Faber and Faber, 1966.

Mayhead, Robin. *Walter Scott*. Cambridge: Cambridge Univ. Press, 1973.

Meisel, Martin. *Realizations, Narrative, Pictorial, and Theatrical Arts in Nineteenth-Century England*. Princeton: Princeton Univ. Press, 1983.

Millgate, Jane. *Walter Scott: The Making of a Novelist*. Toronto: Univ. of Toronto Press, 1984.

Moir, Esther. *The Discovery of Britain, the English Tourists*. London: Routledge & Kegan Paul, 1964.

Monk, Samuel. *The Sublime, a Study of Critical Theories in XVIII-Century England*. Ann Arbor: Univ. of Michigan Press, 1960.

Monod, Sylvère. *Dickens the Novelist*. Oklahoma: Univ. of Oklahoma Press, 1968.

Murdoch, J. D. W. "Scott, Pictures, and Painters." *The Modern Language Review* 67 (1972), pp. 31-43.

Nicolson, Marjorie Hope. *Mountain Gloom and Mountain Glory*. New York: Norton, 1963.

Oppé, A. P. *Alexander and John Robert Cozens*. London: Adam and Charles Black, 1952.

Osborne, Harold. *Aesthetics and Art Theory*. London: Longmans, Green, 1968.

Page, Norman. *Thomas Hardy*. London: Routledge & Kegan Paul, 1977.

_____ . "Thomas Hardy's Forgotten Illustrators." *Bulletin of the New York Public Library* 77 (Summer 1974), pp. 454-64.

Pater, Walter, *Marius the Epicurean*. London: Dent, 1934.

Paulson, Ronald. *Literary Landscape: Turner and Constable*. New Haven: Yale Univ. Press, 1982.

Pevsner, Nikolaus. *The Englishness of English Art*. London: Architectural Press, 1956.

_____ . "Price on Picturesque Planning." *The Architectural Review* 95 (February 1944), pp. 47-50.

_____ . "Twentieth Century Picturesque." *The Architectural Review* 115 (April 1954), pp. 227-29.

Piggott, Stuart. *Ruins in a Landscape*. Edinburgh: Edinburgh Univ. Press, 1976.

Pinion, F. B. *Thomas Hardy: Art and Thought*. London: Macmillan, 1977.

Pollard, Arthur. *Charlotte Brontë*. London: Routledge & Kegan Paul, 1968.

Praz, Mario. *The Hero in Eclipse in Victorian Fiction*. London: Oxford Univ. Press, 1969.

Price, Martin. "The Picturesque Moment." In F. W. Hilles and Harold Bloom, eds., *From Sensibility to Romanticism*. New York: Oxford Univ. Press, 1965.

Price, Sir Uvedale. *An Essay on the Picturesque, as Compared with the Sublime and Beautiful; and on the Use of Studying Pictures, for the Purpose of Improving Real Landscape*. London, 1794.

_____ . *An Essay on the Picturesque, as Compared with the Sublime and the Beautiful; and, on the Use of Studying Pictures, for the Purpose of Improving Real Landscape*. [Vol. I.] New ed. London, 1796.

_____ . *Essays on the Picturesque, as Compared with the Sublime and the Beautiful; and, on the Use of Studying Pictures, for the Purpose of Improving Real Landscape*. Vol. II. London, 1798.

_____ . *Essays on the Picturesque, as Compared with the Sublime and Beautiful; and, on the Use of Studying Pictures, for the Purpose of Improving Real Landscape*. 3 vols. London, 1810.

Radcliffe, Ann. *The Mysteries of Udolpho.* London: Oxford Univ. Press, 1966.

Raleigh, John Henry. *Time, Place, and Idea, Essays on the Novel.* Carbondale and Edwardsville, Southern Illinois Univ. Press, 1968.

Reed, James. *Sir Walter Scott: Landscape and Locality.* London: Athlone Press, 1980.

Repton, Humphry. *The Art of Landscape.* Edited by John Nolen. Boston: Houghton Mifflin, 1907.

Reynolds, Graham. *Constable, the Natural Painter.* London: Evelyn, Adams and Mackay, 1970.

_____ . *Victorian Painting.* London: Studio Vista, 1966.

Reynolds, Sir Joshua. *Discourses on Art, with Selections from The Idler.* Edited by Stephen O. Mitchell. Indianapolis: Bobbs-Merrill, 1965.

Robertson, William. *The History of Scotland during the Reigns of Queen Mary and of King James VI.* 3 vols. 21st ed. London, 1821.

Rodee, Howard David. "Scenes of Rural and Urban Poverty in Victorian Painting and Their Development 1850-1890." Dissertation, Columbia University, 1975.

Ross, Alexander M. "The Picturesque in Nineteenth-Century Fiction." In *English Studies Today.* 5th series. Istanbul: Malbaasi, 1973, pp. 327-58.

_____ . "*Waverley* and the Picturesque." In J. H. Alexander and David Hewitt, eds., *Scott and His Influence.* Aberdeen: Association for Scottish Literary Studies, 1983, pp. 99-108.

Ruskin, John. *The Works of John Ruskin.* Edited by E. T. Cook and Alexander Wedderburn. 39 vols. Library Edition. London: George Allen, 1903-12.

Scott, Sir Walter. *The Journal of Sir Walter Scott.* Edited by W. E. K. Anderson. Oxford: Clarendon, 1972.

_____ . *The Letters of Sir Walter Scott, 1787-1832.* Edited by H. J. C. Grierson. 12 vols. London: Constable, 1932-37.

_____ . *The Miscellaneous Prose Works of Sir Walter Scott.* 30 vols. Edinburgh: Cadell, 1834-71.

_____ . *Waverley Novels.* 24 vols. London: Frowde, Oxford Univ. Press, 1912.

Shaftesbury, [Third Earl of], Anthony Ashley Cooper. "The Moralists." In *Characteristics of Men, Manners, Opinions, Times.* 3 vols. 2nd ed. London, 1714.

Shorter, Clement. *The Brontës, Life and Letters.* 2 vols. London: Hodder and Stoughton, 1908.

Smart, Alastair. "Pictorial Imagery in the Novels of Thomas Hardy." *The Review of English Studies,* new series, 12 (1961), pp. 262-80.

Smith, Charlotte. *Emmeline, the Orphan of the Castle.* Edited by Anne Henry Ehrenpreis. London: Oxford Univ. Press, 1971.

Stainton, Lindsay. *British Landscape Watercolours, 1600-1860.* London: British Museum Publications, 1985.

Steig, Michael. *Dickens and Phiz.* Bloomington: Indiana Univ. Press, 1978.

Steigman, John. *Victorian Taste, a Study of the Arts and Architecture from 1830 to 1870.* London: Nelson, 1970.

Stein, Richard L. *The Ritual of Interpretation, the Fine Arts as Literature in Ruskin, Rossetti and Pater.* Cambridge: Harvard Univ. Press, 1975.

Stephen, Leslie. *Hours in a Library*. 3 vols. New ed. London: Smith Elder, 1892.

Stevenson, Robert Louis. *The Works of Robert Louis Stevenson*. 35 vols. Tusitala Edition. London: Heinemann, 1923-24.

Sypher, Wylie. *Rococo to Cubism in Art and Literature*. New York: Vintage, 1960.

Templeman, William D. *The Life and Work of William Gilpin (1724-1804)*. Urbana: Univ. of Illinois Press, 1939.

Tippkötter, Horst. *Walter Scott, Geschichte als Unterhaltung: Eine Rezeptionsanalyse der Waverley Novels*. Frankfurt am Main: Vittorio Klostermann, 1971.

Torgovnick, Marianna. *The Visual Arts, Pictorialism, and the Novel, James, Lawrence and Woolf*. Princeton: Princeton Univ. Press, 1985.

Turner, 1775-1851. London: Tate Gallery, 1974.

Vigar, Penelope. *The Novels of Thomas Hardy: Illusion and Reality*. London: Athlone Press, 1974.

Walpole, Horace. *On Modern Gardening; an Essay*. New York: Young Books, 1931.

Watkin, David. *The English Vision, the Picturesque in Architecture, Landscape, and Garden Design*. London: John Murray, 1982.

————— . *Thomas Hope 1769-1831 and the Neo-Classical Idea*. London: John Murray, 1968.

Watson, J. R. *Picturesque Landscape and English Romantic Poetry*. London: Hutchinson Educational, 1970.

Williams, Ioan, ed. *Sir Walter Scott on Novelists and Fiction*. London: Routledge & Kegan Paul, 1968.

Wilson, Angus. *The World of Charles Dickens*. Harmondsworth: Penguin, 1972.

Winner, Viola Hopkins. *Henry James and the Visual Arts*. Charlottesville: Univ. Press of Virginia, 1970.

Witemeyer, Hugh. *George Eliot and the Visual Arts*. New Haven: Yale Univ. Press, 1979.

Wölfflin, Heinrich. *Principles of Art History, the Problem of Style in Later Art*. Translated by M. D. Hottinger. New York: Dover, 1950.

Woodbridge, Kenneth. *Landscape and Antiquity, Aspects of English Culture at Stourhead, 1718-1838*. Oxford: Clarendon, 1970.

Woolf, Virginia. *The Common Reader*. 2nd series. London: Hogarth Press, 1959.

————— . *Walter Sickert, a Conversation*. London: Hogarth Press, 1934.

Wordsworth, William. *The Poetical Works of Wordsworth*. Revised by Ernest de Selincourt. London: Oxford Univ. Press, 1904.

Index

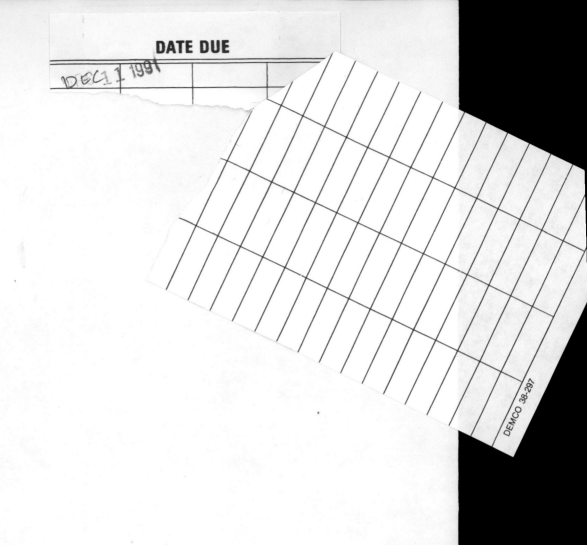

DEMCO 38-297